TO EACH HIS OWN
DOLCE VITA

BEARCLAWBOOKS@YAHOO.COM

To Each His Own
Dolce Vita

BY JOHN FRANCIS LANE

To Each His Own Dolce Vita

© John Francis Lane, 2013

John Francis Lane is identified as the author of this book.
The moral rights of the author have been asserted.

First Edition (April 2013)
Published by Bear Claw Books
Cambridge, UK
bearclawbooks@yahoo.com

ISBN: 978-0-9572462-4-9

Printed in the USA

Acknowledgements

I must thank Paul Sutton who asked me if I'd let him publish a selection of my articles from *Films and Filming*, but when I told him I was writing a memoir of my 'dolce vita' life during the first decade I wrote for the magazine, he was enthusiastic to publish it.

The cover photograph from the set of *La Dolce Vita* was taken by Gianfranco Mingozzi with my camera and is my copyright. The other illustrations are taken mostly from my collection and/ or with my camera. These have been supplemented with photographs from the Cineriz/Sutton Collection and from promotional material provided by the relevant copyright holders. All attempts have been made to credit individual photographers and companies where possible. If any additional crediting and referencing is found to be needed it will gratefully and gladly be added to future editions of this book.

JFL

PROLOGUE

As a reporter for several British newspapers, I had followed the real-life 'dolce vita' of Rome during the 1950s before it was to become a media cult thanks to Fellini and the title of his film. Like the Marcello of that film I too nurtured aspirations to become a serious writer, but was resigning myself to remaining a mere chronicler of sometimes ludicrous events which obliged me to gallivant round town, after royal princesses or Roman playboys, from one nightclub to another, or to attend fashionable weddings such as that in Lugano of a Swiss millionaire to a Scottish model, or that in Florence of the new love goddess of the screen, Anita Ekberg, to the British cinema's glamour boy of the moment, Tony Steel. At the last event, I was the only Fleet Street reporter to treat it as a brazen publicity stunt for the film that Steel was shooting in Tuscany. My account of that wedding, where the 'guests' were newspapermen, and photographers not yet dubbed "paparazzi", amused Fellini when I went to interview him when he was preparing to make *La Dolce Vita*. Fellini said he would include me in the film among the journalists at his make-believe press conference that would be held by the movie star in his film, to be played by none other than that same Swedish 'screen goddess' whose 'Hollywood fairy tale' wedding I had been so sarcastic about.

Thereafter I would soon be able to give up being just a 'dolce vita' reporter and dedicate myself to being a journalist and critic reporting not only on Italian cinema and theatre but also on the political and social changes taking place in Italy. I also succeeded in appearing in Italian films, even if only in cameos, and I did act in Italian on the stage with some success. Unlike the Marcello of Fellini's film, I wouldn't be distracted by the beautiful females on the 'dolce vita' circuit. My distractions were to be found more on the masculine circuit such as those who coloured the life and, unfortunately the death, of Pier Paolo Pasolini, who was a friend, and for whom I would do cameos in *La Ricotta*, with Orson Welles, and in *The Canterbury Tales*, in which I played a friar being led to damnation by a satanic angel who looked like a youth from a painting by Caravaggio.

My remembrance of things past does not aspire to rival the colourful memoirs of distinguished writers whose paths I crossed in Italy, such as Tennessee Williams, Gore Vidal and Edmund White, but is rather more in the line of that written by a friend and colleague of my newspaper days, Michael Davidson, with whom I spent many ribald drinking and eating hours when he was passing through Rome. In his book, *The World, the Flesh and Myself*, he mixed his professional experiences as a journalist with those of his erotic life. The objects of his amorous attention were much younger than those who interested me. The risks we both ran were of a different nature but in Italy in those years they were minimal. The people who crossed Michael's professional path were also very different. His were the survivors of the disintegrating British empire. My professional life took me into a more glamorous even if, at times, a more degrading world.

John Francis Lane being taken to Hell by a satanic angel in
Pier Paolo Pasolini's *The Canterbury Tales* (1972).

Chapter 1

During the years when I was trying to pursue careers as both an actor and a journalist I often risked running into obstacles. When I found myself acting in films with famous stars some would be either ignorant of, or indifferent to, my 'second' profession, while others, on finding out, would resent having a reporter around on the set. My most clamorous mishap occurred with Richard Burton during the filming of *Cleopatra*, for which I had been signed to play Bacchus. Italians were less surprised by my double career because non-professionals, including journalists, often appeared in Italian films. So much so that on one occasion when I had to go to the foreigners' bureau of the Central Police Station in Rome to apply for a work permit to play in a film, the policeman who received me looked at my temporary 'residence permit' and saw that I was registered as a journalist and asked, in what sounded like a menacing tone, "But Mr. Lane, are you an actor or a journalist?". I gulped and replied timorously, "Both". To my relief, he smiled benignly and exclaimed, "Complimenti!", and had no difficulty stamping my papers with the necessary permission. I didn't think that an English official would have treated an Italian in a similar situation with such disarming courtesy.

To explain why I was trying so hard to carry on being an actor and a journalist at the same time, I have to go back to my years as a teenager. I was living in Orpington, a dull town near London, where my father had moved, in the mid-1930s, after selling the businesses he had nourished in East Kent where I was born. In the early years of the Second World War, I was sent as a boarder to a school in Worcester. At Worcester I had what could be described as my introduction to homosexuality. At half-term most of the boarders from nearby counties went home. But the few us who lived far away would stay on and we were free to roam around at our will. One mid-term Saturday night I went alone to a local theatre to see a music hall show and stood at the back because it cost less. A man in uniform felt me up from behind. He didn't insist too much which was perhaps a pity, as I might have learned certain things sooner rather than later. But at least I was aware it was not displeasing to be touched. Back at school when I told another boy what had happened he was shocked. He told me to be careful because there were 'dangerous' men chasing after young boys. It was all right, he said, to play around with boys of our own age. I knew that strange things did indeed go on in the dormitory at night, especially during air-raid alarm rehearsals when we had to put our mattresses on the floor and sleep out of sight. I was intrigued when I heard panting squeals coming from other parts of the room and was a bit dismayed that nobody called on me. Maybe I was too pale and skinny to interest anyone at the time? But from then onwards I was no longer disturbed by the fact that I was attracted to other boys, especially a handsome prefect who was aware of my interest and not disinterested in getting to know me better. He was older but, like me, he was too shy to follow it up, even when we took walks together, an invitation to romance, on the banks of the River Severn opposite the lovely cathedral.

In Worcester, my Aunt Madge, my mother's sister, a spinster schoolteacher, would take me to visit the Cathedral and explain Gothic architecture to me. She had been to Italy before the war. She enthused about Renaissance painting. Hers were the only art history lessons I ever received as a boy.

After my father's death, during but not because of the war, my mother brought me back from Worcester and I went to Dulwich College, a posh public school founded by the Elizabethan actor, Edward Alleyn, but the atmosphere there was more inclined towards the playing fields than to the theatre. Mother and I were fortunate enough to survive the rest of the war. The last wave of German V1 and V2 rockets, aimed at London, often exploded near us, but we found only slight damage when we emerged each morning from the concrete shelter my father had transformed our sitting room into. After a year at Dulwich, I persuaded my mother to let me leave the school and take exploratory trips to London concerning my future. These were mostly dedicated to the theatre. I saw memorable performances above all by John Gielgud and Laurence Olivier among others. In my first sixteen years, apart from a model theatre as a boy in which I 'staged' musicals for the amusement of my family and friends, my passion for the theatrical had only found expression in some amateur dramatics in Orpington, and previously at Worcester when I was lucky that one of the subjects for the English essay was 'The best film you ever saw'. I had been wildly enthusiastic about Anthony Asquith's film of George Bernard Shaw's *Pygmalion*, starring Leslie Howard and Wendy Hiller. Having ransacked my aunt's bookshelves, and read the play and prologue, my teachers were impressed by my knowledge of Shaw. They gave me top marks and I even won a prize. My aunt rewarded me with a book of the Complete Plays of GBS.

After the war, more to honour my father's memory than out of political conviction, I accepted the role of secretary of the local Young Conservatives. In the election campaign of 1945, for which I was still too young to vote, I heckled at a rally by the Labour candidate when he was praising the Soviets for helping us win the war. I reminded him that Stalin had made a pact with Hitler. I was lucky to get out of the hall unscathed. When the first election results were coming in, I telephoned the wife of our Tory candidate. She told me in tears that he had been re-elected but Churchill had lost the election. In the days that followed, I started thinking seriously about my future and I asked myself what was I doing getting involved in politics in this dreary conservative town. My asthma and flat feet had meant I was not accepted for military service, and I knew that my thrice interrupted education would not give me qualifications for a university. I knew for certain that

I didn't want to stay in Orpington. I didn't see myself as a shop-keeper who would become a respectable citizen, a freemason like my Dad, vote Tory and bring up a family. I had already visited Paris, where I had seen René Clair's new film, *Le silence est d'or*, and, in the theatre, I had seen Jean Marais and Edwige Feuillère in Cocteau's play, *L'aigle à deux têtes*, and I had discovered that the French capital, unlike London, had recovered from its post-war doldrums. On that occasion, with a few francs left, I decided rashly to take a look at the Cote d'azur and, when in Nice, booked for a couple of days into an hotel with full pension. It was my first real introduction to good French cuisine. To my embarrassment, when I was served an artichoke, a vegetable I had never set eyes upon before, I realized that, to the amusement of the other guests, an English lady at another table, who had noticed my bewilderment, started gesticulating and shouting as she showed me how I should eat it. When I was ready to leave the hotel, I found I hadn't enough money left to pay the bill. With the audacity of a teenager, I went to the Casino and gambled what I had left in my pocket. I was lucky enough to double what I'd gambled and, rather than gamble again, which the croupiers expect you to do, I pocketed my winnings immediately so I was able to pay my bill and get out of Nice.

In London, I studied for two years at a drama school in Highgate where I shared a house with other students and, though I was not the eldest of them, I soon became the respected boss. At the school I had more success directing student productions than in improving my own elocution, which was an impediment to a successful acting career, and I suffered my first traumatic unrequited love affair, with a foreign student, Toralv Maurstad, with whom I shared a room and who was resolutely heterosexual. He spoke better English than most of us. I had directed him as Oswald in a successful production of Ibsen's *Ghosts*, in which he gave vent for the first time to his emotional potentiality. When, in the 1970s, I was in Olso, on a lecture tour of Scandanavian capitals for the Italian Cultural

Institute, he found me in a restaurant where I was dining with my hosts and he dragged me away. I spent the night with him alone (but still only platonically affectionate!) in his villa. He gave me a copy of his autobiography (in Norwegian, of course!) on the flyleaf of which he wrote: "To my dear friend John, my first director in the theatre, room mate, and I don't know what else...".

I had more romantic success when working with a professional theatre group on a production of Lorca's *Blood Wedding*. The sets were designed by a man who looked a bit like Gene Kelly, one of the sex idols of my teenage years. Though this first reciprocal 'affair' was pleasing, sexually we were not suited to each other as he wanted to be the passive lover. These first two unsuccessful 'amorous' experiences were to influence my future life until I learned to find masculine partners outside the professional or intellectual worlds I frequented who could satisfy my sexual desire.

Since I was not adapting very well to British austerity, nor making much progress in my attempt to break into show business, and in order to get some money out of England legally, I signed up to study French at the Sorbonne and film direction at the IDHEC school in Paris. My first article published in a film magazine was about the IDHEC: 'On Studying the Film' in the April 1950 edition of the British Film Institute journal, *Sight and Sound*. During my period in Paris, I was able to enjoy and learn from all that the city had to offer an Englishman of twenty starved of culture and joie de vivre. It was the time when one could hear Juliette Gréco in clubs and Edith Piaf and Yves Montand, Léo Ferré, Georges Bresson. On the stage I'd see Louis Jouvet and had been among the crowds cheering Gérard Philipe in Jean Vilar's TNP production of *Le Cid*. It was the period when Existentialism was a philosophy to help you to rationalise about your life. The first novels I read in French were Camus's *L'étranger* and Sartre's *La Nausée*. The well-thumbed copies have stayed with me all my life.

In Paris, during the spring of 1949, I had met a blond German with whom I began what promised to be my first truly romantic attachment. Our first meeting was more intellectually than sensually blessed. We were sitting at adjoining tables at the Deux Maggots, one of the cafés in St. Germain-des-Prés that were fashionable in those existentialist years. He was reading the *Four Quartets* by T. S. Eliot, an English poet even if born in America, and I was reading *Requiem and Other Poems* by Rainer Maria Rilke, who was a German language poet even though he was born in what was then Bohemia. The English translator's introduction to Rilke mentioned that the poet had lived in Paris where he worked as a secretary to Rodin. My German friend suggested we visit the Rodin Museum. We made a date there for the next day.

When we met at the entrance to the museum I bought the English translation of Rilke's essay on Rodin. We didn't need a guide book to appreciate statues like *The Kiss* or *The Thought* but, when we came to the garden and saw *The Burghers of Calais*, the extraordinary marble group of male figures in their nightshirts with ropes round their necks, we were a bit puzzled and consulted Rilke. He had read his Froissart and so knew about our Edward III's misdeeds. From my history lessons at school, I remembered only that King Edward III won battles in France and was the father of The Black Prince, whose tomb I had seen as a child in Canterbury Cathedral. I didn't know, until we read Rilke's description of this moving sculpture, that during the period when the English were occupying France, Edward had behaved so savagely to the besieged people of Calais. He had saved the lives of the six burghers who'd offered themselves as hostages only because his (French) queen, who was pregnant, begged him to save them.

"You see", said my new friend, "we Germans are not the only ones who behaved badly while occupying France". Our Anglo-German 'affair' began on that conciliatory note. It lasted in Paris that Spring of 1949 and, after a separation that summer, while I had a job in an English-managed hotel in Menton, and he took off for Italy, I joined him in Rome in early September. But on this, my first visit to the Eternal City, our romantic affair ended dramatically because he had started a German-American affair. Fortunately, I'd soon find Italian *consolations*. I visited Rome again in the 'Holy Year' of 1950 but the city was over-run with pilgrims. I fled first to Ischia where I found charming company with locals and Anglo-American artistic beachcombers, including illustrious ones such as Wystan Auden, who always greeted me courteously in the local café, even if I got to know his companion, Chester Kallman, better. Burt Lancaster was in Ischia shooting *The Crimson Pirate* and all the boys were crazy about Burt (and apparently he with them!).

After Ischia, I went to Venice for my first film festival, accredited as a film student not yet as a journalist. Gavin Lambert, and other Britons I knew from weekend trips to Oxford, where I had mixed with fellow film buffs, joined me to have coffee with Jean Cocteau in Piazza San Marco and console him for the cool reception the Italian critics had given to his *Orphée* which we adored.

By 1951, I had decided that although I'd had stimulating times in Paris and in St-Paul-de-Vence, where I spent several prolonged end of year holidays, I felt I would be happier on the Italian side of the Alps and that it was worth giving Rome a second chance. I lived first in a pension near the Spanish Steps. There, as a loafer, I spent the first instalment of my inheritance, obtained from the sale of the shop in Orpington, and I had to look for work. I did translations of Italian plays for a government-sponsored magazine dedicated to Italian Drama, and I taught English to private pupils of all ages. I also found a job as a sort of secretary to a French journalist who represented a world veterans' association, thanks to which I got the fascinating chore of accompanying international war orphans to a summer camp on the Ligurian riviera. My main problem was keeping apart the warring factions, Israelis and Egyptians, Americans and Yugoslavs (the only communist country present), French and Algerians. I was quite successful as a peace-maker. It was a good thing the boys were too young for me or I might have taken advantage of the affections that many of them developed for me that summer. One tough young Yugoslav boy became very friendly and left me his address. We did correspond afterwards but I never went to investigate how he grew up. As a loyal comrade who'd been chosen to represent the regime he probably became a Tito henchman. The most profitable job I found in those years was with the Food and Agricultural Organisation of the UN, where I proof-read publications about subjects such as land reform in Nigeria and fisheries in Finland, not exactly my cup of vino, but I did feel I was working for people who were doing something useful in our precarious post-war world. Thanks to a good salary I was able to take a nice apartment in a chic residential area, round the corner from where Luigi Pirandello had lived, but near the elegant villa and park of the Torlonia family where Benito Mussolini made his official residence.

My most sexually exciting companion of the time was Salvatore, an attractive but somewhat primitive youth from the Abruzzi mountains, for whom I had been a Pygmalion. He moved in with me and we had a happy six months even if he began to complain that he was being treated as a servant, which was probably true. I didn't want him to think he was being adopted for life, nor did I want to encourage his latent laziness. He found the odd outside job and presumably several lovers of both sexes. I too had affairs, one with an aspiring actor, a handsome Tuscan who looked a bit too much like Vittorio Gassman but without that actor's histrionic gifts. I took him to see Gassman, then the most popular actor of the Italian stage, playing *Hamlet* and my friend shrugged when I told him of his physical resemblance. Gassman's Hamlet was flamboyant and won an ovation from the public but frankly (as his future wife Shelley Winters would comment after she divorced him) gave too much emphasis to the 'ham'. My Gassman look-alike was carried off by a Dutch girl met at a party of mine. She took him to Paris. Their affair didn't last long and he tried to move back into my life. He invited me to see him play Laertes in a poor theatre production of *Hamlet* in a cinema in Tivoli where the actor-manager was so miserly, and the takings so low, that I had to pay for the supper and bus fares back to Rome for my friend and some of his fellow actors. But I felt obliged to discard him because I felt he expected me to help him to get into the film world. I told him he had to fend for himself as I hadn't yet got into films myself. In the 1950s it didn't seem very difficult to break into films in Rome for anyone who was either beautiful or freakish, especially since the neorealist cinema had launched the habit of using non-professionals. They were easier targets for the bullying of egocentric directors and they would often fall victims to illusions about their futures. The traumas this could cause were splendidly fictionalised in films of the 1950s like Antonioni's *The Lady Without Camellias* and Visconti's *Bellissima*.

Being an Englishman in Rome in the early 1950s was not always convenient. In 1953 there had been violent demonstrations over the question of Trieste which, after the peace treaty, had been divided into two areas, one under the governorship of the Slovenes, who became part of Marshal Tito's communist federation after he had defeated the Nazis and Fascists. The other area was under Anglo-American governance with an English general in charge. He became very unpopular. Anyone seen reading an English newspaper on the Spanish Steps, under the window of the room where a much more appreciated Englishman, John Keats, had died, risked being insulted by nationalistic-minded Italians. Fortunately, in October 1954, an agreement was reached to give back most of Trieste to the Italians.

I had been appointed Rome correspondent of a new British monthly magazine *Films and Filming*. The first issue, which would even be on sale at the bookstall on the Via Veneto in Rome, had Marlon Brando in Elia Kazan's *On the Waterfront* on its cover. The editor was Peter Brinson who had written about cinema and

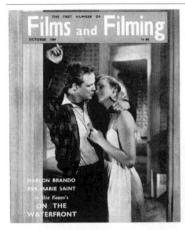

ballet for various periodicals. As the magazine was published in the middle of the preceding month, the first issue dated October 1954 appeared in mid-September, so I had to deliver my first article before going to the Venice Festival at the end of August. I wrote, in an article called 'Italy in London', an introduction to the Italian Film Week due to open on October 25th at the Tivoli Cinema in London in the presence of the Queen and Prince Philip. In it I wrote enthusiastically about Federico Fellini, whose *I Vitelloni*, shown the year before at Venice, was among the Italian films to be screened in London. Fellini had been one of the scriptwriters of Rossellini's *Rome, Open City* (1945) and several other significant post-war films, and was one of those directors who was giving a new creative impulse to the social implications of neo-realism but according to his own aesthetic taste and sensibility. His first film directed alone, *Lo sceicco bianco* (The White Sheik), a spoof on the Italian mania for the photostory magazines, revealed for the first time, in a tragi-comic role, the talents of Alberto Sordi, who was to become the most popular Italian comic star of his generation. Fellini had earlier co-directed *Luci del varietà* (1950) with Alberto Lattuada, a story set in the world of second-rate Italian music hall companies on tour. It was a vehicle for their respective actress wives, Carla del Poggio and Giulietta Masina, the latter destined to be internationally acclaimed in the lead opposite Anthony Quinn in Fellini's new film *La Strada*, which was to première at the up-coming Venice Festival which I would write about for the second issue of *Films and Filming*. *I Vitelloni* was the first example of Fellini's extraordinary gift for combining autobiographical memory with fantastical invention. Set in a seaside town similar to the Rimini of his own childhood and teenage years, it was about a group of provincial 'vitelloni' (Italian for 'big calves' but which, in Rimini dialect, refers to loafers), young men who lounge around the bars and streets of the town waiting for life to come to them. The quietest and most sensitive, Moraldo, was played by Franco Interlenghi, who had been one of the two kids in De Sica's *Shoeshine* (1946) and the juvenile lead in Luciano Emmer's *Sunday in August* (1950). In the last scene of Fellini's film, Moraldo finds the courage to take flight in search of the better life that will never arrive in that town. Presumably he will end up in Rome as Fellini himself did in the 1940s. Fellini had been hoping to make a sequel called *Moraldo in the City*. Instead he had found producers, Dino De Laurentiis and Carlo Ponti, then partners, to finance *La Strada*. Fellini would have to wait until the end of the 1950s to make that 'sequel' to *I Vitelloni*, which would be *La Dolce Vita*.

The London Film Week of 1954 opened with Ettore Giannini's film of his delightful stage show *Carosello Napoletano* (Neapolitan Merry-go-round), in which the up-and-coming new Italian sex goddess, Sophia Loren, was one of the scintillating performers. Her presence in London alongside that of Gina Lollobrigida, and the supposed rivalry between the two, was given much media attention, but for those who admired the post-war Italian cinema, the real scandal was that the organisers of the event had not included *Umberto D.*, Vittorio De Sica's sad but poetic film about the plight of old age pensioners in Italy (the film was dedicated to De Sica's own father, Umberto). The exclusion was no doubt influenced by the Christian Democrat Under-Secretary responsible for cultural matters (and future seven times Premier) Giulio Andreotti. When the film opened in Italy in 1952 he had accused De Sica of "washing Italy's dirty linen in public". De Sica was in London, but only as the co-star of Gina Lollobrigida in *Bread, Love and Dreams*. The National Film Theatre organised a special screening of *Umberto D.* for the critics, who honoured the film and the director of this the final masterpiece of neo-realism.

Carlo Battisti as *Umberto D.* by Vittorio De Sica.

After my brief affair with the Gassman lookalike had ended, Salvatore, who knew how to be humble as well as resentful, returned so that we could enjoy Christmas 1954 together, eating, in the sun on my terrace, the contents of a Harrod's yuletide hamper which my mother had sent me providentially. But when I couldn't stand the office job anymore I lost the flat and, of course, poor Salvatore had to fend for himself again. I moved back into furnished rooms and had mostly bleak times before my fortunes improved. One day while I was drinking cappuccinos with Anglo-American friends at the famous Café Greco, a young man at another table asked if we'd like to come the next day to a studio to appear in a film. We were delighted to do so. The director turned out to be French. I was the only one of our group who managed to say his lines with conviction so I felt it was time I sought work as an actor. I found an agent who got jobs for foreigners and, shortly afterwards, I was signed up to play the role of a British naval officer in an Italian film [*I sette dell'Orsa Maggiore*] about their frogmen who sank a British battleship during the war. But after a week of sitting around in Naples waiting for the arrival of the ship, on which we were to shoot the scene, I was sent back to Rome. When the ship finally arrived, I had other commitments in Rome and couldn't get away. I had decided anyway that I would do better for the moment to get myself a job as a journalist.

I was, in fact, gradually finding my way into the newspaper world by the front door. Thanks to becoming the Rome correspondent of *Films and Filming*, I was accepted as a professional member of the Foreign Press Association, the Stampa Estera, where I soon made friends and useful contacts long before becoming a foreign correspondent myself. Among the journalists I met was one who had been one of the real foreign correspondents standing alongside a 'colleague' played by Gregory Peck when they are introduced to 'Princess' Audrey Hepburn in Wyler's *Roman Holiday*. I asked him what Italian stories could get into the British papers. He told me: "Now that the Trieste situation has been settled, only the Pope and Gina Lollobrigida". The second issue of *Films and Filming* had La Lollo on its cover, and my profile of her inside, but I hadn't yet written anything about the Pope! I managed to work first as a 'stringer' for the *Evening Standard*, for which I would indeed write about the Pope, none too successfully, then I was hired by Stephen Barber, the staff correspondent of the *News Chronicle*. Barber was nearly always travelling to hot news spots in the Mediterranean and needed someone, informed about Italian affairs, as stand-in.

The only other job I had at the time was collaborating on the Italian translation of Marie Seton's biography of Sergei Eisenstein, entrusted to me by Luigi Chiarini, one of the most respected (but often also criticized) intellectual giants of Italian cinema. He had been the founding director of the Centro Sperimentale film school in fascist times, and even directed some films himself, but had been consistent in his liberal views without becoming militant in politics either on the right or left. The work on Seton's fascinating book was a great stimulation for me. Thanks to her personal memories of the great director in her book, I was able to revive and enrich memories of Eisenstein whose films and ideas on cinema had done so much to influence me after the war in London.

In the Spring of 1955, I got myself involved with another passionate but foredoomed love affair, this time with a Neapolitan medical student I met while visiting the ruins of Herculaneum. It turned out I was his first lover and he became very sentimental which I found flattering but a bit suffocating. He'd tell me one day that he had often meditated killing me and then himself. I admit that one of the things I would always adore most about the Neapolitans is their theatricality. Their pagan traditions have been transformed into Catholic ritual ceremonies and these often inspire impressive musical and theatrical performances far beyond the mere picturesque. I'd learn to be wary about getting too involved in further Neapolitan love affairs, even if I wouldn't always succeed in avoiding the inevitable obstacles that arose in a relationship between a Northern rational and empirical thinker and an emotional, even sentimental, Southerner. It would take me some time to learn to judge if the person who appealed to me was, at that moment, on stage or off. I would prefer the performances on real stages and I'd try not to upstage them myself. For this I'd often be accused of being a chilly Englishman. Probably true. Our passionate affair lasted idyllically through the Spring and early Summer of 1955. During that period I took him with me to Sorrento, where I had gone to interview Sophia Loren while she was making *Scandal in Sorrento*, the third of the *Bread, Love and...* films, and introduced him as my photographer. I had to restrain his somewhat naïve excitement as a fan being in the presence of movie stars, and the photos he took with my Leica, of me with Sophia, were disastrous. By August there were the first strains in our relationship. He was becoming too possessive and this was interfering with my professional life. I had commitments in Rome, while Stephen Barber was away, and then I had to go to Venice for the festival. As I couldn't take him there with me I thought it a good idea when he said he wanted to go to Ischia. He had relatives in the island's principal town, Porto d'Ischia, where he was born. Only later would I discover that he had gone to Forio, where he knew my Foreign Press Club bar friend, Patricia, was staying and she introduced him around as "John's friend".

Patricia and the Neapolitan student in Forio d'Ischia. Summer 1955

I was in Venice that year not so much as a critic but mostly as a gossip-seeking columnist covering the festival for Reuter's agency, thanks to whom I was staying at the Hotel des Bains of Thomas Mann memory (not yet of Luchino Visconti's). The festival paid half the bill. The agency paid the rest and my expenses. It was the first time I had worked for a news agency. I had to report on the reaction to the films for dispatches to the countries who had films in competition and, inevitably for a news agency, I had to keep up with the gossip. And there was plenty to write about that year. Sophia Loren was mobbed on the entrance to the inauguration and was seen sobbing inside the cinema, not because she had been hurt but with satisfaction at having made the grade, like her rival La Lollo, who was mobbed the year before. The British cinema was making a big show, more with its stars (above all Diana Dors in a mink bikini) than it's films (*Doctor at Sea* pleased the public, less so the critics, but *The Deep Blue Sea* was at least appreciated for Kenneth More's performance). There was a glamorous cocktail party for the Royal Navy and its Mediterranean Commander in Chief, in the presence of Linda Christian and Edmund Purdom, the latter an old friend from my London theatre days. On another day, I was entertained on the lower decks by some young sailors, one of whom was being dressed up elegantly in gentlemanly attire (the other lads lending what he needed) as he had a date, apparently with a rich American gent in a hotel on the Grand Canal. I also inspected the Greek luxury liner on which the popular society hostess, Elsa Maxwell was inviting celebrities for a cruise. I made the shameful gaffe of not recognizing one of her guests as she arrived on the quay. She was an elegant French-looking lady whose initialed luggage was being carried on board. She looked familiar but I had to ask her name. With a disarming smile she replied with a French surname I didn't know. Only later, when we press were invited on board for a drink by Elsa, did I hear the 'French' lady speak in English, or rather American, and I realized she was none other than Olivia de Havilland!

Back on the Lido, in the gardens of the Hotel des Bains, I met a charming young man who turned out to be the Cultural Attaché of the Soviet Embassy in Rome. We discussed films and he was pleased to hear that I was enthusiastic about the Soviet competition entry, *The Cicada*, by a new director, Serge Samsonov. The Russian diplomat and I would become friends, but only in Rome would I find out why he was so interested in 'picking me up'.

John Francis Lane at Venice behind Clare Booth Luce (Photo: G.Moise)

In Venice, it was American not Russian diplomacy that was the centre of newsmen's attention. The American ambassador, Clare Booth Luce, playwright (*The Women*) and wife of Time-Life mogul, Henry Luce, objected to the festival showing of the American film, *Blackboard Jungle*, which insinuated there were fascist-style teaching methods in a New York school. The rather conformist festival director, Ottavio Croze's refusal to accept the film caused a rumpus among the leftists present. The film shown in its place, *Interrupted Melody*, didn't exactly honour Hollywood. The Americans also cut a poor festival showing with the much publicised premiere, in the open-air in a Lido park, of Burt Lancaster's *The Kentuckian*, which only embarrassed the guests. Even more ridiculous was the valiant attempt to keep the cowboy party alive afterwards with Dawn Addams and Rossano Brazzi doing a square dance.

Before the festival ended we saw Fellini's new film *Il bidone*, which had Broderick Crawford as a phoney priest cheating poor mountain people out of their savings. Instead of feeling vindicated by the cool reception given to him this time, after the triumph the year before of *La Strada*, which I hadn't admired as much as most other people, I felt sad. I believed that the Fellini of *I Vitelloni* and *The*

White Sheik still had a great future. The Golden Lion was won by Carl Dreyer for *Ordet*, the only masterpiece shown on the Lido that year.

Back in Rome, and hearing from Pat what my Neapolitan lover had been up to in Ischia, I decided there had to be a confrontation. I organized a trip down and got off the train at Caserta just north of Naples. He had agreed to meet at the railway station in front of the magnificent royal palace, designed by Vanvarelli, which I had hoped to visit. But it was closed that day and that only helped to create further tension as we waited at the station for the next train to take me back to Rome. I suppose I was lucky we didn't come to blows. At least I chose romantically theatrical backgrounds for this love story's beginning, at Herculaneum, and here at Caserta for its end. We'd see each other again, cordially if a bit pathetically, before he emigrated to Australia with the friend he'd met in Ischia that summer, a gentleman suffering from polio who needed a nurse as well as a lover. Later in the century, long after the Australian had died, my friend would pay visits to Europe and would one day find me hospitalized on the Tiber island. I'd let him stay in my flat and visit me every day to wheel me out into the open air while I continued my convalescence. Neither of us had any regrets, only memories of the good times.

In the autumn of 1955, I would become involved in a more sober relationship with a young man from the North whom I had met when he was a soldier in Bergamo. He suddenly turned up in Rome, now a policeman and in need of a friend and sensual consolation. For his first week in Rome he was not allowed out of the police barracks near the railway station, so I was summoned to visit him and, to my embarrassment (but also with a certain pride!), found myself embraced while the other young policemen were embracing their fiancées or relatives. My cop was good-looking and good-hearted but a simpleton and fortunately had no ambitions to become a movie star. Our brief affair kept me consoled for the Neapolitan's departure but a grim winter was on the way.

Chapter 2

The *Films and Filming* dated November 1955 had Anna Magnani
and Burt Lancaster in *The Rose Tattoo* on the cover and was the
first issue edited by Peter Baker. It contained articles signed by
Ken Tynan and Michael Powell and a report on the Venice Festival
by Dr. Roger Manvell, the distinguished British film historian who
had been on the jury. My contribution was a diary gossip column
reporting some of my adventures at Venice, excluding my gaffe in
not recognizing Olivia De Havilland but including the report that
Fellini's *Il Bidone* had left the audience at the festival screening in
embarrassed silence. I hope I didn't sound too triumphant!

In the same issue there was a letter of complaint about what I
had written about Rossellini's Italo-German film, *Angst*, based
on a story by Stefan Zweig. Rossellini had made it under stressful
conditions in Munich during periods between his European tour
with Ingrid Bergman in his Naples San Carlo Theatre production
of a dull opera about Joan of Arc. (In Italy, Bergman acted the
speaking role of the saint in Italian, but when it was presented
at the Stoll Theatre in London she'd act in English). I had been
scathing about *Angst* which I'd seen in Italian, entitled *La Paura*
(Fear). The film would later be re-edited with a new title, *Non credo
più in amore* (I don't believe anymore in love), and would prove to
be a flop for the second time. I was also not very kind about
Bergman's performance. The reader, who had seen the film in
German in Austria, had reproached me, asserting that Bergman
was "as always brilliant". It was the last film Bergman and
Rossellini made together. It had been made when their marriage
was breaking up (like that of the couple in the film). Rossellini's
attempt at an Antonioni-like treatment of a declining relationship was dismal. Gianni Rondolini, in a very respectful biography
of the director published in 1989, would write that the autobiographical reflection in the film had caused much "angst" to

Rossellini. The young Francois Truffaut, who adored Rossellini, would write that after making this film Rossellini had meditated abandoning the cinema. However, after an 'Indian' period, during which he made some interesting if not exceptional documentaries, Rossellini would return to feature filmmaking, mostly for TV. His best big screen feature would be *Il Generale della Rovere* (1959), with Vittorio De Sica in the lead. The best of his many TV films was made in France for ORTF, *La prise de pouvoir par Louis XIV* (1966), a masterpiece of the historical genre. But Rossellini was destined to be remembered most for *Rome, Open City, Paisà* and for his lasting influence on world cinema.

After moving from one furnished room to another in different parts of the city, and few landladies approved of my life style, I finally found a humble but agreeable room in the home of a young male nurse who worked at the Rome hospital. He and his wife were to prove friendly and patient when I was not earning much as a freelance journalist and would often be late in paying the rent. Our street, between Piazza Navona and the Campo de' Fiori, where Giordano Bruno had been burned at the stake, was the Via del Governo Vecchio, where the 'old government' of its name was apparently once the seat of the Vatican's temporal power. It runs from the palazzo, where the Pope of those years, Eugenio Pacelli, Pius XII, was born, to the palazzo of the Prince Massimo whose marriage to the English actress, Dawn Addams, had been celebrated in the City Hall on the Capitoline Hill with Chaplin as the chief guest. This was the area which the Roman dialect poet of the mid-19th century, Gioachino Belli (anticlerical but also anti-liberal) called "That of the 6 Ps": Papa (Pope), Preti (priests), Principi (princes), Poveri (the poor), Puttane (prostitutes) and Pulci (fleas). It was more or less the same when I lived there, perhaps with less fleas but with another more appealing 'P' added, 'Pizzerie'.

The Winter was proving to be the coldest that the Eternal City had experienced for half a century. In February 1956 it even snowed, which certainly added new charms to the Baroque part of town where I lived, even if it caused urban chaos and domestic discomfort. But a dramatic story coming out of Sicily made us forget our picturesque Roman freeze-up, reminding us that the icy winter in the South was so much more tragic for the many people there who were without work and lived in more pitiable conditions. Our attention was brought to their plight by news from Palermo concerning the social worker and humanist writer, Danilo Dolci, who had been arrested because, with some of his helpers, he had chosen to do a manual job that nobody had asked him to do, or would pay him for, to start repairing a road which was in a disgraceful state. It was a symbolic gesture in defence of the Italian constitution in which it is decreed that citizens have a right to work. The police thought otherwise and, when Dolci called them 'murderers', when they tried to stop him working voluntarily, he was arrested, manhandled and put into the terrifying Ucciardone jail where he shared the space of one cell, and its lice, with forty other 'criminals', many of them connected with the Mafia to which they continued to give orders from the jail. When Dolci was

Danilo Dolci, humanist and social worker.

provisionally released on bail, while awaiting trial, he organised a fast not only by himself but alongside a thousand others, unemployed or underpaid fishermen and peasants included, and this caused a nationwide uproar. For the foreign press it was a good story and I had short pieces about it in the *News Chronicle* but it needed a man on the spot to follow what was going on and to do justice to Dolci. It was a story which merited the pen of a James Cameron, the *Chronicle's* star columnist whom I had met when he came through Rome. But I was getting plenty of consolations as a journalist. I had several pieces in the *Chronicle*, including one for the fashion pages, a subject I would never have thought I could write about, and I got a call from BBC television asking me to help on a *Panorama* programme about Italy with interviews of film stars. Jenny Nicolson, the writer Harold's daughter, wife of Patrick Crosse, the Reuters bureau chief, had given them my name. We interviewed Sophia Loren on the terrace of the fabulous Crosse apartment overlooking the Forum. As the interpreter, I shared the screen with a ravishing looking Sophia and the pompous and rather voluminous Richard Dimbleby. He was a bit peeved that the camera couldn't keep the view of the Forum in the background and frame him and me with Sophia when I was

translating his questions and her answers. The next day we went to Ciampino airport to interview Anna Magnani, who was now the rage in America thanks to her success in *The Rose Tattoo*. She was making what looked like an awful Italian weepie in which she played a nun. This time I had to cope with two prima donnas, Magnani and Dimbleby.

In April, Steve Barber was appointed Assistant Editor of the *News Chronicle* and would soon return to London. For the moment I carried on in Rome as correspondent. Frankly I was not sorry to see Stephen Barber and his wife go. I respected him as a journalist and had learned a lot from him but on a personal level there was no love lost between us. My lifestyle was so different from his own hearty ways. As I was his protégé, however, I had hoped he'd support my appointment as his replacement. I counted on the likelihood that they wouldn't be able to afford to keep up a staff man in Rome. Indeed, I was soon to prove my worth.

In May, the paper decided to send me to Florence to cover the wedding of a British movie-star, Anthony Steel, to the Swedish bombshell, Anita Ekberg, whom I'd interviewed for *Films and Filming* on the set of Dino De Laurentiis's *War and Peace*. It seemed that the publicity office for a motor racing picture which Steel was shooting in Tuscany had arranged for all the leading British showbiz columnists to cover the event. Arriving in Florence I felt a bit anxious. It was my first real commission from the *News Chronicle* on which I would be working alongside professional columnists from Fleet Street. We were all booked into the Excelsior Hotel at the expense of the film company and though I was obviously the least important of the columnists present in the eyes of the publicist I was given the royal treatment too. Of course I felt at home in Florence and this gave me the whip hand, although I knew I had to be careful not to show off too blatantly my knowledge of Florence. The story was to be about the wedding of two movie stars, not about the city of Leonardo and Michelangelo.

The wedding was to take place in the City Hall, the impressive ancient Palazzo Vecchio. On arrival I got a moral uplift from seeing the copy of Michelangelo's David outside it. I had adored the statue since seeing the original indoors in the gallery of the Accademia on my first visit to Florence in 1949. For the wedding, there were about thirty reporters and twice that number of photographers. Because we were so many 'guests', the ceremony took place in the grandiose hall known as the 'Salone del '500', dating from 1495. The dear old white-bearded gentleman officiating the civil ceremony was, I learned, an elder Florentine councillor, a member of the small but important Republican Party. I was probably the only one among the foreign press to understand the significance of his gift to the bride and groom, a copy in English of a selection from the works of Giuseppe Mazzini, the 19th century political philosopher who had lived for many years as an exiled patriot in London. I doubted whether Mr. and Mrs. Steel spent their wedding night reading Mazzini!

When the wedding ceremony finished, the reporters and the star columnists for the London papers (most of whom were female), all scurried to their rooms where their portable typewriters awaited them. It was getting close to deadline time for the first editions in Fleet Street. Having already had some experience of the Italian telephone system I thought it would be prudent to enquire how the situation was for getting a collect call through to London. The girl at the hotel exchange told me she could give me a line immediately. I hesitated. My typewriter was waiting in my room but could I possibly ad-lib the story? Steven Barber had told me: "If you have to ad-lib, be sure that you know what your pay-off line will be and you'll be OK". I had already decided I would send up the event and that I'd end it with: "Tomorrow Tony Steel will be back on the real film set". So I accepted the offer to go into the minuscule phone booth (in those days you had to use them even in de luxe hotels as you couldn't make collect calls from the phone in your room). I had a harrowing twenty minutes, sweating it out as I not only had to improvise my copy but also spell out foreign names for the rather sceptical typist who was taking down my dictation. But I got through to my pay-off line and staggered out. The first of the star-columnists was waiting and already getting angry with the operator who said there'd be a problem in getting a line through to London. I headed towards my room where I had a bottle of whisky. But who should I meet on the stairs but Anita Ekberg herself! Seeing the state I was in, she waved me towards the bar saying: "Darling you look as if you need a drink!". She ordered champagne. I was thunderstruck. She was still wearing the same white dress as at the wedding, latched only to one shoulder, while her blonde hair cascaded over her eyes like the legendary peek-a-boo-bang of Veronica Lake. But to me Anita seemed a Nordic Goddess who had stepped out of one of those lakes I had visited during a magical Swedish summer I'd spent in Värmland, about which I tried to mumble a few memories to her as I sipped the champagne. Suddenly I began to tremble. What had I done? I had made fun of this goddess. Was I once again betraying my misogynistic instincts? I could imagine how sarcastic Steve Barber would be. I didn't enjoy the dinner party which followed, where all my illustrious colleagues, though furious that they hadn't been able to get through to London in time for the first edition, for which their papers were only running a picture, all agreed on how absolutely fabulous this fairy tale wedding had been. I kept silent and got drunk.

Of course I slept very badly. The next morning I got a cable from the paper which at first I didn't dare open for fear that what now seemed like a tactical blunder had cost me my future as a foreign correspondent. Instead, signed by the foreign editor, it read "Thanks for your excellent copy. Just the right touch!". I later learned that I had been the only one to have a by-line splash on the front page of the first edition. I stayed in Florence another two days to recover and to celebrate in the way I had done in this city on my first visit seven years before, glorying in the artistic treasures and finding a new Botticelli-like angel to entertain me.

When the summer of 1956 arrived, and moved into what is known in Fleet Street as the 'silly season', frivolity was the order of the day. The *News Chronicle* let me start a Rome Diary, the only other European city apart from Paris from where they printed one. I went to Cinecittà to watch Ava Gardner shooting *The Little Hut*, a film based on a French farce which ran for years in Paris and London. Ava was the most newsworthy world star of the moment and there was still echo of the fact that, earlier this year, she had been the only Hollywood celebrity to attend Grace Kelly's wedding in Monaco (many had received invitations but only Ava accepted). Though still chasing after Sinatra, who was about to start a picture in Spain for which Ava had been slated but which Sophia Loren was doing instead, (the film for which Sophia was improving her English when I interviewed her in Sorrento), Ava had accepted readily to come back to Rome where she seemed happy to be re-united with Walter Chiari, whom she'd met at the time of *The Barefoot Contessa* (1954). A small role would be found for him in *The Little Hut* even though her current co-stars were Stewart Granger and David Niven. The Italian actor was principally a comedian, but he had been much admired in a semi-dramatic role with Anna Magnani in Visconti's *Bellissima*, and was now helping Ava to forget Frankie. We had all adored Sinatra the singer and were learning to admire him as an actor. As an Italian-American male he was not one of my pin-ups. I only saw him in person once, when he was shooting a film in Italy and arrived in a helicopter at the location where the press had been invited, did his scene, waved at us and took off. *The Little Hut* took place on a desert island but was being shot entirely on a phoney looking film set. The atmosphere, suggestive of a South Sea Island's sweltering heat, was helped by the temperature on the stage at Cinecittà. The air conditioning had to be turned off when the cameras were running because the sound was being recorded live. It made a good story for my 'summer in Rome' column. But during my Roman summer, the *News Chronicle* didn't show much interest in other news coming out of Italy, apart from the arrival there of a forgettable English footballer I was asked to interview. I consoled myself by catching up on some of the new films. Among those I managed to see in English was *Love is a Many Splendored Thing* and, of course, I had a good weep. Patricia told me the story behind the film and the book on which it was based. It was an autobiographical novel by Han Suyin, a Chinese woman who had been the lover of the doomed journalist (played in the film by William Holden). Pat was in Hong Kong at the time because her husband Bill was covering the war in Korea. Hollywood has always been good in taking real-life stories and turning them into tearjerkers especially when allied with a wonderful song like the one that blessed this film.

I also saw in English *The Rose Tattoo*. Though agreeing that Magnani certainly deserved her Oscar, I was frankly disappointed by the film which displayed Tennessee Williams's sexy whimsy at its worst. A much better film that season was Pietro Germi's latest, *Il ferroviere* (The Railway Man), in which he himself acted the lead role (but is dubbed by a more experienced actor). Like Delbert Mann's *Marty*, it is about an old-fashioned but goodhearted working class man who loves his family but doesn't know how to keep up with the way society is changing. Like Paddy Chayefsky's TV play on which *Marty* was based, Germi and his principal scriptwriter, Alfredo Giannetti, were tackling a neo-realist situation with a more fictional approach and even if it inclined towards sentimentality it never went over the top. Germi was truly an off-beat director who moved the Italian cinema in new directions. It annoys me that he was not respected by critics of the left because he was not a communist, he was apparently a social democrat. For the hardline leftists this meant "sold out to the Americans". He made films to please audiences but, from the time of one of his early films, *In nome della legge* (In the Name of the Law, 1949), of which

Federico Fellini and Mario Monicelli had been co-scriptwriters, he had shown courage in tackling social issues. *In nome della legge* was the first Italian film to denounce the Sicilian Mafia.

The *Chronicle's* Foreign Editor stopped over in Rome, on his way to a holiday in Malta, to give me the once-over. We got along well and I showed him the sights, taking him to a Via Veneto night spot, Bricktop's, where the great lady herself greeted me warmly. This impressed him enormously. I told him I'd like to interview the Socialist Party leader, Pietro Nenni, who still had a pact with the Communists but who might be tempted to support a centre coalition with a more progressive programme. He promised to think about it but later told me the *Chronicle's* "diplomatic correspondent" would probably want to write about it when Nenni did decide to break the pact. Obviously I was considered good only for the frivolous side of Rome.

Before the Rome theatres closed down for the summer, I had the chance to see in Italian what was perhaps the greatest European musical of the 20th century, the Milan Piccolo Teatro's first Italian staging of the Brecht-Weill *The Threepenny Opera*. The director, Giorgio Strehler, got inspired performances from a wonderful cast. Jenny was played by the legendary Italian cabaret star, Milly Monti, a cross between Mistinguett and Lotte Lenya. Tino Carraro was Macheath (usually called Mackie Messer). Brecht had been in Milan in February for the last rehearsals and the opening night, and had been delighted with the lighthearted music-hall style Strehler gave to the production, and by Strehler's decision to update it from the 1920s American prohibition years to the present capitalist world. Brecht, who would die during the summer of 1956, had been particularly pleased that Strehler's production made the setting seem more like Chicago than Soho and this also went down well with Italian leftist critics. I was stunned by the four-hour performance. It would be revived in the 1970s with Domenico Modugno, 'Mr. Volare', as Mackie Messer, and with my own favourite pop singer, whom Strehler also adored and whom he turned into a wonderful singer–actress, Milva, as Jenny.

These were exciting times for me but I wasn't earning much from the *News Chronicle*. Even less from *Films and Filming*, but at least the latter gave me the excuse to meet some of the people I most admired in the movie world. On a hot July afternoon, I went to the Titanus studios to interview Marlene Dietrich, who was very friendly and not at all prudish about undressing in my presence (even removing the wig which was replaced by a small beret). Busy as she had been with her recital which had triumphed from Las Vegas to Berlin, Dietrich hadn't made a film since *No Highway* in 1950. She told me she accepted to do this Italian film, *The Monte Carlo Story*, not so much because of the script by Sam Taylor, who had written *Sabrina* and who was supposed to be directing (but an Italian assistant was giving directions on the set) but because it meant she'd be co-starring with Vittorio De Sica, whose films as director she said she admired and whom she considered to be: "The most romantic middle-aged man in the world today". I watched them shooting a scene supposed to be in a Monte Carlo hotel room where they'd slept together. "For censorship reasons", Marlene told me, "he has to come in to breakfast from the outside door but from the way we look at each other as I pour out the coffee, it should

Vittorio De Sica holds the chips. Marlene Dietrich whispers in his ear.

be clear to everyone that we've just made love!". Marlene was sarcastic but not unkind about the chaotic methods of Italian film-making. "All very well for those neo-realist pictures" she smiled, "but for a sophisticated romantic comedy like this a little more polish would have helped". I got the impression that she and De Sica were directing the picture themselves. Apart from the pleasure of meeting the divine Marlene, I was to get a satisfaction that was worth more than a big newspaper fee. I had told Marlene how sad I was that I hadn't been in London when she gave her recital at the Café de Paris. The next morning her chauffeur came by to give me the LP of that show, signed with a charming dedication. It was the LP I would most regret losing when my entire collection was stolen from my Trastevere flat a few years later.

I would be grateful that summer to my landlord on the mid-August bank holiday, a festa invented by the Emperor Augustus, after whom the month itself is named but which the Roman Church had turned into one honouring the Assumption of the Virgin Mary. Most Romans who are not already away on holiday flee from the boiling heat to the coast, as shown in Luciano Emmer's charming little film, *Domenica d'Agosto* (Sunday in August, 1950) where Roman families of all classes have a day of adventure at the Ostia beach. My kind landlord realised that I was broke at the time so couldn't go to the sea or even afford a decent meal in town so he invited me to join him at the hospital where he was on duty. I was able to enjoy a gluttonous meal with him and some of his merry patients which lasted right through the afternoon, a memorable proletarian feast but worthy of the pages of *Satyricon.*

Before going to Venice at the end of August, I enjoyed a few more Roman summertime pleasures. My lover, Salvatore, who had gone off to Sardinia to do his military service had returned a month later, evidently having convinced somebody to get him out as he showed me his 'congedo', a demobbing certificate. Maybe he was considered a bad example for the other conscripts! After a day on the beach at Ostia we went to the ancient Roman theatre midst the ruins of Ostia Antica to see Euripides's *Alcestis*, a play I didn't know but which intrigued me because it was supposed to have inspired Eliot's *The Cocktail Party*. I expected Salvatore to be bored but, amazingly, he became very passionate about this story of a wife who is prepared to sacrifice herself to save her husband. We intellectuals are inclined to treat the classics as mental exercises but simple uneducated people take the 'stories' very seriously, as happened certainly with the audiences in Greek times and, of course, in Elizabethan England where Shakespeare knew how to please the plebs. Salvatore had that kind of instinctive peasant intelligence but, thankfully, never developed intellectual pretensions. That summer I also took him for a weekend to Tarquinia but I didn't inflict on him the Etruscan tombs (which I'd already visited on one of my archeological trips) and we spent our time on the beach or in bed.

John Francis Lane with Salvatore, Summer 1956.

I was invited to Venice a week before the festival began to attend the fashion shows, with all expenses paid because the *NC* fashion editor had preferred to go on holiday. I was delighted because it meant I could stay over in Venice itself in a decent hotel, drink cocktails at Harry's Bar and eat in the good restaurants before being imprisoned on the Lido for the Festival. I covered the fashion shows rather superficially but was lucky to be helped by an old friend from Perugia, Luisa Spagnoli, one of the heirs of the Perugina chocolate firm. We'd met a few years ago when the company sponsored a film critics' convention in that splendid Umbrian hilltop city.

Luisa Spagnoli and
JFL in Venice.

Luisa now had her own fashion house and wasonly too happy to resume our interrupted friendship. I suspected this time she would make every effort not to let me escape her clutches. I was not altogether unwilling as indeed of all my manqué 'romances' with the female sex, from Paris to Rome, she was the one I found the most attractive and intelligent, and worthy of an attempted surrender. It was now or never for me.

Of course it proved hopeless. After a few evenings of Venetian romanticising, even a gondola ride, there came a point when I was unable to take that step further which she was obviously expecting of me. When I tried to kiss her in what we prudish English like to call the 'French' way, it made clear that I wasn't a passionate Don Giovanni even in a Venetian setting. Over dinner at La Fenice restaurant I finally told her my story. She was disappointed but understanding. Clearly it wasn't the first time a man in whom she showed an interest had turned out to be queer. When I put her on the train back to Rome the next night she got in first with the inevitable arrivederci line: "We can still be good friends, can't we?". We would indeed remain friends until she died at quite a young age.

In Venice, I had made friends at Harry's Bar with a fellow critic, Guglielmo Biraghi, a charming and sophisticated person, not at all the usual film intellectual. He had a degree in chemistry and a passion for seashells, and he was also a good film critic without political prejudices. I always read his column in the Rome daily paper, *Il Messaggero*, the paper for which I would one day cover the Academy Awards in Hollywood. He had introduced me to a new Venetian bar, Ciro's, where we'd drink many a gin fizz and be amused eyeing the high-class rent boys on the make for rich clients.

And so I braced myself for twelve days on the Lido, not this time in the de luxe setting of the Hotel des Bains, but in a medium category hotel, the Hungaria, which must have been chic in the Thirties but which was now rather dilapidated and middle class.

During the festival I got to know John Grierson who was President of a very distinguished jury which included Visconti. The meetings with Grierson were to be a landmark in my life. The director of *Drifters*, and the father of the British documentary movement, was an icon of my early film going explorations after the war in London and, though I'd been told that he was growing weary and no longer cared about film, I soon found out that he was very much alert and it was clear that he was bringing some

Scottish good sense to the discussions on the jury. He'd tell me they were the most stimulating he'd had for many a year. Apart from Visconti, the other members of his jury included the radical and influential French critic, André Bazin, and James Quinn, director of the British Film Institute. Visconti organised a showing for Grierson and Quinn of his masterpiece, *La Terra Trema*, which neither of them had seen. Grierson told me that they were both so overwhelmed that Luchino decided to give the print of the film to the archives of the BFI. In 1948, when the film had been presented at the Venice Festival, the jury gave the top prize to Olivier's *Hamlet*. Visconti had been 'forgotten' a second time in 1954 when again there had been political prejudice against a film of his, *Senso*, of which I had been one of the most avid supporters. It would be interesting to see how Visconti, now a jury member, would behave. The festival was closer this year to living up to its name as a 'Mostra', an art exhibition, than it had ever been and this was due to the new director, Floris Ammannati, a youngish Tuscan Catholic intellectual but one who was progressively minded. He had insisted on appointing a selection committee to choose the films. This enraged the Americans, still smarting from the fiasco of last year. So the MPPA, who considered it their right to choose their films to be presented at the festival, had refused to send any official entries and the silly Brits had followed suit, refusing to send John Huston's *Moby Dick*, which had been filmed in Britain (and Ireland) and which counted as a British picture. The only American major to defy the MPPA and enter a film was 20th Century Fox. They sent Nicholas Ray's *Bigger than Life*, which would, I'm sorry to say, only be rivalled as the worst film of the selection by *Suor Letizia*, the Mario Camerini film on the set of which I had helped Richard Dimbleby interview Magnani. To his credit, Camerini, a great veteran director of the 1930s, for whom I'd one day play a cameo (see p147), would say: "It's a purely commercial film. I don't know why it's in the competition".

There would in fact be much criticism of Grierson's jury, even some whistles and boos, when Visconti, as spokesman, read the verdict in Italian at the final night ceremony. The jury decided not to award the Golden Lion, that year the only major prize in the offing. It was generally felt by many of us on the Lido that there had indeed been a film which stood out above all others that year, and that was the Japanese *The Burmese Harp*, by Kon Ichikawa, a pacifist film in which a Japanese soldier in Burma, after his country's defeat, and his distress at having witnessed the savage behaviour of his fellow soldiers, stayed on and became a Buddhist monk. A long and difficult but very poetic film.

Grierson was full of enthusiasm for the new course that Ammannati's Venice had taken and was probably right in claiming that their jury's severe judgment had given extra prestige to the festival. The rejuvenated Scot stopped over in Rome after the festival and we spent a morning in his room at the Excelsior on the Via Veneto working on our festival articles for *Films and Filming* and *Cinema Nuovo*, including one by me about his encounter with a Chinese disciple on the Lido. I hadn't yet finished my own report on Venice, when I got a call from the *News Chronicle* telling me to find my way to Lugano in Switzerland where they wanted me to cover another frivolous event, the marriage of the millionaire, Baron von Thyssen to a Scottish beauty, the model, Fiona Campbell. The marriage didn't offer much stimulation for send-up as they were a handsome couple and it was a quiet ceremony with a small reception for the guests, after which we were shown round the Baron's impressive collection of art which he had inherited from his father. I filed a rather bland story but I managed at least to be a sarcastic about the wedding presents. The new Baroness had been content with "only" £50,000 worth of jewelry, whereas the former Baroness, also a British model, Nina Dyer, had kept her £400,000 worth of gifts as well as her allowance from the divorce. I took the opportunity to enjoy a few days rest in the hotel overlooking the lake and, as I had brought my typewriter and notes with me, I was able to finish my Venice Festival report for *Films and Filming*. When I got back to Rome from Lugano, in late September, the summer's 'silly season' was well and truly over. Indeed, I attended a dinner party in Via Margutta in honour of Jean-Paul Sartre but I was too awed to talk to him. I had been very influenced by him in my first years in Paris but maybe now we were all growing out of Existentialism except to remember it in its historical context. I decided to remember Sartre more for his plays, all of which I had seen and admired, and his novels, than for his philosophical treatises. He still seemed to sympathise too much with the Soviets.

These were difficult ideological times. In October 1956, the world would find itself heading towards events which would change the course of history. My Soviet Embassy friend who had picked me up at the Hotel des Bains the year before, was becoming tiresome as he was not succeeding in enrolling me as a spy. I was trying to disentangle myself from him as he began to ask for names and addresses in return for the bottles of vodka he would occasionally bring me. At the end of October, when the news of the Soviet invasion of Hungary hit the headlines, I used it as an excuse to break with him, but only after ferocious arguments during which he tried to defend Khrushchev by saying that "great changes were underway in the USSR and they couldn't accept rebellions like the one that had taken place in Budapest". I felt he didn't really know what was going on.

Then came the Anglo-French invasion of Suez to defend Egypt against the Israelian aggression (or to defend Western economic interests in the Middle East). We didn't know whose side we were on anymore, particularly those of us who didn't have the problem of political allegiance. I sympathised with the dilemma of Italian communists, and admired the ones who had the courage to take an anti-Soviet stance, but I gave up trying to make judgements. The *NC* did not publish the commissioned feature I'd written on the crisis of Italian Communism because they said I'd dedicated too much space to the personal enmity between Marshal Tito and the

PCI leader, Togliatti, which they felt wouldn't interest our readers. My Scottish writer friend, Ian Dallas, who had visited me in Rome in 1953, and had described our friendship 'as serene as a perfume in still air' in a poem he wrote on the flyleaf of Cecil Day Lewis's *An Italian Visit* which he gave me on leaving, was still trying to convince me to return to London where he was doing well writing for the BBC. But I was determined to resist in Rome. In December, shortly after my 28th birthday, I was offered a job on a big American film and therefore could start looking for an apartment again. The outside world could look after itself.

JFL and Ian Dallas
on the Spanish Steps
in Rome, 1953

By the time the Ides of March 1957 arrived, and I was celebrating the sixth anniversary of my settling in Rome, I had already been living for some weeks in Trastevere. I'd found an attic flat thanks to an ad in the *Rome Daily American*, the English language newspaper for which I was to write, mostly about theatre and films, from the mid-1960s. I was never especially proud of my connection with the newspaper even if it was useful in getting me invitations, particularly at a time when Italians were very generous with hospitality to foreign journalists. It meant I could later show my hosts something in print in return for their hospitality which I couldn't always guarantee them when I accepted on behalf of the

English publications I was contributing to. The *RDA* was founded after the war to continue what had been a paper (*Stars and Stripes*) for U.S. troops stationed in Italy after liberation. It became a daily news sheet for English-speaking residents in Rome. It would fold in the mid-1970s after it fallen into the hands of the notorious Sicilian-American banker, with mafia connections, Michele Sindona, who met a grim end in a Palermo jail. I would continue to write for other English language papers, which would rise and fall in Rome, but I would always be grateful to the *RDA* for helping me to find the dilapidated attic where, first as tenant and then as owner, I would live for the next four decades.

The job which enabled me to earn enough to rent the attic was in the publicity department of a film called *Legend of the Lost*, directed by Henry Hathaway. It was produced by a company owned by John Wayne, who co-starred with Sophia Loren and Rossano Brazzi. I had been offered the job while attending a press conference for *Boy on a Dolphin*, a 20th Century Fox film just completed in Greece and starring Loren and Alan Ladd. I had first met the publicist, a good friend and fellow homosexual, David Hanna, when he was working with Ava Gardner (of whom he would write an honest biography). David needed someone to look after the stills department and to stand in for him at Cinecittà when he was away on location in Libya. I had accepted his offer willingly even though working in publicity was not one of the more dignified ways for a journalist to earn a living. But unlike that previous mundane office job with the FAO-UN, which had permitted me to live for half a year in my own place in an elegant residential area of Rome, this one would at least get me into Cinecittà. I was finally 'inside' the film world of which till then I had only been an outside observer.

I started work in January 1957 and, as soon as I collected my first month's salary, I was able to move into my new home which, for the moment, I could only enjoy in the evenings and weekends because a car came to pick me up at 8 a.m. every weekday and I was at the studios all day. Fortunately my friend, Salvatore, after his brief stint as a military conscript, was happy to re-appear in my life, especially now that I had a new home. He had managed rather well and, not surprisingly seeing his masculine charms and his knack for getting around, he had made many more influential friends than me. Among his many admirable attributes was an instinctive flair for coping with domestic problems. Our new 'home' was not as comfortable as the one we had before even though it was in an historically more fascinating part of Rome. To say it was dilapidated was an understatement. It was an environmental disaster. At the time, the miserable dwellings on the first three floors were let on blocked leases to Roman families who had been there for decades and I'd see the elder folk die one by one. The first to go was an old lady on the third floor whom we never saw but some relative came to visit her every day. Next to go was the husband of the polite but inquisitive lady on the first floor. The two rooms on the second floor (one with a small kitchen and a toilet on a precarious balcony like all the old houses in Trastevere) were inhabited by two sisters, one of whom had a companion who worked until late at night and she'd start cooking his supper around midnight so that the stink of frying oil filled the stairs all night. We also had to endure the noise of the colourful dialect obscenities they shouted at each other and sometimes at me or my friends when we passed by on the stairs, catching the ladies in their underwear going backwards and forwards from one room to the other. Usually however they were respectful towards me and they became accustomed to, even perhaps envious of, the flow of often glamorous young men visiting me. A bakery on the ground floor which often spouted soot on to our terraces from a chimney up the back wall would eventually be closed. When Trastevere became fashionable, later in the century, it would be turned first into an arts and crafts shop and then into a yogurt milk bar. When I moved into the attic it was divided into two small flats, one of which was let to me. My side had an adequate bathroom but I had no kitchen. Near the entrance door, which led straight into the bedroom, there was, however, a gas main so I was able to install a 'cooking corner' under the stairway which led to the second floor. I'd leave my door open when I was cooking, adding my culinary odours to those coming from below. My half of the terrace overlooked the many times rebuilt church dedicated to San Crisogono, a martyr beheaded under Diocletian. Stephen Langton, Archbishop of Canterbury from 1207, had been titular cardinal of the original church before it was rebuilt by a Borghese Pope. I welcomed this link with my native East Kent, but would come to curse Langton's church when its bells sounded the hours and played a monotonous tune at mass times, particularly disturbing on early Sunday mornings. Salvatore soon found friendly local painters, carpenters and electricians to make improvements to the flat. It wasn't exactly a domestic paradise but for me it was a 'home' across the Tiber.

On his terrace in Trastevere, John Francis Lane and a visitor from Norway, the actor Toralv Maurstad.

Chapter 3

When I had free time, I began to get to know Trastevere and learn about its past. It was the oldest part of Rome still inhabited by descendants of the plebs of the Caesars' times and was the only area habitable in the Middle Ages. Presumably Dante would have slept there and Francis of Assisi would have found a pigsty to sleep in while waiting to be received by the Pope. There are buildings named after both of them. The Trastevere district begins at Porta Portese where, in the time of the Victorian English traveller, Augustus Hare, there were still vineyards under its arches, but now every Sunday there's a flea market. During my years as a theatre critic, I'd see the birth under one of the arches of an avant-garde theatre managed by a talented young director, Giancarlo Nanni, and his actress partner (on stage and off) Manuela Kuster-mann. I'd dedicate a lot of praise to Manuela in 1972 when writing a review in the Italian magazine, *Europeo*, of Nanni's production of Wedekind's *Spring Awakening*, which I'd seen at the Venice Theatre Festival. In that article I described Manuela as: "the Duse of the Underground". I would be severely reproached for that description when the production was brought to Rome by the city's leading traditional theatre company, housed in the Argentina Theatre. The management put up posters all over the city with quotes from my article and the title: "How the Duse acts today". Unsurprisingly this upset leading stage actresses of the time. I had complemented Nanni and Kustermann with that misquoted phrase at a moment when the experimental theatre groups were concentrating so much on visual effects that the presence of actors often didn't seem to count any more. Manuela was one of the new generation of Italian actresses who made their presence felt even when performing for directors using classic plays as pretexts for their own fantastical ideas. Good acting performances in unusual theatrical spaces would always help audiences feel they were in a theatre not a madhouse. She had been able to gain from (and survive his sadistic treatment) the experience of playing Ophelia in the first *Hamlet* of the most egocentric, but creatively inspired, actor-director of the new Italian theatre, Carmelo Bene (who earlier had opened a theatre club in Trastevere where he staged and acted in his outrageously daring 'play' called *Christ '63*, which I didn't get to see. The police closed it after the first performance). I'd one day see Manuela herself play Hamlet and acquit herself admirably in the vast open-air venue of Taormina's Greek theatre. But in my early times as a Trastevere resident, the Fede theatre, which she and Giancarlo Nanni had managed courageously, not only for their own productions, would become the focus point for the Italian contribution to the movement that was changing theatrical tastes round the Western world. Between the 60's and 70's some of the most significant experimental theatre groups found space there and I was pleased to be living in the area that had become the off-Broadway of Rome.

The central area of Trastevere, where I had come to live, can be reached by various bridges, of which only two of those remaining intact have antique stones. One was built by Caligula to lead to his garden on what is now the Vatican side. The other leads from the embankment of what was once the Ghetto, and is still the Jewish district (and has excellent restaurants). It reaches our side by crossing the Isola Tiberina, the island on the Tiber. This island has mythological connections to a son of the prolific Apollo. Ovid tells the tale that the Romans in 291 BC, desperate because the city was being depopulated by a plague, sent its emissaries to Delphi to seek the God's advice. He told them to go to Epidaurus and seek out Apollo's son (by Coronis), Aesculapius, who had a reputation as a healer and who might consider helping them. The legend goes that Aesculapius turned himself into a snake and boarded their ship. When the ship reached the Tiber at this point, the snake took refuge on the island and the plague ended abruptly.

The grateful Romans built a temple to his memory, parts of which remain under the church later dedicated to Saint Bartholomew, whose relics are buried there. Bartholomew was also associated with healing and is the patron saint of the medical profession. Years later, on a visit to Rome, when I was no longer a resident, I entered the church for the first time. It was full for Sunday mass, mostly with young people whom I learned were from a good-willed charitable community. I bought a booklet in English which told the story of "a thousand years of history and art" but which, inevitably, only gave a brief mention to Aesculapius who had landed there two thousand years earlier.

In the mid-17th century, a hospital was built on the island and it is still today managed by the friars known as the Fatebenefratelli, the 'do-good-brothers'. I didn't enter the hospital until the early 1990s, when I was carried into it on a stretcher, the victim of a careless woman driver who had knocked me down and snapped my fibula and tibia in two. The do-good-brothers nursed me at a price, and, the surgeons who liked to think they'd inherited the healing powers from Bartholomew rather than Aesculapius, performed a rather clumsy job mending my broken leg. It was this accident, and the effect it had on my climbing the four flights to my attic, that would prompt my decision to abandon Rome in 1997.

It seemed appropriate to me that in addition to the ancient bridges there should also be a modern bridge leading to Trastevere named after Garibaldi, of whom there is a statue (which I could espy from my terrace) on the Janiculum hill where the great Risorgimento hero had begun his defence of the ill-fated Roman Republic of 1848-49. Those who cross the Tiber today by the Ponte Garibaldi arrive first in a piazza where there is a statue of the modern Roman poet, Gioachino Belli, whose verses I had first discovered when I was living in the district he called the "6 Ps". I was always pleased to find this white marble statue of the top-hatted Belli greeting me every time I crossed the Tiber. The

Roman dialect of Belli's witty and often irreverent sonnets was that spoken in Trastevere, the 'cockney' of Rome, a language I would soon begin to understand even if I never succeeded in speaking it because I lacked a rolling 'r'. I heard it spoken often enough by my neighbours who sometimes showed some of Belli's humour even if none of his poetic gifts. The most chic house on the island is the one where Princess Margaret's friend, Judy Montagu, lived. Its front door would be used by Antonioni in *L'avventura* when we see Lea Massari leaving for the cruise where the girl she plays will disappear. There was also a simple family trattoria on the island which, in my time, was still quite cheap and I often ate there. I remember that when my Neapolitan friend was in Rome for Easter we ate there on Good Friday and, perhaps out of disrespect towards the Christian tradition of not eating meat on that day, we ordered an entrecôte steak. They served us but the steak was probably not fresh. We had stomach ache that evening.

In those first months in my new home, while Salvatore was still trying to put the place in order, I continued to write for the *News Chronicle* and *Films and Filming*, even though I was stuck out at Cinecittà studios all day and couldn't attend press conferences in town. I'd only been able to escape from Cinecittà for a few days to cover the end of the trial of the Montesi scandal which had wracked Italian society since 1953. Some leading figures of Italian society, including a well-known film composer, Piero Piccioni, the son of the Christian Democrat Foreign Minister, had been accused of drugging the Montesi girl and leaving her naked corpse on the beach. They were acquitted for lack of sufficient proof. While on that trip to Venice for the trial, I managed to get to the La Fenice theatre, where I was lucky enough to see Laurence Olivier and Vivien Leigh in Peter Brook's bizarre production of that least appealing of Shakespeare's tragedies, *Titus Andronicus*. Nevertheless, it was an enthralling theatrical experience. Sir Larry was in great form but I'm afraid that Vivien, bless her heart, who I had always adored, was more impressive after Lavinia's tongue had been cut out. Her squeaky little voice, which had been fine for Scarlet O'Hara and Blanche du Bois, was inadequate for even the Bard's least inspiring verses. This time I didn't send roses backstage as I had done as a boy in London after seeing her for the umpteenth time in Thornton Wilder's *The Skin of Our Teeth.* I still treasured the memory of her graciously receiving me in her dressing room and I preferred to remember her that way.

Of course from my daily contacts at Cinecittà with film people working there, and the gossipy grapevines, I could provide some film stories to the *Chronicle* without needing to betray my promise to David Hanna not to report gossip from our set. In Rome, frivolous stories were never difficult to find. Thanks to Salvatore, who took me there on his vespa, I succeeded in gatecrashing an exclusive press invitation to the villa of Gina Lollobrigida on the Appian Way where she announced her pregnancy. I also interviewed Dawn Addams, who had been my neighbour in the '6 Ps' area. Dawn had just come back from London where she'd been playing the female lead in Chaplin's new film, *A King in New York.* I called on her at the Palazzo Massimo and, after we'd exchanged a few giggles, she gave me colourful details about working with the great Charlie, whom she had first befriended in Hollywood in the 1930s, and who had come to Rome for her wedding to the Prince at the church of the Aracoeli on the Capitoline Hill. I got an item about her in the *Chronicle* and my interview would be published in the special Chaplin issue of *Films and Filming* (August 1957). A pity the film was such a let-down.

When the Spring came, my Roman attic began to seem a little less ramshackle and we could invite friends to eat and drink on my half of the terrace. I had acquired a record player on which we could listen to the first rock 'n roll records from London which pleased the local boys but my Anglo-American friends preferred those of musicals like *The Boy Friend* and my treasured LP of

Dietrich's Café de Paris recital. I didn't have a TV set as it was not yet a domestic necessity. One could go to a local pizzeria to watch important events, particularly big soccer matches when the fellow pizza devourers were usually good company.

The *Legend of the Lost* unit came back from Libya to shoot interiors to Cinecittà. I got on very well with Sophia Loren. She remembered our meeting in Sorrento, when she was acting with De Sica in the third of the *Bread, Love and...* films and taking a crash course in English. She laughed when recalling the BBC interview with Richard Dimbleby. By the time she made *Legend* Sophia had no need for an interpreter, having all but mastered the language. She kept everyone happy with her good Anglo-American-Italian humour.

I became very friendly with Rossano Brazzi and his adorable chubby wife, Lidia, a happy middle-class Italian couple unspoiled by his Hollywood successes. I interviewed them for an Italian magazine and took a photographer to their terrace. I got on less well with John 'Duke' Wayne. I had never thought much of him as an actor (except under John Ford's direction) but he was a Hollywood icon even if off-screen he was rather too hearty and too politically reactionary for my taste. Even so, I did appreciate the professional self-irony he showed when he came to my office one day to inspect the photo contacts to make sure I was eliminating those which revealed the lines on his neck. "That's why I always wear a scarf in my movies", he confessed quite frankly. As for Hathaway, he was a competent Hollywood craftsman but considered something of a joke by the Italian crew. When he arrived on the set every morning he'd bellow out the only words he knew in Italian: "Buon Giorno! Tutti contenti?" to which in unison they'd reply not without sarcasm: "Siiiiii!"

When I finally wrapped my job on *Legend of the Lost*, I found time again to travel for my own pleasure. I went to Milan to see the new international opera star, Maria Meneghini Callas, at La Scala in Visconti's stupendous production of Donizetti's *Anna Bolena*, an opera which seemed to have been written specially for a diva of her calibre. The other principals had their big moments and space for applause but she had the big stage all to herself for the tragic finale and the neverending curtain calls.

In June of 1957, I saw Fellini's new film *The Nights of Cabiria* which seemed to me his best so far. Dino De Laurentiis had given me the script to read when I had interviewed him the year before. He was asking opinions on it from others because he didn't seem very convinced by it but was eager to make another film with Fellini whose *La Strada* had won an Oscar for the company of De Laurentiis and Carlo Ponti, each of whom was now going his own way. I had told Dino that I thought it well worth making even if I refrained from telling him that I didn't care much for Giulietta Masina who was obviously going to play the pathetic prostitute. But I was very pleased that the film turned out so well and that this time Federico succeeded in removing some of the sentimental pathos from his wife's acting. I was so impressed by the film that I wrote an article for *Films and Filming* in which I tried to explain to the readers, who had written letters complaining about my severe treatment of *La Strada*, why this time I felt Fellini had succeeded where, in my view, he had failed with *La Strada*. I would see *La Strada* often, impressed always by Anthony Quinn's performance. He was well dubbed into Italian. Maybe Quinn's Mexican blood helped him to convey the brute insensitivity and the subsequent remorse of Zampano. For years I would be reproached by Fellini and his admirers for my negative reaction to the film at the 1954 Venice Festival, when I had openly sided with those defending Visconti's masterpiece, *Senso*, which had been deliberately forgotten by the jury more for political than for artistic reasons. That was the occasion where, to my dismay, I discovered that in Italy you always have to take sides. It had started in the Middle Ages with the wars between the Guelfs and Ghibellines and then moved into the artists territory: Michelangelo or Raphael, Bernini or Borromini, Rossini or Verdi, and had continued through to our

Fellini with Giuletta Masina

times when we were obliged to choose between Visconti and Fellini, and more frivolously, Lollo and Loren. Though I had been on Visconti's side over *Senso*, I would find myself taking sides with Fellini in choosing between *Le notti di Cabiria* and *Le Notti Bianche*. But I still loved both these great directors and they both knew it, even though they did get angry when I was less enthusiastic about one of their films.

During the last week of July, Trastevere celebrates its big summer festival which they call the Festa de Noantri which means the feast of 'us others'. I had been over to the festa once or twice in previous years but now that I could consider myself one of 'us others' there was a reason to follow it more closely. The festa starts on a Saturday afternoon with an almost ceremonial procedure in the presence of the mayor and those whom the Italians love to call "the authorities". The famous plumed-hatted Bersaglieri, who have a small barracks in Trastevere, do their traditional run down the main street blowing their bugles to the delight of the crowds who come out of the shops to applaud, while the clerics and the womenfolk gather for the religious procession which winds its way round the whole ward. The ladies gathering in the square in front of Sant' Agata, under my terrace, are less interested in applauding the inauguration of the civic ceremony with the plumed hated soldiers than in the next stage of the afternoon's events. The 'authorities', priests and carabinieri, line up for the procession. When the statue is finally carried out of the church, the bells ring and the statue is lifted up three times, applauded by the ladies as if she were a popular singer. The heavy tier on which the statue is placed now starts its long journey round all the streets of Trastevere. Obviously this was a 'show' which could be particularly appreciated from my grand balcony viewpoint. Less spectacular was the very early morning mini-procession which took place on the Monday morning eight days later when the 'Madonna' was brought home, carried in the opposite direction through the streets. When the statue arrives outside the Sant'Agata church it is received with tears and rejoicing by the ladies who shove their way into the small church to welcome their Madonna back. She's only been a hundred yards away across the piazza to the big church for the week but her devotees behave as if she'd been to America. After a brief blessing from the archpriest of the Carmelites Confraternity, the ladies move out to the café under my terrace which, for the morning, puts out a score of extra tables so the devotees can devour a good cappuccino and croissant for their breakfast. A locally posted carabiniere told me that coping with these devout ladies is the annual local 'duty' they dread most.

Although the festa is prompted by religious celebrations, for the people of Trastevere, there is inevitably also a homage to the district's pagan traditions with many events in the 'panem et circenses' style, such as competitions of virile prowess, amateur theatricals with obscene improvised verses and poetry recitals in homage to Belli and the more recent Roman dialect poet, Trilussa, as well as concerts by the popular singers of the day.

In modern times, Trastevere had always been considered something of a socialist even secular area, so much so that I was told Mussolini never dared make official appearances there for fear of a hostile reception. The piazza in which I lived was named after the 19th century heroine, Giuditta Tavani Arquati, who died fighting to save the short-lived Roman republic of 1848. I would soon feel very much at home in these surroundings and I'd be treated as "one of us" by the local lads whose fortunes and misfortunes I would share. They even found a nickname for me, "Er delfino". I thought being called a dolphin in dialect was flattering though probably in spite of the affectionate intentions they were often sending me up. Though at that first festa as one of 'us others' I was only able to admire the Bersaglieri with their plumed hats from a distance during their run down the streets blowing their bugles. On another occasion I'd meet some of them roaming around with red berets replacing the plumed hats while not on duty. I offered them wine and we finished up inside the dormitory of their barracks which was next door to the church of Saint Francis. It was an exhilarating even if exhausting (and expensive!) experience. When I dropped by a bit drunk a few nights later and rang the bell I hinted to the sleepy sentinel who opened the door what had happened when I had been 'entertained' in the dormitory on another night and wondered whether he or any of his pals would be interested in a repeat performance. He very politely said "No, thank you" and closed the door with a bored but civilised smile. I wondered if the Royal Horse Guards in London, also famous for this kind of indulgence, would have behaved so politely to a tipsy midnight visitor who rang the barrack bell?

That summer I was perhaps being too generous with my entertaining. The money soon began to run out so I had to look for a new job. I found one, again in a publicity department, this time on the remake of Hemingway's *A Farewell to Arms*, starring Jennifer Jones and Rock Hudson. It was to have been directed by John Huston but he had quit just before the shoot began in the Dolomites, having objected to receiving pages and pages of Selznick's famous 'memos', detailed demands telling the director how to do his job. The film was directed by Charles Vidor, who had made *Gilda* and *Cover Girl*, two of the favourite films of my teenage years. But it was a David O. Selznick production and Selznick was The Boss. I started work when the unit got to Cinecittà after the location shooting. When Jennifer Jones, Mrs. Selznick, threw one of her tantrums she'd come storming along the corridor past my office and I'd poke my head out in curiosity. Rock Hudson would also emerge from his dressing room quizzically. After Jennifer had slammed the door behind her, we would wait to hear the first notes of *The Ride of the Valkyries* coming from her room at full blast. Rock and I would exchange a nod and a smile and knew that the rest of the day's shoot would have to wait until the Wagnerian storm subsided. When important foreign journalists came to lunch I'd be invited to join the stars, the director and Mr. Selznick himself who never stopped reminding us he had been producer of the most successful film of all time, *Gone With The Wind.*

Rock was an enchanting person and very discreet. The only time we met outside of the studios was when we happened to be visiting at the same time the Turkish Baths near the Trevi Fountain, a famous haunt for homosexuals. Naturally we pretended not to see each other. But the morning after, when Rock said his usual jovial "Good morning, John", there was a special twinkle in his eye. Not surprisingly he had had more success than me in the baths. It was the first time I realised he was what Americans then liked to call one of 'Dorothy's friends'. The world would only find out when he was dying of AIDS.

I finished my chore with the Selznick company just before the Italian mid-August Ferragosto holiday. Before our 'farewell to arms' at Cinecittà, Mr. Selznick showed us a rough cut of the film and though it was clear it was not gong to win Oscars, and was no match for Frank Borzage's impressive 1932 version of the novel, it promised to be a commercial success. Certainly this first cut was overlong (three hours) and I presumed at the time that there'd be cuts before it was released but, alas, that was not the case! After the screening we complemented everyone concerned. When you work in publicity you don't make critical observations, especially when you are employed by a David O. Selznick. But when he said formal goodbyes to the crew, and I was waiting patiently for the long-promised interview, the first thing Mr. S. would say to me after his visitors had left, would be: "All these guys are thrilled to be associated with this picture but every one of them has been angry with me at some time during the shoot". I asked him how he felt if one of them turned out to have been right to be angry. "My ego protects me" he rebutted honestly. In order to give me this interview a few hours before he and Jennifer left Rome, he ignored two secretaries who were waiting to receive the dictation

of his last memos from Cinecittà. He told me he believed that his
reputation for giving orders by memorandums was one of his
major virtues as a producer, adding: "I think it saves people a lot
of trouble and gives me time to get other things done." He brushed
off the story that John Huston had abandoned the film because he
was not used to receiving a five-page memo telling him how he
should direct the picture, but admitted it had cost him six hundred
dollars to send a cabled memo to New York to explain why Huston
had quit. The interview was published in the January 1958 issue
of *Films and Filming* with Jennifer and Rock on the cover.

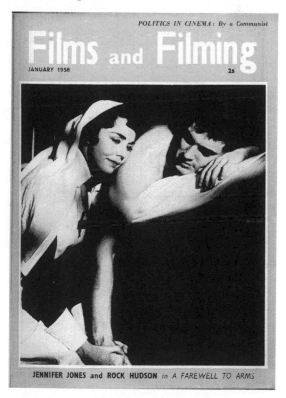

JENNIFER JONES and ROCK HUDSON in *A FAREWELL TO ARMS*

I reminded readers that the producer of GWTW had also made *Duel In The Sun* which, though cynically referred to by the press as 'Lust in the Dust', was superbly filmed by King Vidor and had become a cult movie. In his autobiography, *A Tree Is A Tree* (Vidor had given me a copy when I interviewed him during the making of *War and Peace* in Rome), Vidor wrote that Selznick's drivers went on strike when they were shooting *Duel* on a mountain in Tucson, Arizona because, in order to deliver the memos, they had to drive several times a day up treacherous mountain roads. I also wrote that Selznick deserved credit for some of his other achievements as a producer, notably that he was the first to sign Fred Astaire for a film when the future star was only known as a Broadway dancer, and it was Selznick who brought Ingrid Bergman to Hollywood after seeing her in the Swedish film *Intermezzo* which he remade in English with her and Leslie Howard.

In the summer of 1957, I went back to being a full-time journalist. I wrote an article about the Angry Young Men for a new Italian magazine in which I admitted I was sorry to be missing the movement in which some of my former pals, like Lindsay Anderson, were a part. I hadn't read any of the books or seen the plays that the English press continued to praise or argue about. However, I did find time to read a book just published in America, *On the Road* by Jack Kerouac, the literary sensation of the moment to which the Italian papers were dedicating a lot of attention. I enjoyed Kerouac's language but frankly didn't feel much sympathy for his beatnik characters. I was not the kind who had ever wanted to join the rucksack brigade, as I called these adventurous lads who, unlike the British 'Angries', were not protesting against our sick society but enjoying being part of it.

I hadn't got much lineage in the *News Chronicle* that summer but I did manage to convince them to let me cover the Venice Film Festival. I got hospitality for the full two weeks and double accreditation for *News Chronicle* and *Films and Filming*. During the many years I would live in Italy, as a journalist interested in cinema, attending film festivals would be one of my major professional duties. I would be asked to sit on, even preside over, festival juries, and enjoy the hospitality in beautiful places I would otherwise probably never have visited. Often the events were made memorable by non-filmic occurrences, such as at a festival of anti-fascist Resistance Films at Cuneo in Piedmont in the 1960s, where, as President of the Jury, I had to make a diplomatic speech at the last night ceremony to calm down tempers rising within opposing political factions in the audience. Though very few of the films in the official selection of the 1957 Venice festival were worthy of inclusion, a fact the jury presided over by René Clair would comment upon in its final verdict, there were consolations, particularly from the East. The first of these was Akira Kurosawa's Japanese version of *Macbeth*, which he called *Throne of Blood*, starring the extraordinary actor of *Rashomon* and *Seven Samurai*, Toshiro Mifune. I was introduced to Mifune during a Soviet delegation party and I took him into a corner with his producer, Mr. Toho, and an interpreter and got a good interview. Mifune was a great charmer, a sort of oriental Marlon Brando.

The most memorable event of the 1957 festival was the invitation to the press to attend a special Mass for the cinema given in Saint Mark's Cathedral by the Archbishop of Venice, Cardinal Angelo Roncalli. The year before, many of us had missed the somewhat low-key mass held on the Lido by His Eminence, but we were glad of the excuse to take the trip over to Venice and, in the inspiring setting of the wondrous cathedral, hear this lovely old gentleman, with the face of a peasant, speak endearing words about the mission of the cinema. The next time I saw Cardinal Roncalli would be a year later when I'd be present as a newspaperman in St Peter's for his enthronement as Pope John XXIII.

The most eagerly awaited film of the festival was Visconti's *Le Notti Bianche* (White Nights), an adaptation of Dostoevsky's story set in St Petersburg. Visconti's film was faithful only in its Italian title (in English it was translated literally as *Sleepless Nights*). The film was a courageous production enterprise by Visconti and his producer, Franco Cristaldi, who set up a co-operative with actor, Marcello Mastroianni, and the scriptwriter, Suso Cecchi d'Amico. When I was working at Cinecittà on the John Wayne film I had admired the creative atmosphere surrounding the Franco Cristaldi production even though Visconti was shooting on a closed set. I had managed to peep into the largest of the studio's stages, Teatro 5 (the sound stage which became famous as Fellini's favourite working site) where Mario Chiari, assisted by Mario Garbuglia, had reconstructed the neon-lit modern streets and the less illuminated back alleys, bridges and canals in the seaport of Leghorn to which Visconti had transferred the action. But on the screen, in spite of the splendid black-and-white cinematography of Giuseppe Rotunno, it all seemed so artificial. Visconti failed to mix effectively the dream-like literary artificiality with moments of realistic modern life: the scenes of the denim-clad youths roaming the streets on motor cycles or dancing rock 'n roll in the back room of a late night bar. Marcello Mastroianni had joined the production co-operative to play a role which he hoped would get him away from his typecasting as a romantic lead in Italian lightweight comedies. He gave a convincing performance as the shy daydreamer and, even though there were moments when he slipped back into that identity, he let his hair down in other scenes such as in the dance hall sequence where we glimpsed a more offbeat Marcello. He played a young man under the illusion that a young woman, he picked up during one of his 'sleepless nights' wandering the streets, will give up waiting for the return of a foreigner with whom she had fallen in love a year before. The man is back in town and she is trying to find him. In flashbacks, he turns out to be Jean Marais who gives the impression of having escaped from a 1930s French film.

There's a lot wrong with *Le Notti Bianche*, but perhaps the main weakness was the performance of Maria Schell. She had impressed us all as Zola's heroine in René Clément's *Gervaise* for which she had won the 1956 Venice Best Actress award, given by the jury of which Visconti had been a member. But this time she overplayed the whimsy. I was never forgiven by Visconti for later describing her as a "Swiss Giulietta Masina". It was an unkind thing to write. At her press conference I had been irritated to hear her reply with a smirkish smile when asked her nationality: "Je suis Suisesse".

A few days after *White Nights* we saw the Indian film, *Aparajito*. I shared the enthusiasm of my fellow Britons for the work and person of Satyajit Ray. His film made us re-live the excitement of the discovery of the De Sica and Rossellini neo-realist films which, in fact, had been Ray's inspiration. *Aparajito* was the second film of a trilogy which began with *Pather Panchali*, a revelation at the Cannes Festival two years before. The new film was not such a total masterpiece as the first, it was clearly an intellectual's film and was rather cold in its treatment of feelings, but it was a beautifully refreshing lesson in simplicity. Based on an autobiographical novel by Bandopadhyay, the two films, and a third which Ray told us he was preparing, would tell the story of a Hindu boy's growing up. The three films were scored by the iconic sitar virtuoso and composer, Ravi Shankar, who, in the 1960s, would become friends with George Harrison and John Coltrane, among other Western musicians and would teach them to play the sitar. The jury presided over by René Clair voted unanimously to give the Golden Lion to the Indian. At the prize-giving ceremony Visconti behaved disgracefully in accepting his Silver Lion, which was only second prize, and made a sarcastic remark that offended Clair. Luchino knew that Clair had hated his film. Penelope Houston, editor of *Sight and Sound*, and the British representative on the jury, joined me with other British colleagues to sit with Ray at the café outside the Palazzo Del Cinema with the Golden Lion on the table in front

62

of us. Penelope told me that Ivan Pyryev, the Russian jury member, also hadn't liked Visconti's film and had only agreed to give it his vote for the Silver Lion if the jury also gave the award for best actress to a Russian (Dzidra Ritenberga as a fishwife in the Maxim Gorky adaptation, *Malva*). Ray told me he was glad he had saved his film for presentation at Venice after reading what I'd written in *Films and Filming* the year before about Grierson's admiration for how Ammannati was reforming the festival. Everyone (including Luchino and his clan) saw us sitting with Ray when they came by on their way to the end of festival party at the Excelsior Hotel which we all snubbed. It wasn't surprising that my chances of becoming an honorary member of the Visconti clan were now definitively shattered. I would one day go to Calcutta and be invited to dinner at Satyajit's modest home in what was considered the middle class district of that tragic city but, in all the years I was to live in Rome, I'd never be invited even for a coffee at Count Visconti's splendid villa on the Via Salaria.

Satyajit Ray's *Aparajito* (1956)

Chapter 4

In Venice, I had been hearing a lot from British friends about the 'angry' new English writers and I felt the need to catch up. When I got back to Rome after Venice I went straight to the English bookshop in Via del Babuino to buy Kingsley Amis's novel, *Lucky Jim*, published three years before, which I felt ashamed not to have yet read (I see my copy was the 18th reprint). I could understand why the Amis novel was a bestseller. It was a very enjoyable read and its satire of provincial cultural life in Britain made me squirm while I laughed. I wasn't sure how Amis's rather unsympathetic Jim could be considered worthy of respect as a rebel against the educational system in the UK. From what I had read I suspected that another Jim, the one invented by John Osborne, was probably more topical but I hadn't yet seen *Look Back in Anger* nor even read the play. I was now more than ever convinced I had to try to fit in a visit to London this autumn.

Though I was rather broke, I decided to take the plunge and go to London, persuading my mother to fork out my fare from the money we had in a Swiss bank "for emergencies". With the excuse of the screening of Visconti's *White Nights* at the London Film Festival, where he would be present with Mastroianni and Suso Cecchi d'Amico, I flew over for my first visit since 1952. This visit was to prove quite traumatic but fruitful for me even if after a month I was glad to get back to Trastevere. After a warm good-bye from Salvatore in the Roman sunshine, I was met at a cold and melancholy London airport by my Scottish writer friend, Ian Dallas, who, for some time, had been trying to convince me to give London a new try. I was very glad to see him again, but I felt very much like a tourist in London. On arrival at Heathrow, I immediately became a very angry young man because the customs made me pay what amounted to all the English cash I had in my pocket as duty on a leather handbag I had brought for my mother. In London

I was an outsider again even if Ian was putting me up in a friend's home in Chelsea, in a lovely street overlooking a cricket field.

The first night we went to dinner in a Greek Cypriot restaurant and ate well, but I insisted in ordering a bottle of Italian vino rather than drink that awful Greek stuff they dare to call wine. I realised that London was changing at least in its eating habits as people now seemed more interested in eating decently, but preferably in foreign restaurants. The next morning we went to the Savoy for Visconti's press conference and I felt cheered by being with Italians again. We went to the Italian embassy for a reception in his honour at which Sophia Loren was also present. She was in London for the opening of *The Pride and the Passion*. She insisted on my going to see it (I would do so the following week. Her English was okay but the film was a dud).

The early evening screening of *White Nights* went down well at the wonderful new National Film Theatre under the Waterloo Bridge. I remembered how, as a teenager, I used to wander down to the embankment, while waiting to catch a train from Charing Cross to our home in Orpington, and I'd look across the river and wonder why there was such a barren space on the South Bank. Many things were indeed improving in London! During the screening, I felt Luchino's penetrating eyes piercing me from two rows back, eager to see if I was betraying a more positive reaction than I had shown at Venice. Of course I gave him the satisfaction of seeing me react favourably, at least to the scene in the dance hall when Mastroianni goes wild. I did in fact appreciate the film more this time, in spite of still hating Schell. He gloated about it when I saw him later at the dinner which was given at a fashionable Italian restaurant. Afterwards we all went to a party Ian had laid on for Luchino and the others. As he and I bundled Mastroianni into a taxi, Marcello quite excitedly asked me: "Who are we going to meet?" He, of course, was not yet as famous as he would be when he next came to London, for the opening of *La Dolce Vita*, but it was already clear by then that he was a somewhat more offbeat Latin Lover and a better actor than Rossano Brazzi who, at that moment, was the Italian male star most admired in London. The only 'star' I was able to introduce him too was the charming up-and-coming young actor, John Fraser, a good friend of Ian's who would become a good friend of mine when he came to Rome the following year. John was to play Bosie in Ken Hughes's film about Oscar Wilde. He was learning Italian so he and Marcello enjoyed themselves trying to talk shop.

Marcello Mastroianni in Visconti's *White Nights*.

On my first Sunday in London for five years I enjoyed a quiet day roaming around the city where I had had many joys and sorrows before I was twenty. It was a sunny day and this made London seem more agreeable. I was amused by the speakers at Hyde Park Corner. They were more fun to listen to than political speakers are in the Italian piazze who take their politics so seriously. Sunday dinner in a pub with roast beef and two veg almost reconciled me to English cooking! On Monday I went to the *News Chronicle* office and was given a warm welcome by the foreign-desk people who finally saw me in the flesh. I was taken to lunch by my godfather in the newspaper world, Steve Barber, now the paper's assistant editor. He seemed somewhat less arrogant than he had been in Rome. We ate in a Fleet Street pub where I gluttonously devoured another worthwhile English dish, steak and kidney pie, but instead of ordering a cooled lager I wanted to show I was 'one of the boys' and drank a pint of lukewarm mild and bitter. Though my father was from Faversham in the heart of the hopland county, I had never really enjoyed English uncooled beer. We were joined by Jimmy Cameron who, as always, had important things to say. This time he talked passionately about the anti-nuclear campaign. It was the 'cause' of the moment among British intellectuals. He told me he was writing a book about 1914, on the madness of wars. (When published I'd read it eagerly and I'd find it very inspiring). They both kindly complemented me on how I was covering Italy for the paper. They didn't know that I'd been playing truant with my publicity stints but as I earned so little from the *Chronicle* I don't think they could have reproached me.

That evening, Ian had arranged for us to take the Visconti gang to see Olivier in John Osborne's *The Entertainer* at the Palace Theatre. I felt that Suso and her daughters appreciated it more than Luchino but we were all more enthusiastic for Larry's dazzling music hall performance than we were for the play. Ian knew the Oliviers very well and took us backstage afterwards. It was rather embarrassing for us all. Luchino and Larry had never met before, though Larry told him that Vivien was a good friend of Luchino's brother, Luigi, the future Duke of Modrone, and had stayed with Luigi and his actress wife, Laura Adani. Luchino didn't speak English and Larry's French was not very good so Ian, Suso, and I did most of the talking, while Suso's bright daughters Caterina and Silvia silently ogled at Larry. Sir Larry, still in his make-up and wearing a beautiful oriental satin dressing gown, offered sherry and cigarettes from a box which revealed they were a new brand named after him for which he apologised. We were all relieved when the meeting was over. When Ian and I slipped back to thank him, Larry made his excuses and campily said: "Darlings, I'm sorry, but I'm not very good at being Noel in the dressing room".

When I reflected on the play, I admitted that I had been impressed by the sheer theatrical force which Osborne put into it. As an actor himself he knew how to write good parts for actors. It only weakened when he must have started thinking he should live up to his newly won fame as the demagogue of the Angry Young Men and try to say something important, he added in a bit about the war in Suez. During the week, I finally got to see *Look Back In Anger* which was still playing but with a new cast. It was a bit of an anti-climax to see a play that had already become something of an historical landmark. I could appreciate why it had won praise and controversy, for it did in fact touch raw sores in contemporary British society and showed the difficulty the new generation were having in adapting to a Britain that was no longer Great, something our Upper Class Establishment refused to be resigned to. But I could also understand why others, like Ian, found its theatrical form and even the 'angry' dialogue rather second-rate. Noel Coward and Galsworthy had written 'angry' plays earlier in the century. One felt that Jimmy Porter and his pal, though they ran a sweet stall, behaved like frustrated repertory actors bored with their provincial life, which was Osborne's own background.

I had to tell Ian again that I wished he could put some of his own resentments into a play. In reply he gave me to read his latest play, about Rimbaud, which I read during the coming weekend when I finally got to Eastbourne to visit my mother. I had first read Rimbaud when I was a student in Paris, thanks to a short but passionate affair with a sixteen year old who picked me up when we were watching a programme of avant-garde films in a Quartier Latin cine-club. He wrote poetry and thought he was a new Rimbaud and that I'd be his Verlaine. It's true he had a scruffy appearance and an angelic face but the only other thing he had in common with the author of *Une saison en enfer* was that he didn't care for hygiene. Fortunately, unlike the real Rimbaud, he didn't have lice in his hair as Mme Verlaine discovered when she had to clean up the bed where the young poet had slept while staying in their Paris home. 'My' Rimbaud had been very helpful when, at the film school in Paris, I had to prepare in French what they call a *découpage* of a film scene. Having just read Enid Starkie's very fine biography of the poet (which I see on the flyleaf I dated 'Spring 1949', the time of my brief 'saison en enfer' with that boy), I reproduced the first evening's disastrous dinner when the disreputable young Arthur arrived Chez Verlaine. That occasion wasn't included in Ian's play, which concentrated on the more violent exchanges between the two lovers during their travels, first in England and then to Brussels, where the elder poet almost killed his young friend. Ian also used the far from poetic violent language they exchanged during their lovemaking and fighting, including four letter words which wouldn't be accepted on the London stage for many years yet. Indeed, as far as I know, this play would never be performed or published and, though I have copies of all of Ian's early plays, I don't seem to have kept this one. This is a pity because it was the best play Ian had written. In those theatrical times it was better to be sub-Brecht than sub-Eliot. We had both read and appreciated Eliot's lecture on 'Poetry and Drama' but only a poet of his quality could get away with writing family dramas in verse and make them enthralling theatre.

The reunion with my mother in Eastbourne was very moving. The last time I'd visited her she'd been living in a semi-detached house on the Sussex Downs and it had been possible to take lovely windswept walks towards Beachy Head, but she had recently moved into a flat in the town where a room had been prepared for me and what belongings of mine remained were stored there. My mother had evidently destroyed some of my teenage diaries which she had probably read, and had not liked my salacious fantasies, but I found a naive diary I had written at the age of ten during the first weeks of September 1939 when I had been evacuated from my school in London to Reigate in Surrey, the first time I had ever been separated from my parents. In those childhood pages I was a bit startled to find early traces of the 'JFL egocentrism' which I am sorry to say would stay with me throughout my life. Though Eastbourne seemed just a rather posh resort for upper middle class elderly people, I went out alone to explore the town on Saturday night where, to my surprise, indeed alarm, there were plenty of signs of the 'new permissiveness' that was sweeping through England. Though I was not yet thirty myself, I felt very old in the midst of these youngsters of the rock 'n roll generation and I felt no kind of sensual curiosity to get to know them better. I would probably have enjoyed myself more if I'd been in Brighton but, on that night out in Eastbourne, I felt very nostalgic for Trastevere where 'The Dolphin' felt more at home.

During my second week in London I had lunch with Tom Maschler who was a rising star in the publishing firmament. For MacGibbon & Kee he had edited the manual of the Angry Young authors, *Declaration*, which I had bought and found fascinating, even if the most readable pieces were not those by the more famous new authors, such as my friend Lindsay Anderson. At the time, Anderson had only made documentaries, one of which, called *Thursday's Children*, had won him an Oscar, but he had not yet made a feature film and was resentful (as he'd be all his life) against the British film industry. I preferred the essay by a lesser known 'Angry', Stuart Holroyd, who insisted that the philosopher should above all concern himself with the religious dilemma. Tom agreed that Holroyd's essay was interesting even if its author was despised by the other 'Angries'. I asked Tom what he thought would have emerged if the young romantic English poets of the early 19th century had written their *Declaration*. Tom was amused and replied frankly: "It would certainly have been better written!"

We discussed ideas for books on Italian subjects. He was interested in Italy and I was surprised to hear he had once tried vainly
to break into the Italian film industry himself. He said he was
preparing for publication a book by Danilo Dolci and this impressed
me. I had followed as closely as I could the noble but at times tragic
destiny of this impassioned and selfless social worker who had
taken on the Sicilian Mafia and the politicians involved in its
macabre refusal to give Sicily a decent face. The Mafia and their
political cronies had ruled on the island since the liberation after
the Second World War when the Americans, perhaps to please
Lucky Luciano, who had helped them with the landings, or maybe
just ingenuously because the Mafiosi had been anti-fascist. The
fascists had done their best to suppress the Mafia because they'd
considered it a risky alternative power on the island. Dolci justly
believed it was time that Sicily woke up. The introduction to the
book had been written by Aldous Huxley. I was pleased to see
that he began by describing Dolci as "a new Gandhi, a modern
Saint Francis with a degree in architecture and engineering". Tom
showed an interest in the idea of publishing Cesare Zavattini's
diaries or maybe a book on the neorealist movement. But I'd never
follow up the encouragement he gave me.

I went to the film studios at Elstree to have a coffee with Ken
Tynan who had an office there. We concluded nothing on that
first occasion but, in time, we'd prove to be useful to each other. At
Elstree, which had been taken over by ATV television, I also met
some of Ian's more amiable friends and they confirmed what I had
already sensed during this London visit, that television was the
medium at this particular moment which offered the best outlet
for creative attention. New ideas could find space in television more
easily than in the British cinema and theatre where things were
still moving slowly. It was no surprise that the new generation of
English filmmakers, led by John Schlesinger, Ken Russell and John
Boorman would start their careers by making films for television.

I spent half a day exploring Savile Row, where I had been asked to look for contacts for my weirdie Sicilian friend, Angelo Litrico, who had a chic men's tailoring place in the Via Veneto area and who wanted me to find a fashion house in London which might be interested in doing an exchange deal with him. Rather than in Savile Row itself, where they are all so posh, I aroused the interest of the management of a more middle-class establishment round the corner in Regent Street, Hector Powe. They made me a gift of the glamorous silk waistcoat I admired while visiting them. They were intrigued by the news that Angelo had offered to dress the new Soviet ruler, Nikita Khrushchev, who was not exactly one of the world's best dressed public figures. But the 'story' was a good media gimmick and indeed would be the basis for launching Litrico when I'd return with him later in the year.

I spent another weekend in Eastbourne but this time didn't venture into the town. However, I did manage to convince mother to let me have some more money from the trust fund. It was the capital which brought in her only income but she agreed it would be a good idea for me to buy a car and try to learn to drive, though she did remind me that when I was a teenager the instructor had given up on me after two lessons, and said I'd never learn to drive. I knew he was probably right but I wanted to try again. Salvatore could be my teacher, or chauffeur if I failed. Mother didn't know that Salvatore was still in my life. She had met him on a visit to Rome and not surprisingly had disapproved, especially after the boy, hoping to make a good impression, had driven us out to Tivoli in a 500 Fiat he'd borrowed but had forgotten to fill with petrol, so we were stranded on the way. I'd never learn to drive and I'd never buy a car, not for myself anyway.

In London, I went to the *News Chronicle* to say goodbye and arrived opportunely as the news had just come through that Ingrid Bergman and Roberto Rossellini were now officially separating though, in Rome, we'd all known for sometime that their love affair was over. I was able to help the columnist put together a piece about The End of their love story. Their separation in professional, and perhaps private terms too, had begun in 1956 when she came to London to make *Anastasia* (for which she'd win her first Oscar since *Gaslight* in 1944) and he had gone to India where he'd met Sonali Das Gupta. While in Paris to make *Tea and Sympathy* (1956) Ingrid had met the Swedish impresario, Lars Schmidt, whom she'd marry after the annulment of her marriage to Rossellini.

My goodbye to London was rather sad not because I was really sorry to leave but because on my last night Ian took me to a concert by Judy Garland. It was a total disaster. Poor Judy was, by now, in bad shape physically, and vocally a faint shadow of herself. It was a case of 'A Star is Dead'. Fortunately I had the records of the 1954 George Cukor film of *A Star Is Born* and I'd prefer to remember that Judy.

I returned to Rome by train with no particular emotion as I left the White Cliffs of Dover behind at sunset. On the way to Paris I enjoyed the company of a rather camp Cuban, who lived in Canada, who offered me champagne with the excellent genuine French meal we ate on the way to the Gare du Nord where he got off. The train transferred to the Gare de Lyon and, when eventually it was about to depart, I was witness to a touchingly dramatic farewell scene between two handsome young Italians who kissed each other passionately and wept as the train pulled out. The younger, and most attractive, of the two was the one leaving and by chance we were alone all night in the second-class compartment (I didn't have a sleeper as I was travelling 'on the cheap'). We soon got into conversation. He was a Sicilian living in Rome and while in Paris had met his friend who worked in a restaurant. Before the night was over, and we reached Turin, I did my best to console him for having left his great love behind. It was a pleasant way to welcome myself back to Italy.

The train reached Rome four hours later than I had announced in a telegram to Salvatore. He had given up waiting for me at the station. We were reunited at home. It was mid-November and our rudimentarily heated flat was beginning to feel chilly, but he soon warmed me up. In a letter to Ian, of which I kept a carbon copy, I see I tried to sum up my London visit. I didn't feel I'd achieved a great deal except to exorcise from my mind the dread that I had of returning, after so long away, to the city where perhaps I could have had a successful career in show business. But I now knew for sure that, whatever became of me, I was better off in Rome. I also realised I had to concentrate more seriously on writing something worthwhile. In London, I had read Colin Wilson's *The Outsider* and hadn't been particularly enthusiastic about it, apart from an admiration or perhaps envy for his ability to have seemingly consumed every book ever written, and I needed to be able to confess, as he does, that writing: "is a convenient discipline for subduing my stupidity and laziness". But would the temptations of my Roman life allow me this expediency?

During the last days of November, I struggled to write a news story about the war between the Italian state-controlled oil company's president, Enrico Mattei, and the Seven Sisters of petroleum power who objected to the Italian proposal of a 60–40% deal with, and in the favour of, other oil-producing countries, including the Iranians. When I interviewed Mattei and asked him how he had been able to do a deal with China, a country still not diplomatically recognised by Italy, he had replied that he didn't need to ask permission from the Rome Government. The Italian President, Giovanni Gronchi, had recently paid a state visit to Iran where he had been warmly received by the Shah, who was grateful to the Italians for having given him and Soraya hospitality during his exile in Rome. But now back in power, the Shah wanted to keep on good terms with the Americans too. It was a mistake for which the young Shah would soon pay heavily. Clearly Mattei, in spite of being honest (not always an advantage in the Italian power game), and in spite of his assertion to the contrary when he spoke to me, didn't really seem to have enough political influence in Italy to impose his will.

Something more absorbing for my attention than the Iranian oil industry was the Russian novel, *Dr. Zhivago*, just published in Italian, a world scoop for Giangiacomo Feltrinelli, the left-wing publisher (who also published Guido Aristarco's *Cinema Nuovo* to which I contributed). He had succeeded in smuggling the manuscript of Boris Pasternak's forbidden novel out of the Soviet Union. Though I have read, in Italian, some of Moravia's novels, and some of the stories by Cesare Pavese, the 700 pages of the Russian's novel were forbidding but worth the effort.

When I was still only half way through it I went, one evening, to the annual spree for the national day at the Yugoslav Embassy. Among the colleagues from the Foreign Press I met there were the Russians, already loaded with slivovitz, the Slav vodka. I joined them and, before long, we were arguing heatedly about Pasternak. The first one to get angry was the man from Istvezia who said that the novel had already been published in the Soviet Union which I told him wasn't true. I knew that only excerpts had been published in a literary magazine which soon disappeared from the bookshops, sold out but never reprinted. Another of my Soviet colleagues, the jovial man from TASS, a good drinking companion, had a car with an Italian driver (a communist who was not supposed to understand Russian but I suspect that he did. He was probably a member of the Italian communist party whose job was to spy on these guys). When there were no more bottles of slivovitz or tasty titbits on the embassy tables we took off for dinner at Gino's fish restaurant in Trastevere, where I was always given friendly treatment (and would be even in future years when it became chic and much more expensive). Over dinner we continued to argue about Pasternak. The only reproach they could make about it being published in Italian that I could agree with was that they wondered why Pasternak's poetry wasn't published in the West, which they admitted to having read and liked. They didn't seem to realise that the Russians, the stupid Soviet regime, should be proud to publish such a novel because it proved that the country's great literary traditions were continuing even under Communism. We were all very drunk at the end of the evening and, while I only had to stagger 300 yards along the street, they had their driver to take them home. He had eaten with us and though he got more and more sullen as the evening wore on, obviously bored with hearing us discuss literature, at least he hadn't been drinking. Anyway the Russians paid the bill and fortunately my rather tame offer to pay my share was brushed aside.

The paper only published a paragraph of my story on Pasternak but, shortly afterwards, they sent me to cover the funeral of the tenor, Beniamino Gigli, the kind of commission I enjoyed doing, even if it was a sad event because I was a Gigli fan. I was amazed to see how many people turned out to follow the hearse from the singer's bizarrely ornamental home in the elegant Parioli district to the church and cemetery on the other side of the town.

In mid-December, I went to London again, this time with Angelo Litrico, and I decided to make the most of the occasion being offered to participate in London's version of what in Rome would soon be called the 'dolce vita'. We stayed at the Savoy where Angelo and I shared a suite with a double bedroom. I was rather startled, to say the least, when, before getting into our (separate) beds he unscrewed one of his legs. I knew he limped but didn't realise why. The press office of the Savoy did their best to help us out with his 'suit for Khrushchev' angle, and it aroused much interest in the media, even if the TV appearance I thought I had set up at the BBC fell through when they found out that Angelo didn't speak a word of English. He got on well with the Hector Powe people and they managed to make an agreement for some kind of exchange, but

I did my best not to get too involved as it just wasn't my scene. Angelo, of course, paid all the bills but I still spent a lot of money out of my own pocket and, when back in Rome with Christmas approaching, I realised that the nest egg I had obtained from mother to buy the car was already beginning to dwindle.

The Trastevere boy with whom I had begun a new relationship seemed a character from a polemical new novel which I had managed to read in spite of it being mostly in dialect. This was Pier Paolo Pasolini's *Ragazzi di vita*, about boys like those I knew in Trastevere, though the world Pasolini was writing about was more that of the 'borgate' the Roman slum periphery where I never ventured. I suspected that my 'ragazzo di vita' might be a delinquent (which indeed he'd turn out to be, even if only part-time) but he was very cute and obliging, not so lazy as Salvatore, and he'd be useful as a contact with the local underworld when I had robberies or needed the services of the shrifty but useful local money-lenders.

The *Chronicle* showed an interest in my doing a story about T. S. Eliot who was in Rome. I telephoned the great literary patroness, Princess Marguerite Caetani, because I knew Eliot was staying in her palazzo. She told me he had gone to the country for the weekend but would be giving a lecture-reading the following week. She promised to invite me to the event and the party she was giving for him afterwards but she'd forget to do so. I'd only hear about it when it was over. I did a story anyway but the *News Chronicle* didn't use it as it seemed one of the posh Sundays had got in first. They published a piece about the poet's Roman stay and about Princess Caetani's literati friends who contributed to the cult magazine she published, *Botteghe Oscure*, named after the street where her palazzo is situated, not far from the communist party headquarters. I had no difficulty getting a story into the *Chronicle* about another Princess, the Queen's outrageous sister, Margaret, who was gallivanting around Rome with her socialite friend,

Judy Montagu, who lived on 'my' Tiber island. To get the story I had to go to one of the most chic (but boring) Roman night clubs, the Hostaria dell'Orso (The Bear's Inn); a cavernous medieval style tavern. It is in the Altemps palazzo near the theatre named after Goldoni where, with an English-language company, I was to have a success playing the title role in Chekhov's one-act play appropriately called *The Bear*.

JFL in *The Bear*
with
Patrick Persichetti

I ended 1957 feeling that I had had a good year professionally, though I still hadn't achieved much in a creative sense. I was still too easily distracted by the uniformed offerings in Rome. I had just discovered the sailor trade available in the gardens of Piazza Mazzini near their barracks. One of them, a well-built but rather dumb blonde lad from Sicily, had a splendid physique and per-formed quite well even if he was inclined to giggle while making love which was rather irritating. He would one day be arrested by the military police while cruising in the Piazza Mazzini and stupidly (perhaps proudly?) admitted that the phone numbers in his address book were those of his 'clients', among whom was yours truly. Fortunately there were no embarrassing follow-ups for me anyway. But as this 'scandal' got a lot of attention in the Rome papers, the sailors (and their 'clients'!) had to be a little more-discreet from then onwards. I couldn't help remembering this blonde Sicilian rather irreverently when I attended the opening night of what was the major theatrical event of the new season in the Rome theatre, Visconti's stunningly realistic production of Arthur Miller's *A View from the Bridge*, in which two brothers, immigrant cousins from Sicily, of the longshoreman Eddie Carbone's wife, have jumped the ship on which they are merchant seamen and want to stay illegally in Eddie's Brooklyn home until they find work. One of the brothers is dark-haired and the other (played by an excellent young actor of the time, Corrado Pani) has long blond hair. When this boy is asked how come he's blond, he says "Maybe because a thousand years ago the Danes invaded Sicily". He meant the Normans of course. Occasionally one does find fair-haired people in Sicily. My blond Sicilian sailor would not be the only blond Sicilian among my uniformed lover boys. The butchy longshoreman, Eddie, in Miller's play, who scathingly hints that the blonde Sicilian must be queer was played by Paolo Stoppa, the leading actor of Visconti's company. Visconti's production lifted a rather melodramatic play to the level of a Greek tragedy but with that touch of melodramma (with two 'm's it becomes the word for opera in Italian) which deliberately coloured all of Visconti's work in cinema as well as theatre.

Though I had begun to discover the work of the other leading Italian theatrical directors, from Giorgio Strehler in Milan to Eduardo De Filippo in Naples, Visconti was still for me the one whose work most impressed me. On my first visit to Italy in 1949 I had arrived in Florence too late to see what was considered to be the most extraordinary theatrical event of post-war Italy, a sumptuous production that summer, in the Boboli Gardens, of *Troilus and Cressida* with a cast which was a Who's Who of Italian acting stars, names that at the time meant nothing to me when I saw the faded poster still on the walls around the Palazzo Pitti (one of the names was that of the set designer, a young Florentine, then Visconti's boyfriend, named Franco Zeffirelli). I made up for it after I settled in Rome in 1951. My first experience of Italian theatre was at Rome's Eliseo where I saw Visconti's production of

Arthur Miller's *Death Of A Salesman*, a play I knew well because I'd seen it in London with Paul Muni as Willy Loman, the part played in Italian by Paolo Stoppa. Among the other actors in Visconti's early productions were future film stars, Massimo Girotti, Vittorio Gassman, Marcello Mastroianni and Franco Interlenghi. Visconti had been responsible for revolutionizing Italian theatrical tastes after the war, not only in his choice of controversial new plays like Sartre's *Huis Clos* (in a double bill with Anouilh's *Antigone*) and Hemingway's *The Fifth Column* (with sets and costumes by the communist painter, Renato Guttuso) but also 'scandalous' works (particularly for Italians) such as Cocteau's *La machine à ecrire*, Marcel Achard's *Adam* (about homosexuality) and Jack Kirkland's *Tobacco Road*, from Caldwell's novel - all three plays with leading roles played by Luchino's future sister-in-law, Laura Adani, and the young Vittorio Gassman. Visconti was also the first in Italy to stage plays by two American dramatists for whom he'd direct many more plays in years to come, Tennessee Williams and Arthur Miller. He abolished the prompt box, of which actors of the new generation like Gassman had no need, but which, as I'd often see, ageing actors depended on. Indeed, before settling in Italy, I had seen a more traditional Italian performer who did. In Paris, I had seen the legendary Emma Gramatica, who almost saved from ridicule a ghastly D'Annunzio melo, *La città morta* (The Dead City). I would be privileged to see the equally aged Ruggero Ruggeri playing the roles he created for Pirandello plays in the early Twenties, in productions which Sir Laurence Olivier, indifferent to the inevitable financial burden it cost him, brought to the St. James's Theatre in a London not yet ready to see foreign companies acting in their original language.

Early in 1958, I watched the San Remo Song Festival on television. It was won by a song called *Nel blu dipinto di blu* ('Blue painted Blue'. The lyricist, Franco Migliacci, said it was inspired by Marc Chagall) but which everyone was already calling 'Volare' after its lilting refrain. Soon afterwards, Domenico Modugno, the song's composer-singer, came to give a concert at the Reale, the big cinema across the street from us. I went with my new Trastevere boyfriend and, like everyone else, we joined in the 'Volare' refrain, throwing our jackets in the air wildly (but I removed my wallet first!). Modugno was born in Apulia and was a traditional Southern type and I had heard him sing some beautiful Sicilian folk songs. There was nothing particularly sensual about him but he had the charms of a pater familias and he had a great humorous vein without being a clown. His singing style provoked what seemed to me a much more healthy form of strictly Italian musical excitement than the rock 'n roll stuff which some young Italian singers were already trying to emulate. The Beatles were only just starting out in Liverpool so that mania was yet to come. I offered a story about Modugno to the *Chronicle* but, with all the 'new music' emerging in the UK and the USA, they were sceptical about the potential of a hit song from Italy. They'd soon find out I had been right. The song was to become an international hit, and indeed the best-known Italian popular song after *O sole mio*. Anyway, in the years to come, I would have many occasions to admire and write about Modugno's musical and theatrical flairs.

After five years during which I hadn't set foot in England, early in 1958 I found myself there for the third time in four months, again in the company of Angelo Litrico. This time we didn't stay at the Savoy and I was glad to avoid sharing a hotel room with him. Ian Dallas put me up but instead of in a romantic Chelsea venue it was in a dreary flat in Primrose Hill, looking over bleak rooftops. I recorded that on a grey Sunday morning in February, after an English breakfast, as we read the papers and argued over art and religion, and our love-hate feelings about the English way of life, it seemed we were acting a scene from the play Ian hated so much but which I realised was very close to our generation's predicament, *Look Back in Anger*.

Chapter 5

My journalistic life in 1958 offered me several enjoyable filmic trips out of Rome. I was invited to the Riviera, south of Genoa, where Germans and Italians were shooting a film in a picturesque fishing village called Camogli, near the larger fashionable resort, Portofino, where the company put the press up for the night. The film was called *Kanonen-Serenade*, directed by Wolfgang Staudte, the only director of the two post-war Germanys who had so far won an international reputation, above all for *The Murderers Are Among Us*, a compelling film shot in East Germany and still at that time the only German film to denounce Nazism. The star of the new film was none other than Vittorio De Sica. We journalists were present at the launching of the ersatz "ship" to be used in the film which, in reality, was a no longer seaworthy trawler reinforced with plywood for the exteriors in the film. Not surprisingly the bottle of champagne swung by a German starlet didn't break when it hit the plywood prow.

In the evening, at a lively dinner party in a good restaurant in the harbour of Portofino, after we had eaten an excellent fish soup washed down by the Italians with good wines from Liguria and by the Germans with authentic Bavarian beer, Staudte did his best to convince me that he hoped his film would be seen as another anti-militarist work. I had my doubts. It seemed too much of an Italian comedy.

Not long afterwards I was invited to the 'launching' of another ship for a film, this time closer to Rome. This 'ship', also rather cardboard-looking, was being launched by my favourite Hollywood actress, Bette Davis. The film was called *John Paul Jones* and was about the man who sailed the Mayflower II across the Atlantic. The great Hollywood star, who had famously played Elizabeth of England, was about to play what she described to me as a three-minute 'vignette', the role of Catherine the Great of Russia.

Bette was very courteous to us all and seemed to be enjoying herself immensely. I enjoyed myself too but unfortunately wasn't committed to doing an interview with her. I did, however, get my photograph taken with Bette, and Peter Baker pleased me by publishing it in his diary column in *Films and Filming* (August 1958) perhaps to show I was having such a good time in Italy that I couldn't complain that our playboy publisher, Philip Dosse, didn't pay much for our contributions.

VIGNETTE : Bette Davis, with FILMS AND FILMING *Rome correspondent John Francis Lane, at the launching, near Rome, of a ship used in* John Paul Jones, *in which Miss Davis has a vignette part.*

The Ides of March of 1958 'came and went' and I began my eighth year as an adopted Roman by seeing an impressive first film by Francesco Rosi, a Neapolitan, who had been assistant to Visconti on *La Terra Trema* and *Bellissima*. His film *La Sfida* (The Challenge) is about a small-time crook (played by handsome Spanish actor José Suárez, and as Neapolitan-looking as any real Neapolitan I'd ever seen!) who moves from cigarette smuggling to one of the biggest rackets of Naples involving the fruit markets. Suárez wants to hit the big times so he tries to branch out on his own. This arouses the ire of the Big Boss who has him killed shortly after his marriage. The bride, a widow on her wedding day, was powerfully played by an 18 year-old newcomer, Rosanna Schiaffino, for whom I predicted a bright future. It was a directorial debut that while clearly under the influence of neo-realism also had the feel of American gangster movies like John Huston's *The Asphalt Jungle*. Franco Rosi brought a stylistic contribution of his own to the Italian Cinema and tackled the contemporary social scene of his Naples even if, like Eduardo De Filippo and many others, he himself had to flee from that afflicted city in order to find work. Naples seems to me a mirror of all that is wonderful and at the same time terrifying about an Italy trying to pick itself up from defeat in the war and the strife of the civil war which followed. Rossellini had illustrated this beautifully in an episode in *Paisà* (1946). Rosi was lucky to have, as his cinematographer, Gianni Di Venanzo, who captured in black and white the magical lighting contrasts of sunlit Neapolitan back alleys, tenement block rooftops and market places. The same Di Venanzo had photographed Visconti's *White Nights* (it was one of the best things about that film) and, another important film of 1957, Antonioni's *Il Grido* which I had considered with Fellini's *Nights of Cabiria* to be the best Italian film of the year. I went to see *Il Grido* again, in a fleapit cheap cinema ('third vision' as they called them then) and though the film impressed me even more second time round, it was depressing to see how the audience reacted, becoming restless and bored with Antonioni's way of telling a story of a man suffering in love. The man was played by an American star, Steve Cochran, who had had the courage to accept such a complex part in a foreign film and who, I think also took a risk in involving his own company in its production. Cochran plays a working man, not one from the bourgeois class like most of the characters we'd so far seen in

Antonioni's films. Many reproached Antonioni for this but I felt it was his strength that he didn't confine himself to one class or to a rigid Marxist approach to a proletarian's problems. The question of how people communicate, or fail to communicate, their feelings was not necessarily conditioned by their social class. I had talked to Michelangelo about this when I had been to interview one of the actresses in the film. I eagerly awaited his next film (which would be *L'avventura*). He had promised to invite me to the location in Southern Italy.

In May, I had to deal with the rather inconclusive outcome of the Italian general elections which resulted in the dynamic mini-sized Tuscan, Christian Democrat secretary, Amintore Fanfani, forming a pre-Centre-Left government without the right-wing Liberals but still also without the real Left. It wouldn't last long.

There were few intellectual stimulations in the Roman Spring of 1958. One was a recital by Peggy Ashcroft at Palazzo Caetani which, this time, the Princess remembered to invite me to. The great actress was in Rome to do a film with Audrey Hepburn, *The Nun's Story*. I did a story about her for London and also for the Leftist Rome afternoon paper, *Paese Sera*, for which I'd been asked to write, and I managed to do it in Italian.

I would get another glimpse of a Hollywood myth that summer but a rather more banal and mercenary one. I was asked to be the interpreter at the press luncheon of the Chief Executive of M-G-M, Joseph Vogel, who was in Rome to see how *Ben-Hur* was proceeding. Vogel was very proud that M-G-M currently had two prestige pictures, *Ben-Hur* and *Gigi*, in production in Europe and waved off a sarcastic question as to why they had made such a mess of *The Brothers Karamazov*. "We make pictures to entertain the public. You can't make entertainment and also be faithful to a Dostoevsky," was his pragmatic studio boss reply. He dismissed rumours that William Wyler and Charlton Heston were fighting but I heard on the grapevine that that there were problems with the script even though Christopher Fry and Gore Vidal had been brought in, without being credited, to give it a more literary flavour. In later years, when I became friendly with Gore, he'd tell me that his idea of hinting that the relationship between Heston's Jewish Ben and Stephen Boyd's Roman patrician had not been as hearty, when they were younger men, as it was now when they are re-united after many years and embrace warmly before becoming bitter foes. This hadn't gone down well with either Wyler or Heston. Gore's literary assistance on the script didn't last long. He would claim it was also his idea that the Romans should speak in English-English and the Jews in American-English.

Much bigger script problems were facing the other mammoth film shooting that summer in Rome where, at the Titanus studios, the producer, Goffredo Lombardo, was making *The Naked Maja*. It seemed that director, Henry Koster, and his stars, Ava Gardner who played the Duchess of Alba, and Anthony Franciosa, who played Goya, were complaining that the script was being changed every day. Even the casting director didn't know which characters would still be in the script the week after. One doubted that this film about a famous painter would be as 'serious' as *Lust For Life*, about Van Gogh which Mr. Vogel told us sadly had not made money. But Ava's presence as the 'naked maja' should have at least given this one box-office appeal. It didn't.

Another big Hollywood star in Rome was Gloria Swanson, in town to play Agrippina in a comedy about Nero. Here it seemed the only problem about the script was that it didn't exist, either when the film started or when it finished. When the film wrapped, Swanson was given a glamorous press party in a Via Veneto hotel. The 'scriptless' film that Gloria was making would be called in English (but hardly ever seen!) *Nero's Big Weekend (Mio figlio Nerone)*. At the reception, while the Italian comic star of the moment, Alberto Sordi, who played Nero, was doing a great hand-kissing act with Swanson for the photographers, attention was suddenly distracted to the other side of the room where someone had just entered. He was an elderly rather shabbily dressed little man who was immediately recognised by the Italian movie connoisseurs present as André Deed, who had been popular in Italian silent films as Cretinetti. Shyly, he told us he had heard that Gloria was in town and wanted to meet the star he had adored thirty-five years ago. He was immediately introduced to her and she behaved graciously, even if the photographers were more interested in getting her to pose with the new sexpot, Brigitte Bardot, who played Poppea, and with De Sica, who played Seneca. A film on such a subject with such star names, even without a Billy Wilder to direct it but at least with a witty script, could have made film comedy history. Instead it turned out to be mediocre and would soon be forgotten. I'd write about it in my contribution to a series that *Films and Filming* was publishing on 'laughter makers' in the great film-making countries. The article, published in the May 1958 issue, gave me the excuse to write about the greatest Italian comics of the time starting with Totò who uses the facial and body language of the Neapolitan version of Commedia dell'Arte, which is not always appreciated by non-Italians. I also wrote about another great Neapolitan, the actor-dramatist, Eduardo De Filippo, who had also left his mark on the post-war Italian cinema. He had appeared in and directed two extraordinary films, both adaptations of his own post-war theatrical successes, *Napoli Milionaria*, the play he'd one day revive when he was invited to bring his company to London for one of Peter Daubeny's World Theatre Seasons, and *Filumena Marturano*, which De Sica would film with Sophia Loren and Marcello Mastroianni as *Marriage Italian Style* (1964). But those two early films by De Filippo, which had such profound things to say about the people of Naples, are rarely remembered among the great films of post-war Italy, maybe because they seemed more theatrical than filmic. They deserve to be appreciated alongside the films of Rossellini and De Sica. They had much better scripts.

Meanwhile, I was invited to another location shoot in the South. This was a visit to the Royal Palace at Caserta where Alberto Lattuada was making *The Tempest* for Dino De Laurentiis, adapted from two Pushkin stories, *The Captain's Daughter* and *The Pugachev Rebellion*, with a bearded Van Heflin as the rebel hero. During the lunch break I sat with Dino to eat a box lunch. He chose the one prepared for the Americans and I chose the one prepared for the Italians, and he chose well as mine had lukewarm pasta. I hoped he was also making a good choice with this new super-production but I had my doubts. This latest attempt to make a big costume picture, which mixed Italian and American talents, and which would have a soundtrack that inevitably would end up a hotch-potch of accents, would have to be post-synched with voices, few of which would belong to the original actors.

Thanks to Dino I got an exclusive interview with his wife, Silvana Mangano, who didn't like speaking to journalists but who agreed to see me because I was English. She quite frankly admitted that she hated the cinema. As the star who had become a world famous pin-up girl thanks to her sexy roles in *Bitter Rice* (1949) and *Anna* (1951, the latter also directed by Lattuada) I could see why she was getting bored, even if her husband had tried to keep her happy with the occasional more dramatic parts in films like René Clément's *The Sea Wall* and, above all, in her episode of De Sica's *Neapolitan Gold*. Silvana's father was a Sicilian railway worker who had married an English lady. She told me she was sorry she'd never been on the stage. It didn't seem that her part in this *Tempest* was going to add more laurels to her reputation. She would have to wait years to give her most memorable perform-ances in films by Visconti and Pasolini, not produced by Dino.

Visiting Caserta reminded me that it had been the place where I finally broke up with my Neapolitan student lover. We had not been able to visit the Vanvatelli Palace Museum because it was closed for the day, now I at last saw its interior, but it had been transformed into the imperial palace at St Petersburg, for which hundreds of sexy-looking cadets from the local military academies had been recruited.

The summer of 1958 was the one that Fellini would tell me had inspired much of the content of his Roman "sweet life" which he was about to make. Apart from some of the dreary social events that I had been obliged to follow, only one of the boys I knew was of 'dolce vita' stature, a hot subject for those gossip columnists who covered the Via Veneto society and movie scene. He was Maurizio Arena, the most sexy young Roman actor of the moment, and known as 'Il fusto', the muscle boy. I had published a tantalising picture of him in tight jeans in *Films and Filming* in an article on 'Italian Male Curves' (March 1958). Subsequently, getting to know him in person, I'd succeed in placing a photo of him in the *Daily Express* with his current girl friend, the luscious blonde actress, Linda Christian, who had married Tyrone Power in the most spectacularly press-covered wedding of post-war Rome, which took place in the church inside the Roman forum. I tried to help Maurizio upgrade his professional image and even proposed a film story for him which we discussed at length over enormous lunches he served generously to 'us' Trastevere friends in his home on Monteverde, near to where Attilio Bertolucci (and his sons, the future directors Bernardo and Giuseppe) lived. Unfortunately Linda, usually having drunk too much when we saw her, monopolised Maurizio's amorous attention.

But before the big heat of summer really settled in, I took off to Naples for my 'return to the stage'. A British (indeed Scottish) actress, Audrey Macdonald, who had settled in Rome (and would be one of the girls courted by Mastroianni's journalist in *La Dolce Vita*) asked me to play the solicitor in *The Millionairess* which she was presenting in Naples at the famous Teatro San Ferdinando, the theatre of Eduardo De Filippo. She believed, too optimistically, that the American soldiers stationed at the nearby NATO base

Arena in *Poor But Handsome*. Macdonald & Lane in *The Millionairess*.

would be eager to flock to see her. She was wrong. Apart from the First Night attended by a handful of officers she managed to rope in, and some local celebrities, whom I suspected De Filippo had invited, helping to encourage her (he had a soft spot for Audrey and lent her his theatre rent-free), we would play mostly to empty houses. It turned out that the American GIs, for whom a play by Bernard Shaw was probably not a draw anyway, were also wary of venturing into an area of Naples which certainly was off the tourist map and a bit dangerous. Audrey's charm was great but she didn't have anyone who could have rounded up an audience for her and brought them to the theatre in a coach with an escort. And I had no connections then with the Naples press so couldn't be her PR. So money was short. We could only afford to eat the occasional take-away pizza and, of course, I couldn't allow myself the luxury of accepting the many enticing offers that came my way every time I stepped out on the street, either from local youths, or from the sailors who abound in Naples. We slept in a

house in the square overlooking the Royal Palace and soon realised
that the traffic going in and out of the house during the day was
because the landlady was renting rooms by the hour. Still we all
had fun and, the Englishman who did a good job in directing us,
John Karlsen, would become a good friend and would be one of
the first tenants of my 'second' attic in Trastevere when I got
round to taking on the rent of the whole top floors, even if I still
couldn't afford to pay a double rent.

It had been wonderful to act again on the stage, even to half-
empty houses, in such an historic theatre, where I'd subsequently
see Eduardo himself act many times. But even so I was glad to
go back to being a spectator and catch up on my journalistic
commitments. I had missed the opening week of the first Festival
of Two Worlds which Gian Carlo Menotti had just launched in
Spoleto, a city I had adored since my first trip outside of Rome
during the autumn of 1949, on my way to Florence, driven by
my German ex-lover. I managed to get up to this promising new
arts festival for the last days and caught several theatrical events,
including the first play by the Neapolitan who'd become a good
friend, Giuseppe Patroni Griffi, and his excellent company of
young actors. I saw ballets by Jerome Robbins and John Butler.
And I saw several great musical events, the major one of which
was Visconti's production of Verdi's *Macbeth* conducted by the
Adonis-like Thomas Schippers, which had inaugurated the Festival.
Visconti used transparent painted gauzes which created different
effects depending on the lighting and which disappeared when lit
from a different angle. This kind of effect is used a lot today but
then it was a novelty. In her affectionate biography of Visconti,
Gaia Servadio says she asked Luchino if it was the first time this
kind of effect had been used in Italy and he replied sarcastically
"Zeffirelli says he was the first". Though Spoleto had immediately
established itself as the most important event in Italian cultural
life since the war, even if the Milanese snobs felt that nothing

culturally important could happen south of Florence, it took a great Milanese aristocrat and artistic icon like Visconti to convince them it could. Italy finally had its Edinburgh even if there was some conservative political abuse aroused because it was clear that a majority of the performing artists were blatant homosexuals. A hearty fascist-minded Italian intellectual flew over the city with D'Annunzio-like flamboyance dropping leaflets warning the local population that the virility of their sons was being threatened by these intruders. The locals just laughed. For them the festival meant that their lovely city was at last on the tourist map and, anyway, their young men could look after themselves, which of course they managed to do, not altogether disdaining the flattering attention bestowed on them by the visitors. At the last night party given by Menotti I ran into Visconti and this time I had only praise to offer for his Verdian *Macbeth*. "Glad to hear that you like something I do!" was his surly comment. I deserved as much.

I went to Ravenna, invited by ENI, the national petroleum agency, where I was shown round their methane refinery and I got an interesting article for the paper out of this new meeting with Enrico Mattei. And the city of Ravenna was a great discovery. Dante had died and was buried there. Lord Byron had adored the city. It had once been the capital of the Holy Roman Empire and of Byzantium from which remain its celebrated mosaics, one of the great artistic treasures of Italy, a new aspect of Italian creative art for me, of which I had only had a small taste from the impressive but somewhat more modest mosaics on the facade of Santa Maria in Trastevere, just along the street from my home. I decided from then onwards I would seize every opportunity that came my way for the generous offers of hospitality which were offered to foreign journalists if they gave me a chance to visit the so-far unseen beautiful places in Italy which I couldn't afford to explore at my own expense. I didn't mind joining the scrounger brigade. I was tired of going around on the cheap.

A chance to get out of Rome again cropped up immediately and I was invited to Apulia to visit the location of a film which Jules Dassin was shooting there with Gina Lollobrigida. It was an adaptation of the novel which won the previous year's Goncourt literary prize, *La Loi*, by Roger Vaillant. The "law" of the title is a strange symbolic game played in parts of Southern Italy, which used to be played in Rome where it was called 'passatella', and is now forbidden because the players are obliged to drink a lot. If you win you become the Boss and are entitled to humiliate the other players who, before long, bring out their knives. This 'game' is the psychological as well as the passionate theme of Vailland's novel which Dassin, the most famous of Hollywood political expatriates, was filming in the Gargano, a peninsula jutting out of the Adriatic coast, an area where emperors and princes built their castles on hilltops, many of which still stand majestically in view.

To get to Apulia I had to take a train to San Severo, a prosperous market town, where a production car met me and took me into what is called the Umbrian Forest, where I slept the night in a hotel which had been a hunter's retreat. It seemed I was spending a night on Mussorgsky's (or Disney's) Bald Mountain. It was mid-July but it was rainy and quite chilly. The next morning, I was driven through olive groves to the village of Carpino which Dassin had chosen as the setting for his film. There seemed to be more flies in this village that day than one sees in a whole summer in Trastevere. Dassin found time to give me a long interview in which he talked frankly about the problems he had faced with the Un-American Activities Committee as a result of which he had left the U.S. in 1950. Now, after two projects in Italy, neither of which materialised (one was an adaptation of the Verga novel, *Mastro Don Gesualdo*, which D. H. Lawrence had translated into English), he took up the project of filming the novel by Vailland, who had been a communist when *La Loi* was published but who had left the party after the Soviet invasion of Hungary. Dassin told me he'd done a lot of research on the Italian South when preparing the Verga film project and this was helping him with the adaptation in which, he said, he was emphasizing the story of the visiting agronome (played by Marcello Mastroianni) who had been sent to the area to advise on how to modernise agricultural methods, but who finds that the local mafia control everything. "He'll also redeem the local girl who is a victim of the local Boss", Dassin told me, "but I haven't changed this because the part is played by Gina who is the star and who is also partly involved in the production". Dassin added that "even though in the book she loses her virginity to one of the local lads, in the film it happens with the agronome whom she'll marry at the end. As the story is so negative about the people in this poverty-stricken area I wanted to show that there are positive forces at work in a region of this kind".

The making of the film seemed to be causing a turmoil locally. La Lollo was being treated as a sort of Goddess, like Padre Pio, the saintly priest of nearby San Giovanni Rotondo. Here too, people brought their sick for blessing by the diva. Gina was embarrassed but she told me that she has to accept it and be patient. A boy in the square asked me if I thought their village will become famous and people would come to visit it as they do to the village where Lollobrigida made *Bread, Love and Dreams*. Also starring in the film was Yves Montand who also got treated as a divine being. I found more divinity in the young Italian actor, Raf Mattioli, who plays Montand's son, the young intellectual of the village who wants to flee the town with a beautiful local married woman, played by Dassin's lady friend, the Greek actress, Melina Mercouri. During the interview with Dassin she reproached him for being so frank with me about his political feelings. I suppose I saw *La Loi* when it was eventually released in Italy but it would be a forgotten work. Dassin is remembered more for his best American films, *Brute Force* and *The Naked City* and for the commercial success of *Rififi* and *Never On Sunday*, the latter made in Greece with Melina.

The 1958 Venice Festival would remain memorable less for the Golden Lion winner, the Japanese *The Rickshaw Man*, than for the double Silver Lion winners: Rosi's *La Sfida* and the French director Louis Malle's *Les Amants*. *Les Amants* caused a scandal but merited attention for being an impressive follow-up to his debut, *Ascenseur pour l'échafaud*, and was a confirmation that something new was emerging from the cinema on the other side of the Alps. But for me that year's festival would be remembered most because it gave me the chance to catch up on the most significant film of the year, shown in what was called the Information Section because it had already won the Berlin Festival earlier in the year. This was Ingmar Bergman's *Wild Strawberries*, an absolute masterpiece.

I must quote the exact words I wrote in my diary because they seem much more important to me half a century later when they have an almost frighteningly prophetic relevance to my own life: "This film made me wonder about my own future. Can I go on with this kind of existence? I am too depressed by having to follow film festivals where we often end up pretending that certain films are more interesting and important than they really are. Then one sees an inspiring film like *Wild Strawberries*. Victor Sjöström was poignantly convincing as a very old man who suddenly suspects that all his life he has been an egoist and that people hate him for it, in spite of his charm and brilliance." I was only on the eve of my thirtieth birthday and felt afraid that this might be my fate but it was comforting to find that by the end of the film, the old professor did not have such a pessimistic view of his life as he had felt at the beginning, after a depressing but cinematically extraordinary dream sequence. The old man discovers he is loved and respected more than he had thought. This film and the debut of new directors like Rosi and Malle permitted me to leave the Lido feeling there was a future for the cinema after all.

Chapter 6

In September 1958, after Venice but before returning to Rome, I stopped over first in Bergamo and then in Milan. Bergamo was a fascinating 'discovery' for me. The city had a well-preserved hilltop ancient city and a modern lower town with an opera house named after its most famous son, Donizetti. I went to Bergamo for a handsomely subsidised festival of art film shorts. Shorts on artistic themes were given generous financial support by the government, though I'd often notice audiences getting very restless when they had to sit through their obligatory inclusion in cinema programmes. In Rome I had met Luciano Emmer, best known for his first feature *Sunday in August*, but he won international respect before that for the excellent art films he made with Enrico Gras. He liked to make 'narrative' art films which told a story whilst illustrating an artist's work.

Though Bergamo was a very clerical city, the festival was prepared to give space to a film about a 'subversive' artist like the communist, Picasso, but the top prize of a million lire that year was won by a film about a more politically harmless modern artist, Henry Moore, made by a British TV documentarist, John Read, the son of Sir Herbert, the art historian and theorist, several of whose books were already on my shelves. I got to know John very well during the week, at the end of which we travelled together the 50 km distance to Milan, driven by the British Institute director, a very civilised chap with a great knowledge of art. He gave us a privileged look at Milan's most important art collection, the Brera, which I had already visited to see the great works by Raphael and Caravaggio, but where I was now helped to appreciate works by lesser-known artists. We also went to Santa Maria delle Grazie to see the recently restored Leonardo's Last Supper. I'm always glad to see it again as I fear it may not last forever.

I decided to stay on a few more days in Milan because I found the city stimulating, even if its citizens seem too intent on trying to out do the Americans in being obsessed with money. Certainly it is in strong contrast to our lackadaisical Rome. I remembered the wonderful De Sica-Zavattini fantasy *Miracle in Milan* (1951), with the smiling boy, Toto, coming out of the orphanage where he'd grown up to find that his eagerness to say "Buon Giorno" to the Milanese people scurrying by is not appreciated. Yet, in Milan, one can't help admiring the city's eagerness to move into the mid-20th century's progress towards a real industrial strength. On a previous visit, to see an opera at La Scala, or a play at the Piccolo Teatro, there had been only one skyscraper, the Pirelli. Now others were springing up. The Milanese were not content to bask only in the relics of their past glories which certainly exist here too. I saw the 'economic miracle' emerging, and would soon interview protagonists of it such as Enrico Mattei.

In October, I went to Florence, invited to a conference organised by the mayor, Giorgio La Pira, a somewhat eccentric Utopist but a progressive Christian Democrat who had been hoping to bring Catholics together with Jews and Arabs for a peace conference. Naturally, with the critical situation in the Middle East, the *NC* showed an interest in the story and were prepared to pay my expenses, even if my food and board were already being covered by the organisers of the event, which was sponsored by the Italian company which had most interest in good relations with the Middle East, the petroleum agency ENI of which Enrico Mattei was the chief executive.

Just when it seemed that a big news story was about to break, the French delegation walking out in protest against the official presence of the Algerians, and it was clear that Muslims and Israelians were not going to sit at the same table, in spite of La Pira's rather mystical ecumenical proposals, I was summoned back to Rome as it seemed that the Pope was at death's door.

A few days later, I think I was the only British journalist actually phoning in from Castel Gandolfo, seat of the papal summer residence, within minutes of the Pope's death, though all those who had been sent out from London, comfortably installed at the Foreign Press Club, were phoning their stories even if the dateline on their by-line reports were 'from Castel Gandolfo'. From a professional point of view I was still a rather naive journalist. Indeed, the day before Pope Pius really died, I had gotten into trouble with the *Evening Standard* for which I was still a stringer. As an afternoon paper they were ready to go out onto the streets with a special edition if the Pope died during the day. I had an agreement with a Rome daily paper reporter who had a contact inside the papal palace who had promised to open a certain window when the Pope died. We saw the window being opened and both of us got on the phone immediately to our papers. Several Rome papers were already out announcing the death. But His Holiness had not yet started his journey to the other world. We'd discover that a nun had opened the window to let some fresh air into the probably ill-odoured papal apartment. Naturally, the *Standard* got a bit hysterical because the wire services were refusing to confirm the death. At a certain point I was put through to the editor himself who shouted angrily: "But Lane is the Pope dead or not?" I hesitated a moment and then said: "We don't know for certain but may I suggest you write 'Mystery over Pope's death: Vatican's denial'. The editor spluttered and put the phone down but that's probably what he printed. I never saw the paper. They sent out a staff reporter within hours and he was able to cover the event when it really happened. He didn't know a thing about the Vatican so he was dependent on me for help. The Pope would, in fact, die during the following night but we weren't officially informed for some hours. It proved to be a terrible night in Castel Gandolfo. Fortunately I was paid quite well for my suffering and, of course, I was working for 'two masters'. With the *Chronicle* it was left to me to cover the death and the funeral but their religious experts filed the stories out from London. During the Thursday, when the Pope had really died, I was witness to some pretty grim happenings in Castel Gandolfo. After his death there had apparently been an immediate but rather inexpert attempt to embalm him. It seemed that the Vatican's official embalmers in Rome had not been summoned. When the body was finally laid out for the faithful to come and pay their respects it was already beginning to decompose. The gendarmes on duty protested so, after a few hours, the body was enclosed in a coffin. Hundreds of people had been waiting outside to get in and when the doors were finally opened I fought my way in beside them. I was impressed by the signs of devoted adoration by the people who filed by but there was something very macabre about the whole thing. As a non-believer I felt no particular emotions myself but I couldn't help remembering how, the year before, when Salvatore had taken me in his borrowed 500 Fiat on a trip to the Alban Hills for a wine festa in Marino, we had stopped at Castel Gandolfo on our way back to Rome. Pope Pius was in his summer residence there and he made an appearance in the courtyard in the late afternoon. We were standing at the back of the crowd. Salvatore had been rather cynical about the enthusiasm of the devotees. Then Pius started to rail against the sinful ways of the young people of the day and how his 'sacred' Rome was being defiled by one scandal after another. He pointed a finger over the heads of those present shouting: "They are possessed by the Devil". We were far away but his eyes seemed to penetrate in our direction and poor Salvatore suddenly began to tremble, saying: "He's looking at me!" I too felt a bit uncomfortable, but was more philosophical because I knew that the Pope's clean-up campaign was encouraging the government to increase censorship on what he considered obscene films and plays. Anyway, we got out of the papal palace quickly.

Feeling exhausted after visiting the decomposing corpse of the Pontiff, I went to my favourite restaurant overlooking the lake to enjoy a good meal and lots of local wine. But a new horror story awaited me. At another table I saw a gaggle of obviously high-ranking prelates who, I'd learn from a waiter, were Swiss. They were enjoying a hearty meal and having a good laugh. They had obviously just come from visiting the corpse, but it seemed to me that whereas I had earned the right to eat and drink well they perhaps should have been more respectful. I didn't understand their German but, in the midst of the laughter, I heard them mention the name of the Swiss monkey-gland specialist, Paul Niehans, who had been giving the Pope (and the West German Chancellor, Konrad Adenauer, and the painter, Georges Braque), a rejuvenation cure. He was there in Castel Gandolfo that day but none of the press had succeeded in getting him to speak. There was even speculation that this 'cure' might have had something to do with the mess-up over the embalming. Obviously this was what caused the merriment of my fellow diners. They finished up the meal by smoking cigars. I ate my meal rather soberly and slunk away. I am not a moralist but I couldn't help thinking that maybe Pacelli's "cleaning up" campaign should have begun in his own parish.

I didn't put this episode into my story from Castel Gandolfo but kept a record of it in my diary, thinking I might try to write an ironical piece about it and maybe send it to *Punch*, something on the lines of those written by a fellow *Standard* stringer, Peter B., who wrote under the pen name of Anthony Carson, but I didn't want to fall foul of the Vatican press office to which I was now officially accredited, thanks to which I could go in and out of the Vatican gates whenever I wanted to, and even use their duty free shop. Looking back, I have to recognise that what I cared about at that moment was surviving in Rome in the most comfortable way possible, even if it meant missing many creative opportunities, as I lived through history in the first person.

In October 1958, on the day the white smoke emerged from the chimney over the Sistine Chapel, where the Cardinals had gathered to elect the new Pope with the centuries-old ritual that had not been seen since Pius XII was elected in 1939, I was once again 'on the spot'. This time in St. Peter's Square. I hadn't understood the name spoken in the Latin announcement by the Cardinal from the balcony when he announced "Habemus papem", but a young American seminarist standing nearby, and who had admitted to me he was praying that Cardinal Spellman of New York should not be chosen (either because he didn't want him to abandon New York or because he didn't think he'd make a good Pope) was glad of the choice made and explained to me that the new Pope was Cardinal Roncalli, the Patriarch of Venice, who had taken the name of 'Johannes'. It took me a few moments to realise that Johannes was 'John'. "That's my name too!" I told him as I rushed out of St Peter's Square to a nearby café, where I had already made a reconnaissance, saying I would be making my collect call through to London from their booth. In the office they already had the news. Everybody was watching it on television! It was the first time that television had covered a papal election live. I was only useful to the *Chronicle* in providing 'local colour'. Though we had put Roncalli on the 'papabili' lists as a likely outsider if the Holy Ghost (i.e. the cardinals in conclave!) needed to make a compromise choice, we had not put him on our short list of the most likely candidates, but I had a personal trump card. I could add that I had 'met' the new Pope during the previous year's Venice Festival when he delivered a homily in St. Mark's Cathedral to the film festival crowd. He had seemed like a jolly type with the comforting looks of a peasant grandpa. It seemed to me an original note that probably no other correspondent would be able to add but it got lost in the official story in the paper. However, both our by-lines were printed so at least they could write truthfully that one of the paper's reporters was in St Peter's Square when the news was announced and the 77 year old new Pontiff appeared on the balcony.

I'd be left alone to cover the enthronement of Pope John XXIII later in the month. Again too much of what I wrote got lost in the editing and they used a picture on the front page with a caption 'from our correspondent'. But I did have the satisfaction of seeing a 'personal angle' by-line story from me in print the day before the enthronement. I described the arrival, at Rome's railway station, of the new Pope's relatives, greeted by Vatican officials and the carabinieri in full dress uniform. A red carpet had to be quickly laid down in front of the compartment exit as the train was pulling in once they had certified from which carriage the illustrious visitors would be descending. It was a bit like that scene in Chaplin's *The Great Dictator* when Chaplin's Hynkel (Hitler) receives Jack Oakie's Mussolini-styled Napaloni on an official visit and there are many gags concerning where the red carpet should be put down. But it was a very moving moment when Roncalli's family finally got out of the train. The Pope's brothers and other relatives were real peasants from that Bergamo countryside which I had only recently viewed from the city's hilltop. They were wearing their Sunday best and, the real touch of colour for my story, was that I reported they were carrying bags full of appetising and genuine country food, cheeses, fruit and vegetables. I quoted one of them saying: "Who knows what they serve him in the Vatican kitchens?". My by-line story made the front page of the *Chronicle* and they gave it a good title: 'Old folks at Rome'.

The enthronement itself was less colourful, though a 'one-off' event in my life that I felt privileged to have attended, even though the seats given to the press were on a raised dias near the high altar, where we were only able to watch the last phase of the ceremony, and so missed the spectacular entry on the Gestatorial chair. Having been obliged to get up very early in the morning in order to reach the entrance long before it all began, I was feeling rather tired and bored by the time the papal procession arrived, the old boy with his papal tiara now firmly planted on his well-blessed peasant head. I'd passed the intervening hours scribbling notes for what would be another idea for a book that would probably never be written. But it was a good idea. I wanted to call it 'Rome against Rome'. It would tell the history of how the Romans had over the centuries turned against the Popes especially when they were politically evil. I knew about Boniface VIII being sent to the *Inferno* by Dante when he was still alive. The misdeeds of the Spanish Borgia family and their Pope were well known, as were those of the Inquisition, such as the humiliation of Galileo and the burning at the stake of Giordano Bruno in the Campo dei Fiori, where a statue now stands in Bruno's memory. But there are many other occasions when the Popes had aroused the anger of the Roman populace. Still, I had an inkling that this new Pope would prove more popular than recent pontiffs had been and, when I set eyes on him, I felt I'd have to suspend for the moment my 'Rome against Rome' anti-clerical crusade. The foreign press were received in audience by the new Pope. I was very impressed by him. The most striking thing about Angelo Roncalli's physical appearance were his enormous ears. He told us he'd been reading the papers these last days, not out of 'amour-propre' he insisted but because he was having problems sleeping and told us that our speculations about what happened at the conclave were all wrong. "Silence has been successful after all", he said almost teasingly. The Vatican officials looked a bit shocked that he should be so frivolous with us but I noticed one or two of them began to smile, perhaps relieved that after the severity of Pacelli they now had a boss who behaved like a human being.

I began to realise it would be foolish of me to give up such a 'serious' paper as the *News Chronicle*, though it continued to be in a precarious state and was often on the verge of closing down. But the stories out of Rome in the weeks after the Vatican were no longer front page news and were mostly rather silly season copy even if we were now at the end of October. There was the case of the Indian Prince whom a film actress had said she would marry in preference to her fiancé, an Italian Marquis. The paper sent me to Naples to find the Prince even though I suspected he was hiding in Rome (which turned out to be true). On a lovely autumn day I went to Palestrina, south of Rome, to see the exquisitely preserved pre-Roman temple to the goddess Fortune, but I didn't feel that the goddess was with me when I got back to Rome. That same evening I was obliged to cadge a lift from a colleague in his car to rush back to the same area, to the seaside town of Anzio near to which a BEA jet had collided with an Italian military plane. It was a most unpleasant story to have to cover, the sort that is a nightmare for a reporter. It dampened my enthusiasm for continuing my career as a foreign correspondent.

Back in Rome, I did my best to catch up with the cultural scene. I'd missed many of the opening events of the new season, but I did hear Aldous Huxley give a talk in which he revisited his *Brave New World* in a very superficial vein for the benefit of society ladies who had nothing better to do with their afternoons. There also was a visit from Jean Babilée whose ballets seemed to have improved since I last saw them. I was impressed by one called *Balance à trois* in which two muscular young men show off their prowess for a girl's benefit. Luchino Visconti had introduced the performance. I had also seen Luchino's new production, an adaptation of a play based on Thomas Wolfe's *Look Homeward, Angel* in which this early 20th century American author seemed to anticipate Tennessee Williams, but maybe Luchino was responsible for that.

I often visited Maurizio Arena. Linda Christian was no longer around but there was always a pretty girl in attendance. I no longer had any illusions to vie for his amorous attention but I still thought I might be able to help him with his career as he certainly respected me. The two films he had made in the past season, *Poor But Handsome* and *Poor But Beautiful* were modest artistically but the top

domestic money makers, giving Arena and his co-star and fellow
'fusto', Renato Salvatori, the same kind of box-office rivalry that
had boosted the careers of Gina Lollobrigida and Sophia Loren.
But 'male curves' didn't cast the same media spell beyond the gossip
columns and magazines like *Films and Filming*. Renato Salvatori
was slated for the lead in a boxing film Visconti was planning to
make in Milan this coming winter (*Rocco and his Brothers*) but with
Renato now playing second fiddle to the French actor, Alain Delon,
(Luchino's new heart throb). Maurizio told me he was going to
make a boxing film too and perhaps direct a film himself. One day,
he took me to Castel Fusano the chic beach residential area south
of Ostia to show me the villa he was building there, complete with
swimming pool. I feared it would be the closest he'd come to
boosting his image as a Hollywood-style star, but an affair with
a blue-blood Princess, Maria Beatrice of Savoy, would keep him in
the news for a few more seasons, anyway until he put on too much
weight, and that didn't help him to have success as a character
actor. He'd direct two films himself, both soon forgotten. And he
died at the age of forty-five.

Renato Salvatori, Marisa Allasio and Maurizio Arena
in Dino Risi's *Poor But Handsome*.

The 50th issue of *Films and Filming* (November 1958) appeared and Peter Baker was proud to continue his claim on the masthead that it had: "the world's largest sale among critical filmgoers". The issue carried my report on the Venice Festival and also my 'Personality of the month' profile of the 33 year-old producer, Franco Cristaldi, whose Vides company was making some of the most interesting new Italian pictures, including Francesco Rosi's debut film *La Sfida*. In the piece, I recounted a personal anecdote. In London, for the festival screening of *White Nights*, whilst dining in Chelsea with Cristaldi, Visconti, Mastroianni and others, I realised that Cristaldi hadn't spoken a word to me since he arrived in England. I couldn't resist asking Luchino if he knew why? He smiled and told me that Franco hadn't forgiven me for not including *White Nights* among the three best films at Venice in the vote by contributors to *Cinema Nuovo*. I knew that Luchino hadn't forgiven me either but he had preferred to tease me about it rather than give me the cold shoulder. But Cristaldi was a younger man and idealistic. It hurt him if he felt his commitment was not being appreciated. This profile was my first step towards showing him that I did in fact appreciate what he was doing for the Italian cinema where producers tended to think that Italian films should be made in English with American stars.

As my 30th birthday approached, I remembered a prophecy I had heard during the winter of 1950-51, when I had been escaping my Parisian whirl as a cinephile Bohemian and had spent the end of year holidays in St-Paul-de-Vence, staying with an American lesbian, a fellow student at IDHEC in Paris, and her Dutch mate. As the 20th century moved past its halfway mark, we were visited by a gypsy who the girls had invited to read our fortunes. I was told that my creative flowering wouldn't happen until I was thirty. So, on the eve of December 1st 1958, I wondered if the prophecy would come true? Or was I condemned to only indulge in my instinctive indolence which I blamed on Rome rather than myself?

Anyway, I decided to spend my birthday in Naples, and splendidly too, thanks to a free press junket for the world premiere, at the San Carlo Opera House, of the Dino De Laurentiis film, *The Tempest*, the set of which I had visited the year before. We were put up at the Excelsior Hotel on the Santa Lucia seafront. An American colleague and I treated ourselves to a good seafood lunch at the Bersagliera restaurant under the Castel dell'Ovo. Among the crude shellfish we were served as 'antipasto' were oysters which I felt was a tribute to Whitstable, the place where I was born. Luckily this was before Naples was hit by a cholera epidemic that made it dangerous to eat shellfish from southern Italian waters, though the oysters of that day were probably brought from more northern shores. Whilst eating that memorable fish meal we were blessed by the presence in the waters around us of another tantalising species of seafood, the rowing team of the Italian navy, flexing their muscles for our benefit, and well aware that we were ogling at them. I'd have to wait another decade before I'd be entertained in the Castel dell'Ovo by the sailors stationed there.

The Tempest was rather as I had expected, spectacular but uninspiring. Lattuada had done his best with the part concerning Pugachev's revolt (Van Heflin was well-dubbed in Italian) but the other Pushkin story on which the script was based, *The Captain's Daughter*, was lacklustre, not helped by the rather unconvincing lovemaking of Silvana Mangano and an actor called Geoffrey Horne. Naturally, Dino was convinced he had an international hit. I stayed on an extra day in Naples, at my own expense, and of course after moving into a cheaper hotel, to see something much more rewarding at the San Carlo, a performance of *Andrea Chénier* with the great soprano Antonietta Stella and, in the title role, Franco Corelli, the most handsome tenor in the world. Corelli has a fine voice and well-deserved the ovation he received from the Neapolitan audience after the 'Improvviso' sung by the young revolutionary poet in the first act. The tribute was spoiled, when the applause was subsiding, by an over-exuberant (male) fan shouting out: "You're a new Caruso!", at which all hell broke loose with jeers and counter-applause. Caruso had been born just across the Bay in Sorrento. It was sacrilege for Neapolitans to think that any new tenor could be as good. But there are those of us who prefer our tenors to be good-looking (which Caruso was certainly not!) as well as vocally gifted. The reaction of the audience was a show in itself, and confirmed to me that going to the opera in Italy is always a rewarding experience regardless of whether or not the performances were good.

For the special issue of *Films and Filming* dedicated to Italian cinema I was having difficulties preparing a piece 'by' Fellini, a first draft of which I had to make up from quotes published in Italian papers which Fellini gave me permission to quote from (He was busy arguing with De Laurentiis who was to have produced the film). He said his new film 'The Sweet Life' would have "a Baroque air", and that it would be "a portrait of Rome at a certain moment in its eternal history, the Summer of 1958", which he would try to reproduce in detail, "as if it were a film in period costume". He was referring above all, I think, to the rumpus that the photographers had caused on the Via Veneto the summer before when they chased after the ex-King Farouk and pursued Ava Gardner from one nightclub to another. Fellini admitted that the character to be played by Marcello Mastroianni would be something like the Moraldo of *I Vitelloni*, who had left his (and Fellini's own) home town, Rimini, at the end of the 1930s and now, twenty years later, had become a journalist, "but the interior problems of a journalist today are quite different from what they were when Moraldo was in his twenties. My Moraldo-Marcello as I have now written him does not set out to be controversial or satirical or moralistic. It is a gay story, intending only to amuse". Obviously at that time I had translated the Italian word 'allegro' as 'gay', which in the English language still meant what Webster defined it as! However, looking up the word I see that 'gay' then could also mean a 'fop or to a person of licentious tendency'. Webster's first edition was of course published in what historians describe as 'the Gay Nineties'.

Before Christmas, I went to see Fellini at his office on the Celio, one of Rome's seven hills, in the studio known as the Safa-Palatino, the production HQ of the new financial backer of the film, Angelo Rizzoli, the Milan publisher and producer-distributor who had taken over from Dino De Laurentiis when the latter wanted the new American star, Paul Newman, to play the journalist. Fellini's refusal to accept the casting of Newman gave Dino an excuse to pull out. In 'my' new article 'written by' Fellini, I quoted him as saying what he was telling everyone who interviewed him at the time: "How could I possibly have conveyed all I see in this character if instead of Mastroianni I had had an American who doesn't even speak Italian, let alone Roman dialect?"

Federico told me that he had nothing against American actors, and was possibly going to make a film with Gregory Peck (which of course he'd never make). I spent most of that morning at the Palatino studios watching scores of aspiring actors waiting to be received. Very few of them were professionals. When I was finally ushered in we had a friendly chat but he interviewed me rather than I him. He asked me questions about my life as a foreign newspaper man in Rome. I told him about my experiences at the Ekberg wedding and he said that he'd put me in the scene of the press conference in the film of the movie star who would in fact be played by Anita. He told me to come back in the New Year.

Chapter 7

On Christmas Day 1958, I went first for cocktails at the home of my dear friend Patricia (whose journalist husband was out of town) and as always we camped it up. I had invited her to come with me for a slap-up strictly English Christmas dinner (pudding et alia) at George's, the very chic restaurant managed by an Englishman, Vernon Jarratt, and his wife in the Via Veneto area. Vernon had first come to Rome with the liberating army and had stayed on, becoming a friend of Rossellini's and writing a history of the Italian cinema and then opening this restaurant. Who should be at another table but Dawn Addams and her father, the Group Captain (who would play one of the travellers in Antonioni's *L'avventura*). They asked us to join them for coffee and liqueurs and we had fun pulling crackers. We were both a bit tipsy so we took a walk in the fresh air of the Villa Borghese gardens, but I could see Patricia was wobbling so I took her home in a taxi, in which I then proceeded to the Valle Theatre, near Piazza Navona, where Eduardo De Filippo had left me house seats for the matinée of his very moralistic new play, its title taken from an Italian proverb, *Lies Have Long Tails*. My 'delinquent' friend, Enzo, joined me at the theatre and we enjoyed the play. Afterwards we went to our respective homes (we'd already exchanged Christmas greetings in the morning), but around midnight he returned, rushing in when I opened the door sleepily to tell me that the cinema across the street, the Reale, where we had sung 'Volare' with the crowd at Modugno's concert, was on fire. We watched from the terrace as the smoke poured out of the windows and the firemen arrived. I thus ended the festive day feeling like Nero watching Rome burn.

I had to get up very early the next morning which, in England, we call Boxing Day but which is Saint Stephen's Day according to the calendars of Catholic countries. I dragged myself across the Garibaldi bridge to the Ministry of Grace and Justice where, with other journalists, I was supposed to pick up a special pass to enter the Rome prison, Regina Coeli (Queen of the Heavens) in Trastevere, just along the Tiber, where Pope John was due to pay a Christmas visit to the inmates. At the Ministry, the policemen on duty didn't seem to expect us and told us to go anyway to the prison. When we got there we found more confusion. My friend, Patrick Crosse of Reuters, bullied them into letting us in on the basis of our press passes issued by the government. When the old boy arrived, looking indeed like Santa Claus, we waited in the central gallery while he made the tour of the cells and finally appeared to give his blessing to all the poor creatures who, well-washed and wearing what looked like new striped pyjamas for the occasion, were clinging to every possible space while Pope John prayed for them and their families. He told the tale that once as a boy he'd been caught poaching and had spent a night in jail. When he was leaving amidst applause I didn't think he or the Minister heard the prisoner who shouted pitifully: "Give us an amnesty!". It had been a very moving experience about which I enjoyed writing. The *Chronicle* published my story on the front page.

Enzo's Christmas leave had finished so I spent New Year's Eve with Salvatore who had reappeared. I saw 1959 in with him and the Trastevere crowd in a noisy local pizzeria. After Twelfth Night and the Epiphany festa had passed, the holidays were over and Rome became again a place where one had to get on with one's work. Peter Baker was pestering me to finish my chores for the *Films and Filming* Italian Special issue. A referendum among world film critics at the Brussels World Fair had chosen Vittorio De Sica as the greatest contemporary director, listing him after the first three of all time, Chaplin, Eisenstein and Clair. Peter particularly wanted a piece 'by' him. It wasn't easy to track down De Sica but I had a stroke of luck. The *NC* fashion editor was in town for the seasonal shows. I always enjoyed helping her because she was a fun person. She took me to dinner at Gigi Fazi's, Rome's best restaurant, in my opinion. Last year, Rossano Brazzi had been sitting at the next table and had given me a warm welcome which had, of course, impressed her. This year, who should be dining there but Vittorio De Sica and his lady friend, Maria Mercader. When he was leaving, he was very courteous as I introduced him to my colleague. He told us he had just come back from London. I told him I had left messages all over town saying I wanted a piece by him for our special issue. He promised to do it and, even though I'd have further problems tracking him down, he would eventually dictate a piece to a secretary who typed it out and sent it to me. In England, he had appeared for the first time in a TV series, *The Four Just Men*, based on tales by Edgar Wallace, and had acted in English. The piece he wrote discussed the difference between British and Italian humour. He felt that the only real difference, in our working methods, is that the Italians speak at the top of their voices, "while in England you speak under your breaths". De Sica said he was hoping to get Alec Guinness for one of the roles in the film he was preparing with Zavattini, *The Last Judgement*.

Photo by G. P. Poletto

John Francis Lane and Vittorio De Sica

In the New Year, I went to see Fellini again, as he had asked me to do. I showed him my version of his article for *Films and Filming* and, though his English was still not very good, he queried one or two points and I corrected them. He allowed me to stay in his office as he received his aspiring performers. It was an illuminating experience. Among the eccentric characters who showed up, everyone is welcome even if they hadn't been summoned for an interview, was a circus performer Federico told me was one of the original artists who inspired his Zampano-Quinn in *La Strada*.

On television, I watched Rossellini's documentaries about India. They were rather tedious with no visual qualities at all and very little original commentary. However, for the Italian issue, I translated a piece about Rossellini and India written by a friend, Callisto Cosulich, the film critic of the left-wing afternoon paper, *Paese Sera*. I didn't like Rossellini's recent work, not even the Bergman films, of which only *Europa '51* was worth remembering. I felt that Rossellini was turning into a guru for other film-makers and that contributed more to his reputation than his features did.

With another *Paese Sera* journalist, Maurizio Liverani, I was trying to write a film story about an Englishman in Rome. One evening, I went with him and his wife to a screening of Antonioni's early documentaries, which were quite brilliant, particularly *Gente del Po* (People of the Po Valley) about the area where he filmed *Il Grido*. Michelangelo and Monica [Vitti] invited us to eat with them afterwards and he agreed to write me a piece for our special issue. He delivered it promptly two days later. His piece began: "It is very difficult to talk about oneself, not a very pleasant thing to have to do. I am a film director and that explains many things. (Otherwise I might have become an architect or painter). In other words I feel I am a person who has things he wants to show rather than things he wants to say. The two concepts sometimes coincide and then we get a work of art. It is not my place to say whether this has happened in my case". I translated it and sent it off immediately to Peter Baker. I was also succeeding in getting some ads which no doubt made the publisher happy.

When I wrote my think-piece for the Italian issue, I tried to sum up how neo-realsm was born and the important role that some of the theorists of magazines, published before and after the fall of Fascism, had contributed to the movement that was now developing into an aesthetically more adventurous and individualistic creative cinema. The article begins: "In all the criticism which has been written about the Italian film renaissance of these last fifteen years, very little has been said outside of Italy about what is perhaps the most significant contribution by Italian film-makers to the history of the Cinema: namely, the cultural value of those Italian critics, many of whom were later to become directors or screenwriters themselves, who have made of the film a definite feature of their national culture, perhaps indeed, now we can take a perspective, as the most important development in the arts of Italy during the present century. Not since the time of Verdi has there been such creative activity in this country."

The News Chronicle sent me to Naples for the Socialist Party congress, where Pietro Nenni seemed to be continuing his 'splendid isolation' in Italian politics. He had broken with the Communists but was not yet in a hurry to join forces with the Christian Democrats. Richard Crossman, one the most left-wing members of the labour party, was also in Naples and was complaining that Nenni had not said anything about Italy's most urgent practical problems, such as how to deal with Mattei's ambitions. The ENI chief was on a visit to London so this question was very topical. The *NC* asked me to do a profile of Mattei in a hurry, so I rehashed the piece I wrote the year before, adding what I'd learned in Milan during a recent visit to the ENI methane refinery Metanopoli.

Meanwhile, in Rome, a much more interesting experience for me than having to write about Italian politics, was organised by The Teatro Club: a Sunday night performance by the English

Stage Company. Anne Guerrieri had asked me to write the programme notes and then help to stage-manage the event, in which George Devine, John Osborne and Joan Plowright would be appearing in excerpts from plays premiered at the Royal Court, including *Look Back In Anger*, with Osborne himself playing Jimmy Porter. They were looking for a local actor to appear in one of the scenes. When George Devine arrived I offered my services. The scene I played in was from Nigel Dennis's *The Making of Moo*, a rather weird fantasy which mocks religion. Evidently I acquitted myself well. It was exhilarating acting with such distinguished professionals. I was captivated by Joan Plowright when I'd been sent to the airport to escort her into town. John Osborne himself was more agreeable than I had expected. He was not at all the conceited pompous young rebel that they made him out to be in the British press. The only time I saw a glimpse of the 'angry young man' was when at the party given for them he was pestered by an Italian journalist and I had to protect him. For years to come that journalist would blame me for not having let him get that interview.

John Francis Lane with George Devine and John Osborne
in a scene from *The Making of Moo* in Rome.

I was eager to read more of the angry young writers. I hadn't yet read John Braine's bestselling first novel, *Room at the Top*, which I bought on one of my London trips in 1958. I was sorry I hadn't mentioned Braine in my article for the socialist magazine *Italia Domani*. It would have allowed me say something else positive about the new British writers, not all of whom should have been grouped under the 'Angries' label. As with *Lucky Jim*, I enjoyed Braine's portrait of a provincial intellectual humbug. But none of the 'angry young' books could stand up to Dostoevsky's novel about provincial life, *The Possessed*, which I had read first in 1947 and was re-reading excitedly. The angry young men of Dostoevsky's times were much more courageous. Still, these new British novels were about the England in which I grew up, even if I was a few years behind Jim and Joe. Re-reading my article, I was relieved I had not been as cynical as I feared, and had dedicated more irony towards the way the Angries had been exploited in the papers than to the writers themselves. As I had seen with Osborne, the writers were professionals who wanted to be heard and who had to accept being part of a 'movement' which, like neo-realism in Italy, had happened at the right moment in history and which, if given press attention, even sneeringly, could help to promote their cause as authors and as trendsetters. Like 'Baroque', the tag of 'Angry Young Men', was intended an insult when it was first used but it became a term of distinction.

In the last week of January 1959, the Italian government of Signor Fanfani had been obliged to resign. The fall was prompted by a scandal concerning a financier named Giuffré who, like the Sicilian-American, Sindona, had been dubbed 'God's banker'. My story in the *Chronicle* on Fanfani's fall was quoted in most of the daily papers here but only because the Italians like to think that somebody abroad cares about their politics.

I saw Renato Castellani's women-in-prison film, *Hell in the City*, (*Nella città l'inferno*) a rather over the top melodrama. I was sorry it got the cover of *Films and Filming*'s Italian issue (April 1959). Of course, Magnani and Masina were both adored in the UK. Magnani gave her regular performance as the strong-willed Roman woman who shouts her head off but can be gentle when her comfort is sought. Naturally she gave her all and almost saved the film.

Early in February, there was a literary-political scandal to write about. Poor old Ezra Pound, who lived in Rapallo, was under fire because an article signed by him had been published in the neo-fascist newspaper saying that socialists are imbeciles and that only Mussolini as an ex-socialist himself knew how to deal with them. Il Duce had given up socialist militancy after the 1917 Bolshevik Revolution. It was surprising that after all the years Pound had spent in a mental asylum to save him from being condemned as a traitor that he could still openly defend Fascism. Those of us who admired Pound's poetry, and who forgave him for some of his ideas and his indiscreet behaviour during the war, preferred to ignore this new outburst which some fascist-sympathising journalist must have cudgeled from the senile old poet who may have thought he was talking off the cuff. Certainly, Pound had not changed his mind about what he considered to be the main threat to the world, Big Finance, and he'd be proved right in so many of his views as the century proceeded. But he made the mistake of blaming the Jews for all the ills of capitalism when they were only 'guilty' of being the most expert at getting their "pound of flesh". Newspapers will always publish the stories that their journalists succeed in twisting out of the people they interview. I had always tried to avoid that kind of reporting even if I'd been guilty of doing some cudgeling myself. But at least I had given Fellini the chance to approve what I had put together to be by-lined by him.

The tenants in the flat next door to my attic finally left and the landlord agreed to let me take it over, as long as I organised the required structural works for which (maybe) he'd reimburse me (of course he never would but his agent would always be tolerant when I was late with the rent which now almost doubled). I would rent the other flat to a charming American girl, Sunny, a friend from Paris, who was studying at the Centro Sperimentale film school. She had been a lesbian but had been seduced by one of my earliest bisexual Italian lovers, a student from Bologna (when I stayed with him and his family he took me for my first and only visit to an Italian brothel. Inevitably I was more interested in the clients than the 'employees'!). His ex-girlfriend paid me six months rent in advance and would move in when the workman had opened up the wall dividing the two terraces. I had to persuade Salvatore to move out as he had been fighting with the cleaning girl and was getting too lazy. I made him give me back his keys and I left them with the workmen while I went away on what would be a merry press junket to Cortina in the Dolomites for the premiere of *Bell, Book and Candle*, starring the new sex idol of Italian men, Kim Novak. Novak's presence had a melting effect on all of us in this snowy landscape where none of us journalists wanted to ski. It was my only touch of wintery weather that year, for when I got back to Rome it was Spring-like even though it was only early March. When it was sunny I could sit outside looking towards the Janiculum hill and try to do some writing while the workmen continued on the other side of the Terrace.

I saw a new Italian play, which was 'angry' in its way, about a female partisan called *La Romagnola*, and was set in the Romagna region during the Resistance against Mussolini's ill-gotten Social Republic. Written and directed by Luigi Squarzina, for his Genoa civic theatre company, one of the best in Italy, the play was a bit rhetorical but impressive. The Leftists were there defending the play because young neo-fascists had been making demonstrations inside the theatre. I was amused however when I heard that these youngsters had been dropping mice on little parachutes from the gallery during the performance. Once again I wasn't sure whether in Italy the best theatre was on stage or off.

Chapter 8

The best 'theatrical' event of early 1959 was not in a theatre but on television. It was a show by Vittorio Gassman, the first attempt by an Italian actor-showman to try and do something original with the medium instead of just accepting a professional engagement. His weekly show, called *Il Mattatore* (which could be translated as The Big Show Off) gave this versatile actor the opportunity to display his eclectic talents in almost every sphere of Italian entertainment, except opera, even though he was often very operatic when performing tragedy. He was at his best in comedy as we'd seen in the film comedy of the moment, *I soliti ignoti*, but his mellifluous voice was also put to good use during the programme in poetry readings, the best of which seemed to me his quiet declamation of Lorca's *Death of Ignatius*.

The workmen put the final touches to my double terrace and, with the archway in between the terraces now open, my American friend, Sunny, moved in just in time for the Ides of March and the celebrations for my eighth anniversary as a Roman resident. The day after the party on the terrace, Sunny told me that she had heard at the film school in Via Tuscolana that Fellini had started shooting his *Dolce Vita* across the street at the Cinecittà studios. A set had built of the inside of the cupola of St Peter's, a stairway which Anita Ekberg is filmed climbing up with Marcello Mastroianni. A few days later, I was summoned to Cinecittà for the scene of Ekberg's press conference for which had been built a set representing the lounge of the movie star's suite at the Hotel Excelsior. The only other foreign journalist in the scene was Henry Thody who, with his handlebar moustaches and very English-style drinking habits, was a familiar sight in the Via Veneto bars, and in our Press Club where he represented the *Sunday Times* and other less serious papers. He'd often asked me to help him with his stories. We had a big row once when he got me into trouble with Sophia Loren because in a tabloid story he had quoted her as saying unkind things about Gina Lollobrigida which she hadn't said so brazenly. She blamed me because I'd introduced Thody to her. Naturally, Federico made him look as ridiculous as possible. I thought I'd probably look pretty silly myself as all I had to do for this first scene was to grab a glass or something to eat every time a waiter passed by. Ekberg greeted me warmly, obviously not connecting me with her wedding in Florence. I was just a news-paperman that she'd met somewhere.

John Francis Lane (bottom right) acting with Anita Ekberg
in Fellini's *La Dolce Vita*.

At a certain moment, when Federico made her behave grotesquely, she turned on him reproachfully and said: "Federico I think you're trying to make fun of me!" He embraced her and said affectionately: "But Anitona", which is what her name had become. "How could I? You're meant to be Ava Gardner". Federico was not lying. It was indeed Gardner he was parodying but Ava was a great star, some times a fair actress and always a Love Goddess. Anita Ekberg was a simple Nordic girl who had become a Sex Goddess. I no longer felt guilty that I'd sent her up in reporting her marriage to Tony Steel which I think had already ended. That evening in Florence, at the bar of an authentic Excelsior Hotel, she had offered me a glass of real champagne. Now in the phoney movie set of the Excelsior lounge, as I sipped the fizzy soda water which passed for champagne, I wondered what this film would be for Anita? I didn't realise it would be the performance which would immortalise her in cinema history.

After Easter, I was called to the *Dolce Vita* set again. This time they were shooting at Ciampino airport. It was the scene showing the arrival of Sylvia (Ekberg) and I was just one in the crowd of milling journalists and photographers. But the scene was great fun to watch shooting. Federico made the press and publicity men look even more outrageous than we had been on the Excelsior set. On screen, I'm not visible in this scene but there exists a photograph of me looking seductively at two carabinieri arresting me (not real ones but two stunning-looking students from the Centro Sperimentale film school hired as extras). This photograph was taken with my camera by one of Fellini's assistants, Gianfranco Mingozzi, who had been hired as sixth assistant. He told me that as the youngest member of the crew he had had the honour of striking the first 'ciak' (as the Italians call the clapper board) for the first shot inside the studio-built staircase of St. Peter's. He was only paid 20,000 lire a week, which was what I was paid for a day as an extra. But for him, just out of film school, it was an incomparable apprenticeship. He'd subsequently be promoted within the crew and would later become a director himself, making some excellent TV documentaries and some classy features. The photo would always hang on the walls of my homes. Gianfranco, who'd become a lifelong friend, would publish it in a nostalgic book he wrote about his experience of the making of the film, and I chose it for the cover of this book.

During the three days I was on the set at Ciampino, I didn't have much chance to speak to Federico but, as always, it was enthralling to watch him at work directing actors in the way they did in silent cinema, giving orders to the actors from behind the camera. One day however, I did manage to give him a copy of the Italian Special Number of *Films and Filming* which had just arrived. I showed him the article with his by-line that I'd put together and he seemed pleased with it, particularly when he found himself saying: "I turned down a fortune to make a film about horses in Hollywood with Anna Magnani". He admitted it was true. The film was *Wild is the Wind*. But the day after, when he'd had time to look through the magazine more thoroughly, he took me aside on the set and said he had been upset by something I'd said in 'A Style is Born', the 'think piece' about Italian cinema. My article was full of praise for Visconti and Antonioni and I had perhaps been too severe with Fellini and *La Strada*. I wrote that *La Strada* was "disputable as a work of art, even on an individualistic level". I realize now that I was too much under the influence of the Marxist ideas of Guido Aristarco and his *Cinema Nuovo* (whom Fellini in fact teased in one of the questions put to Anita at the press conference). Fellini told me like a hurt child: "One day you'll learn to appreciate *La Strada*". I told him I had seen it again several times and though each time I appreciated its qualities more, there were still things about it I'd never accept. As Giulietta was visiting the set and was nearby when we were talking I didn't say more.

I returned to my busy life as a real-life correspondent. It meant covering the visit to Rome of the Queen Mother and Princess Margaret who, of course, called on the new Pope. I was still an Englishman at heart so I was delighted to see the Queen Mum up close, having as a boy worshipped her and the King from the time of their Coronation. All the children of Britain had been given medallions to commemorate the event. During the war, the Royal Family's grace and strength had given us comfort. Now, the Queen Mother's graciousness was sufficient to disarm even the most rabid republican. Less pleasing to meet was Margaret, whose previous Roman visit had seen me obliged to do the rounds of Rome by Night in pursuit of her. She seemed very bored when she had to shake hands with us journalists at the Embassy reception. Somewhat different from Audrey Hepburn's enchanting fairytale Princess in *Roman Holiday*. The press built up a myth about Margaret having a flirtation with the Italian-German royal prince, Enrico d'Assia, a painter whom I'd met in Forio d'Ischia and I knew that his preferences were not for the female sex. I tried to get an exclusive interview with Enrico but he didn't return my call. Obviously it was embarrassing for him. It was all part of the real 'dolce vita'.

The *Chronicle* sent along someone from our diary column who didn't have much success with the story. I was happy to give a helping hand to a colleague from the *Standard*, Anne Sharpely who was apparently a pet of Lord Beaverbrook. She had recently stayed at his villa at Cap-d'Ail. We got along fine and, looking in my diary of the day, I see that we both appreciated the charms of the young man who drove the car she hired. For the receptions in honour of the royals I proudly wore my tails for the first time, the splendid outfit Angelo Litrico had tailored for me. The Embassy affair was rather a bore but I liked the one at the Quirinal Palace, with the splendidly uniformed Corazzieri lining the staircase where once Popes and then the 'Sardinian' Kings (as Augustus Hare scathingly called the Savoy monarchy) had reigned. Now Giovanni Gronchi, the President of the Republic, was trying to deal with the musical chairs of Italian politics.

In spite of all the sympathy that had been exchanged between Britain and Italy during the visit by the royal ladies, relations between our two countries suffered a set-back, even with a few smiles, when there was another silly story for me to cover. Before the start of an England-Italy soccer match at Wembley, the band had played by mistake the Royal March of Augustus Hare's Sardinian royalty instead of the national anthem of the thirteen-year old Italian Republic. The fervent Italian Republicans complained angrily at the careless affront. But the joke was that the No. 1 royalist of Italy, a certain Renato Marmiroli, whom I had recently met with his publisher, chose me to deliver a message to the bandmaster at Wembley Stadium thanking him for his "historic error which had brought a thrilling moment of happiness and pride to millions of Italian patriots who were listening to the match" on the radio. The *News Chronicle* gave much space to my story, somewhat lessening my ironical angle, and running an editorial saying that there should be more people like Marmorili, "who are so loyal to their ideals". Maybe this was intended as tongue in cheek but it seemed a stupid thing to write for a paper that continued to boast that it was "a paper as good as the people who write for it". That applied to writers like Jimmy Cameron (and maybe I liked to think sometimes to JFL) but not to the author of that silly editorial.

I'd wear my tails again that Spring, this time for the reception in honour of President De Gaulle. Real champagne was served (not the spumante of the Quirinale) in the setting of the French Embassy which was housed in the opulent Palazzo Farnese, splendidly illuminated inside and out for the occasion. It was more exciting than anything a film set could offer. One evening, however, before April ended, I heard that they were shooting a key scene for *La Dolce Vita* between Mastroianni and Ekberg at night in the streets near the Trevi Fountain. I dragged myself over to see what was going on but found such a crowd gathered that I couldn't get close to see what was being filmed. I should have been more patient, of course, for they were shooting the scene when Anita goes into the fountain followed by Marcello. I missed watching live one of the greatest sequences in cinema history, where reality and a film set joined forces to create magic.

I was reading D. H. Lawrence's *Sea and Sardinia* in preparation for a holiday in Alghero in May with my mother. Lawrence was right in saying that Sardinia was "left outside of time and history". I didn't get to see the rugged mountain areas, and I wouldn't visit Cagliari until many decades later when I went there to see an opera, but the part of the island I saw with my mother was very suited to tourist travel. I soon found out that the reason for her visit was not only to have a holiday with me but also to ask my 'permission' to marry again. Her husband-to-be was a jolly, retired, merchant sea captain, the widower of her cousin. I was of course delighted because I knew she was very lonely. I had always felt guilty at not being able to visit her more often. She'd say to me rather coyly "Of course we'll sleep in separate rooms. None of that nonsense for me. But at least he will join me in a drink now and then". She had recently been courted by a former boyfriend, a Canadian officer she'd first met when working at the War Office during the Twenties but had preferred my father to him. Now he was a widower. Meeting the much mellowed Canadian again after so many years she was horrified when they spent a 'trial' weekend together in, I think, Ostend. He had been shocked when she wanted to drink a nightcap. She was much better off with the ex-sailor.

Early in June came an invitation to go to Cinecittà, this time as a real journalist, for a party on the set which Fellini had preferred to create rather than shoot in the real Via Veneto. He could thus shoot night scenes without the sightseeing crowds that had turned up when he was filming at the Trevi Fountain. On the tables of the cafés of 'the street' built by the set dressers we were served a buffet. The producer, Rizzoli, was basking in glory and seemed indifferent to how much his 'crazy genius' was costing him. Among the stars present was the legendary Louise Rainer, who had been expected to start shooting her scenes a month ago, but nobody knew, or wanted to say, why she still hadn't shot them, until someone confided to me that she and Fellini didn't seem to be able to agree on the character she'd be playing, apparently a temperamental American writer who treated Marcello as a good lay and who wasn't interested in his literary ambitions. Years later, Tullio Kezich suggested Rainer's refusal to play the part was also dictated by economic considerations. It was not surprising that Federico would finally give up trying to convince her to trust in him. Rainer would be one of the few international stars who Federico didn't succeed in catching in his net. In the end, however, the character was eliminated from the script. Perhaps to the film's benefit.

I was determined to get to Spoleto in June for Menotti's second Festival of Two Worlds which, after the success of the first year, was now a big social event. Visconti was staging a rarely performed Donizetti opera, *Il Duca d'Alba*, another stunning production conducted by Thomas Schippers. A fiery production of Prokofiev's *Angel of Fire* shocked the local clerics; and some splendid Jerome Robbins ballets delighted us all. Above all there was John Gielgud who performed his recital, *The Ages of Man*, which ran the whole gamut of Shakespeare from sonnet to Prospero breaking his staff. It was the sort of theatrical occasion which made me wonder why I ever left London. I soon found out a good reason why. In addition to the artistic joys in Spoleto, I succeeded in making a conquest, a carabiniere who gave me an appointment at midnight near the public gardens which were dimly lit. The couples who were already engaged in amorous activity took flight immediately when they saw two tall men arrive, one in uniform. So we had the place to ourselves for a delightful encounter. He obviously needed the sex more than the exorbitant sum he asked for afterwards which was probably to placate his masculine honour. But as he knew he was risking more than me, and fortunately didn't get violent, I gave him twice what I usually paid for these encounters and we parted amicably. Prudently, after the early years of excesses in Rome I tried to avoid open air encounters, not only for the risks involved but also for reasons of hygiene, but Spoleto was a city which had always cast a magical spell on me since my first visit there at the age of twenty, long before it hosted a chic international festival. Looking back now I remember another 'military' conquest I'd make under those same trees many years later on an historical summer night for Italy. On that occasion I finished making love with a young man in uniform just at the moment in which the population of Spoleto, like those of every Italian city, were making bedlam in the streets to celebrate Italy's World Cup victory.

Back in Trastevere I had a less pleasing encounter with the Italian police than the one in Spoleto in 1959. A local lad who worked in a butcher's shop, whom I had been seeing regularly, had been arrested. In order to convince the police he was an honest boy at heart, he told them he had stolen my Leica camera but had brought it back. This was true, but when I was summoned to the police station, and did my best to put in a good word for him, the police told me bluntly, obviously quite aware of the situation,

"Mr. Lane, let us judge who is honest or not. As a newspaper man you should concern yourself with more interesting stories and above all be a bit more careful about the company you keep!"

I could hardly tell them of the company I had just been keeping in Spoleto! It would be unfair to describe such encounters in the terminology of what today passes in 'gay' literature as 'rough trade'. I was only an offbeat experience in the lives of those young men, but I like to think that many of them, especially those who were doing their conscript military service in Rome, lonely and short of lire, will remember with pleasure even if only privately the times we spent together without feeling their masculine pride had been compromised.

Later in the summer, though my finances were low, I was able to take another weekend in Spoleto thanks to having done a well-paid day's work in a film. In Spoleto, I was glad to see Gielgud's recital again and this time I went backstage where he gave me a warm welcome. I said I'd been shy to come back after the First Night because I expected him to be surrounded by admirers, like he had been when I last went back to say "Hello" after seeing his spellbinding Prospero at Stratford. But now after hearing him conclude his recital with the monologue, "Our revels now are ended". I wanted to tell him how moved I'd been. "It's kind of you" he said somewhat sadly, "but as a matter of fact, my dear, I've had very few backstage callers here in Spoleto". Indeed I'd heard that Menotti and the other festival bigwigs, though very respectful, had not been making a fuss of him. He was quite happy to comply when I asked if I could come and photograph him. He gave me an appointment the next morning in the apartment of Menotti's palazzo in the Duomo piazza which had been given to him for his stay (Menotti had moved to a palazzo in a quieter part of town). I took the photos, and they came out well, but I never succeeded in getting one published, despite interest from *The Observer*, because there was an inkers strike in Fleet Street. The only story I got into the *Chronicle* from Spoleto was about Louis Armstrong who'd been taken ill after his concert. I couldn't even get a story in about two new American plays that I'd seen at the Festival, one by William Inge, the other a first draft of Tennessee Williams's intriguing but complex *The Night of the Iguana*, which premiered there with Actors Studio players.

I found solace in my Roman life. Having stayed for the six months she had paid in advance, Sunny had gone off to San Francisco to get married. Another American girl and her handsome but rather grumpy boy friend moved in. Thanks to them however I was able to set up a dinner party on our terrace for Antonioni and Monica Vitti, an excellent meal cooked by my Trastevere lover, Enzo. Monica was her usual delightful self. Michaelangelo, keeping the theme of alienation out of his conversation, was an enjoyable dinner guest. We all enjoyed a good gossip about the film world.

I attended a fabulous garden party at Roberto Rossellini's villa at Santa Marinella to which I had been invited once before, when Queen Ingrid was on the throne. These were the gardens where Ingrid had tried to strangle the chicken in Roberto's episode of *We, the Women*. However, the reigning queen now was Roberto's new lady friend, the charming Indian intellectual, Sonali Das Gupta. Alas, she was not present that day. There was a great deal of discussion during the afternoon over how far a shooting script should be complete before the cameras start rolling, obviously something essential to the whole concept of Italian post-war filmmaking. The film that Rossellini had just finished shooting, which he said might be ready for the Venice Festival that summer, *Il Generale della Rovere*, was perhaps the first Rossellini had made with a carefully prepared script. It was written by a pungent journalist, Indro Montanelli, author of the original story, together with the Catholic playwright, Diego Fabbri, and Sergio Amidei, the original scriptwriter of *Open City*.

I took visiting friends from London to a restaurant which had just opened in Trastevere and was already all the rage. It was called 'Meo Patacca', the name of a low-life local poet of the 19th century, obviously a hero of the restaurant's owner, Remington, or 'Remy', a jovial Australian who passed himself off as an American. He had come to Italy to study singing but, after a few months at La Scala school in Milan, had discovered that he didn't have a strong enough baritone voice to rival Tito Gobbi, so had come to Rome to look for work in films. He got the odd acting job but, like most American actors who had settled in Rome, he got regular work only in dubbing. Remy spent most of his time and money drinking and exploring the haunts where Roman dialect poets used to recite publicly but were no longer welcomed. He had married a rather frail half-oriental Italian woman who, evidently, had a small inheritance and they decided to open a tavern where friends could gather for a drink and to recite their poems. They went into partnership with a couple of crafty waiters who had helped them to find a place near the Saint Cecilia church, a dilapidated hole in the wall with a cellar which they opened up. From the start it was something more than a tavern. Before that summer was out, it would expand from two to six rooms and would spread up over two more floors. It was such a success that he (and his waiters, proving themselves very competent business partners) would make a fortune and buy up the whole piazza. But during those first weeks it was still unspoiled. The waiters and customers all very friendly. I went every night with friends, drinking that surprising vernaccia wine which I'd so recently discovered in Sardinia. Many Roman intellectuals 'took it over' as the place to go that season. It was there that I first met Pasolini who I found one evening having a riotous time with local lads, a couple of whom I knew.

Among my professional engagements that summer was a request to translate the catalogue for the forthcoming Venice Festival; and a festival invite to Taormina, my only chance to enjoy a summer holiday. The sea at Taormina is something very special. In those years, the festival didn't count for much. It hadn't yet become the glamorous international event of later years. It was a somewhat improvised provincial occasion during which the first films of the up and coming season (the foreign ones already dubbed into Italian) would get their Italian premieres in the open-air arenas of the two hosting cities, Messina and Taormina, the latter of course in the fabulous 'Greek' theatre attended every night by many thousands of Sicilians and tourists. When the films were showing at Messina, however, it meant getting into evening dress at 6 pm and travelling by coach along a road which went through all the villages on the coast. Often men, women and donkeys would be blocking the streets. The final night ceremony in the Greek Theatre is the awarding of the Davids of Donatello. Most that year went to two films which had not enjoyed great critical success: Lattuada's *The Tempest* and Castellani's *Hell in the City* (Magnani winning Best Actress, of course). The only foreign star present was Susan Hayward, star of Robert Wise's *I Want to Live*, retitled in Italian *I Don't Want to Die*.

However, the most interesting event of the week in the Greek Theatre was a stage performance called *The Trial of Orestes*. The defence of Orestes was intriguing. The blame for the killings was put on the Ancient Gods. Among the dramatic excerpts performed splendidly by Vittorio Gassman was a scene from Sartre's brilliant philosophical play, *The Flies*, in which Orestes is an existentialist hero who takes full responsibility for his act and thus becomes a free man. In an Italian public trial, even if only in a stage show, there had to be a victorious Christian morality in the conclusion. In this case, the Christians won but only by a narrow majority from the 15,000 voting spectators. Only in Italy could an audience pay to sit watching lawyers gabbling away for more than two hours and by their thunderous applause show they felt they had got their money's worth.

Chapter 9

Back in Rome from Taormina, I kept up with my newspaper chores. Standing in for the *Evening News* man, I wrote a story about the problems Sophia Loren and Carlo Ponti were having in trying to get their marriage recognised without him being arrested for bigamy. They'd married in Mexico but the Vatican refused to consider his divorce valid. The *News* liked the story and said they had sold it to the *New York Post* who, in due time, sent me a cheque for fifteen dollars.

The News Chronicle had sponsored a quite preposterous expedition across the Alps in Hannibal's footsteps by a group of undergraduates who, alas, did not succeed in getting their elephant through the pass they had chosen. They arrived in Rome rather disconsolately without the elephant, so I cheered them up by taking them to dinner at Meo Patacca's where they all got drunk. Of course, I charged it to the paper including the taxis which took them back to their hostel on the outskirts of the city.

I don't remember much about Venice 1959 because I didn't keep a diary but, from what I wrote in *Films and Filming,* I see, somewhat to my amazement, that I wrote the most damning report so far which showed that, as usual, I was biting off the hand that fed me. In this case literally because they gave me royal treatment. When I'd arrived, I found I was the British representative on three juries which would have entitled me to hospitality anyway so perhaps I had a right to be resentful as it now meant I had done the translation of the catalogue for free. Certainly the festival had started off badly with the opening film, made by a director named Kevin McClory, who hit the headlines less for his mediocre film, *The Boy on the Bridge,* than for his performance at the Excelsior bar when he delivered a left upper cut at the chin of London film critic, Leonard Mosley, who had evidently panned his film in advance.

I had tried hard to defend Ammannati's policy of selecting films rigorously but this year his selection committee had not served him well. Maybe it was just bad luck for Venice that 1959 had seen the birth at Cannes of what was becoming known as the Nouvelle Vague. Francois Truffaut's *Les quatre cents coups* had bowled everyone over even though it had only won the best direction award. Even the British Cinema had made a good showing at Cannes with Jack Clayton's film of John Braine's novel *Room at the Top*. At Berlin, the French had also scored well with Claude Chabrol's *Le beau Serge*, but the same director's subsequent film *A double tour*, shown at Venice, though lavishly filmed, was a chilly unemotional pseudo-Hitchcockian whodunnit. It won the Best Actress award for Madeleine Robinson.

The 20th Venice Festival saved face however with two small American independent films, Lionel Rogosin's *Come Back, Africa*, and a collectively made experimental film, *The Savage Eye*, which had Bunuel-like touches. The industry impressed only with Otto Preminger's *Anatomy of a Murder*. Its clinical candour shocked a bit, but the rather conventional casting of James Stewart as the somewhat dizzy down-on-his-luck attorney, and the wisecracking, Eve Arden as the secretary, made the film seem rather déja vu. Ingmar Bergman's latest film, *The Magician* (Ansiktet, *The Face*) was full of his usual imaginative touches with its curious tale of a travelling hypnotist showman. It had premiered at Edinburgh the week before but it was still considered eligible for Venice where it won the Jury's Special Prize. I went early one morning to a small screening room in the cellars of the Palazzo del Cinema to see the final part of Satyajit Ray's trilogy, *The World of Apu*. Apparently the selection committee had refused to accept it for the competition "because it was too similar to *Aparajito*, the second film in the trilogy, which had won the Golden Lion two years before". What a shameful criterion!

I was proud that the FIPRESCI jury on which I represented Britain had no difficulty in deciding to give the international critics prize, for films screened out of competition, to Andrei Wajda's magnificent *Ashes and Diamonds*, the only masterpiece screened in Venice that year. I felt this director was destined to become another of the European greats. The other jury I was on gave its award to another fine Polish film, *The Train* by Jerzy Kawalerowicz, which was perhaps the best of the fourteen films in the official competition. The Polish cinema was also having its New Wave but was getting less attention than the one from France. In Venice, it had obviously been pre-planned that the Italians should win, so much so that Rossellini's *Il Generale della Rovere* and Mario Monicelli's *La Grande Guerra* (The Great War), two films of distinction but neither a masterpiece, shared the Golden Lion. Curiously, nobody, not even the selection committee, had seen them in advance because both were finished only a few days before being shown on the Lido. Anyway, nobody complained about the Italian victory. Both films were on the honest theme that war-time heroes were not necessarily the stuff that rhetorical heroism decries. I had been appointed secretary of a committee of foreign journalists in Rome to select five candidates for the first ever Foreign Press Film Award. The award, for the best Italian film of 1959 would be presented early in 1960 at Rome's Excelsior Hotel. I realized immediately that the Rossellini and the Monicelli were probable candidates for the prize. Gassman and Sordi gave excellent performances in Monicelli's ironical First World War story; De Sica got away with his gamble on a dramatic role in the uninspired but competent Rossellini film and, I thought, deserved the Best Actor cup. But to keep the Americans happy it went to James Stewart for the Preminger film. Most of the reports from Venice would describe this as the worst festival of recent years, even if we at least enjoyed seeing new films by Bergman and Bunuel (*Nazarin*) as well as the two American independent films and 'our' Polish prizewinners. But there was also the great curiosity of retrospective screenings of German and Italian films of the Nazi and Fascist regimes which had played at Venice between the first festival in 1932 and 1939, and which included Leni Riefenstahl's stupendous *Olympia*. The much-maligned director told me blandly that she never intended her film to be a hymn of praise to Hitler Youth. She also told me that she wanted to make a film about Greek Amazons with herself as the Queen. On the Lido she certainly looked ready for the part. This story about her was the only item from the 20th Venice Film Festival that I got into an English newspaper. Talking of *Olympia*, in 1960 the Olympic Games were to be held in Rome, and at the same time as the 21st Festival. As I left the Lido I wondered which I would choose to attend? I didn't know what fate had in store for me.

On my way back to Rome, after another stop-over in Bergamo for the arts film festival, I decided to explore the Italian city of Vicenza. I had made a passing visit a few years before, when the Venice Festival and the tourist board of the Venetian Region took journalists on a half-day tour of the Palladian villas. I had promised myself to come back to see more of the city, starting with Palladio's Teatro Olimpico. I got the impression that audiences went there more to appreciate the splendour of the theatre itself than to see the performances. I attended a concert performance, in English, of Purcell's *Dido and Aeneas*, with the fabulous black American soprano, Gloria Davy, and seven string musicians. To find out what it felt like for an actor to perform in such a restricted space, I'd have to wait many years, until I'd be engaged to play Sir Politic-Would-Be in an Italian production of *Volpone* for Vicenza's annual theatre festival. Before leaving Vicenza I visited a superb Palladian villa which had not been included on the previous Palladian tour. It had been built for the Valmarana family. It was closed so I rang the front doorbell. Who should open the door but a film critic I knew well from Rome! Count Paolo Valmarana, the son of the house, the critic for the Christian Democrat newspaper. He showed me around, letting me see the stunning Tiepolo frescoes on the ceilings of the rooms where he and his family slept and entertained. This was the home where he had grown up. It was a rare pleasure to visit a beautiful monument that people also lived in.

The new season in Rome began for me with a private screening of Francesco Rosi's new film, *I magliari*, which unfortunately was a bit of a let-down after the promise of his debut, *La Sfida*. It often happens that a director whose first film has been highly praised disappoints with his second. Like his first, it was a film about Southerners but this time Southern emigrants in West Germany. The English title would be *The Swindlers* but a 'magliaro' is a particular type of rag trade swindler who cheats his customers by selling ersatz materials as finery. The Roman 'fusto', Renato Salvatori (dubbed with a Neapolitan accent) plays a basically honest emigrant, stuck in Hamburg without a job, who becomes the lover of a nouveau riche business tycoon's wife, well-played by English actress, Belinda Lee, who combines an almost Latin-style sensuality with sophistication, rare in English-born girls. Belinda had been a Rank starlet, but was now getting better parts in Italian films than she had ever had in England. The other story in the film is about a Roman good-for-nothing, played with his usual comic bravura by Alberto Sordi, who had become Italy's top box-office star thanks to the success of a film I despised for it's over the top slapstick, *An American in Rome*. *I magliari* is superbly filmed by Gianni Di Venanzo. His vividly contrasting black and white cinematography captures the moods of the new neo-capitalist Germany re-emerging in its Northern cities, but Rosi failed to unite the two stories, the dramatic sex melo of Salvatori and Lee with the social satire of Sordi's pathetic Italian abroad trying to cheat his way into survival. Maybe Rosi's producer and distributor, Gustavo Lombardo of Titanus, was too eager to score a commercial success. But it proved to be a flop for them all. Rosi had yet to make his greatest films.

I carried on trying to keep the *Chronicle* happy, but the stories of mine they printed were only little items like the massacre of starlings in the gardens of the British ambassador to the Vatican, and the announcement that President Gronchi had been invited to Moscow, which was causing controversy here because it would be the first visit to the Soviet Union by a Catholic Head of State since the Revolution. The *Chronicle's* holiday supplement asked me to write a piece describing how visitors to next year's Olympic Games would be able to get around and enjoy themselves in the Italian capital. Obviously, I had to be a good tourist guide but I managed to get in a plug for the Meo Patacca restaurant in Trastevere which had now become the most fashionable eating venue in Rome. I was sorry to think of it being filled with tourists but, since it was going to happen anyway, I thought I might as well give it a boost.

One night in October, I went to a cine-music hall housed in a small square behind a main street of central Rome, probably once the entrance to the stables and servants quarters of the palazzo belonging to the Altieri family, but the palazzo now counted Anna Magnani among its chic residents. I usually went to these cine music halls for the (military) audiences attending the early evening variety show but, on this occasion, I was there to see a late night screening of veteran director Carmine Gallone's recent film of *Tosca*. My adored Franco Corelli was singing as well as acting in it. Tosca was played by a pretty American actress with her voice dubbed (not very well synchronised!) by the great soprano, Maria Caniglia. During the interval of the film who should arrive but Cesare Zavattini, with a frankly not very attractive young woman. He introduced her to me as a Mexican singer. It was almost midnight when the film ended. I was preparing to leave but Za recommended I stay for the variety show. I am glad I did. The star attraction was a drag act which was quite extraordinary. Maybe it was something I should put in my Olympic tourist guide? Or maybe not! I was thinking a lot about the 1960 Rome Olympics and the fact it would clash with the Venice Festival to which I had now received a phone call from Ammannati, and an official letter from the Biennale asking me to be the British representative on next year's jury. I thanked Ammannati and provisionally accepted, but I decided I would wait until the New Year to reply officially.

The only theatrical event of October that I recorded in my diary was a production in a Rome theatre of *Caligula*. Camus had refused the rights to Italians after seeing and hating a production by Giorgio Strehler in Milan in 1946 but, fourteen years on, had given the rights free of charge to a company of students who had claimed to have abandoned the Academy of Dramatic Art. A lot of famous actors had walked out from the Academy of Dramatic Art because they didn't think it was teaching them much. I was impressed by the performance, particularly by the very young (and strikingly exotic) actor who played the title role, Carmelo Bene. It turned out that only he and the director had left the Academy, expelled for their rebellious behaviour. Carmelo's type of flashy good looks had no appeal for me but there was something ingenuously exciting about his performance, the way he seemed to be almost parodying traditional Italian histrionic acting. In my diary I praised his "frenzied style of acting" without being aware, of course, how important Carmelo's influence would be on Italian theatre and, later, in films. I knew at once that I needed to see more of this type of experimental performance but several years would pass before I caught up with him again. His work was often considered scandalous (on one occasion, he had peed on a distinguished critic in the front row). I would publish enthusiastic articles about him, including one for *The Times*, which would shock and irritate many conservative Italian theatre folk. I would later accompany him on a trip to London to help him find an actor to play Edward II in a film he hoped to make of Marlowe's play. He chose Oliver Tobias. The film never materialised because the backer of the project had his fortune blocked by the revolution in Libya.

Carmelo Bene, Olivier Tobias, John Francis Lane

At the end of October, with *NC* not interested in sending me to the Christian Democrat party congress in Florence, I accepted an invitation to go to Turin where Dino De Laurentiis was presenting the Italian premiere of *La Grande Guerra*. The flight was harrowing. Somewhere around Genoa, the plane hit a terrifying storm and we all thought the end was nigh. The fact that I was sharing the threat of disaster with some of the most important names in the Italian cinema was little consolation. Fortunately, at the worst moments, Vittorio Gassman gave us an impromptu comic show which helped to calm our nerves. We reached Turin safely. The premiere, the following day at the historical Carignano opera house, was a great success. Dino, who had not enjoyed being caught in the storm on the flight up, hired a de-luxe restaurant car of Italian state railways for the return and had it latched on to the Turin-Rome express. It was one of the most enjoyable train journeys I'd have in all my years of travelling up and down Italy, even if I didn't get a chance to speak to Dino. He was playing cards throughout the whole trip – and winning, of course!

In Rome, I attended a press conference at the Excelsior given by Joe Levine, the American tycoon who had bought the first Italian *Hercules* film, dubbed it into English and spent a million dollars to launch it (successfully) in the U.S.A. and round the world. He was now producing others of the genre. At the cocktail party, I met the star, Steve Reeves, who was quite the most gorgeous hunk of man I'd ever set eyes on in my life, and somewhat more admirable than the Italian muscle boys I rave about. Certainly, Steve was superior

Steve Reeves in *Giant of Marathon*.

to the second-rate American (or bogus American) muscle men subsequently hired as stars of the Italian films of the genre!

Of more cultural interest that autumn were meetings at the British Council, first with Harold Acton, who told me that he was about to publish a book on the history of the Bourbons. Obviously he was going to whitewash the notorious family but I looked forward to reading the book even while doubting he could make me feel sympathy for the outrageous King Bomba. I had adored Harold Acton's *Memoirs of an Aesthete*, a book I'd treasure all my life, though it did leave me feeling I didn't want to become an 'aesthete' myself. There was also a meeting with E. M. Forster, who seemed in an advanced stage of senility, but who still seemed to have an eye for the boys. I was reading his marvellous novella, *Where Angels Fear to Tread*, which I thought someone should make into a film.

At the beginning of November my first-ever article for *The Times* was published under the by-line of 'a correspondent'. I'd soon be promoted to 'special correspondent' and then, one happy day, when the august publication finally agreed to credit its contributors, I too would get my name in print. The first piece was about the current problems in Italian theatre and cinema. The Rome paper *Paese Sera* reprinted the whole article in Italian and that gave me a big boost.

I was summoned to Cinecittà to dub my lines in *La Dolce Vita* but found to my dismay that there wasn't much of me left on the screen, though Federico wanted the lines in English from me and Henry Thody, whose moustache of course got him a bigger close-up. It suddenly occurred to Federico that his movie star, Sylvia, had not been given a surname so I was asked to provide it. As an 'in-joke' I suggested the name of 'Rank' and he accepted it. It was my only contribution to the script of the film which everyone was becoming eager to see. Federico promised that the first rough cut would soon be ready and that he'd be happy to show it to us and hear our opinion. But when we pressmen went out to Cinecittà for a press party for a costume flick about Archimedes, after grabbing a drink and a sandwich, we called on Federico, who had told us that first cut of the film might be ready that week. He apologised, saying it was still not ready and had been "cut up into a hundred pieces again". He was still making changes. We stayed on and watched him doing some more dubbing. He was busy trying to get a real peasant woman to say: "Yes, we've seen the Madonna". After twenty-six takes he was finally satisfied. I asked him why did he bother? Couldn't a good actress have done the line immediately? He looked at me coyly and said: "But I like to have authentic voices when they're available. Didn't I let you dub your line Francescone!"

Before we left Cinecittà, Valerio Zurlini caught sight of us and invited us to see his film, *L'estate violenta* (Violent Summer) which was very elegantly filmed, a quite original approach to the critical moment of the 'violent' summer of 1943 when the middle and upper class Italians were enjoying their holidays on the Adriatic coast, seemingly indifferent to the fact that Italy was losing the war, and was about to be plunged into civil strife between the two Italys, the fascists and the partisans. A young French actor, Jacques Perrin, to whom Peter Baker would give a lot of attention in *Films and Filming*, played the pampered son of a local fascist boss who ends by siding with the anti-fascists. Certainly Zurlini's film would be another which we would take into consideration for our first Foreign Press film award which I was busily trying to get organised.

My autumnal social highlight was the state visit of Prince Rainier of Monaco and Princess Grace and the receptions in their honour. The first invitation I got was from the President of the Republic to the Quirinal Palace, the usual formal affair when journalists don't see much of the distinguished guests. The second invitation was more glamorous and I was one of the few foreign journalists invited. It was to the Grand Hotel. The royal couple greeted us all at the entrance. It was the first time I had seen the former Hollywood star close up, and though this gave me no particular emotion, I was impressed by her beauty and graciousness, certainly more endearing than meeting Princess Margaret at the British Embassy. I would write to my mother that I had shaken hands with Grace Kelly; and Mother would tell everyone in Eastbourne what an exciting life her son was living in Rome.

His Serene Highness

PRINCE RAINIER III
and
MISS GRACE KELLY

A smaller social event was a party given by my friend, Luisa Spagnoli, whom I hadn't seen much of since our abortive 'romance' in Venice. I was glad to finally see her lovely apartment and meet some of her friends, mostly from the art world. She had quite a stunning collection of modern art works, none of which I would have been particularly eager to hang on my walls. A late arrival to the party was Alberto Moravia, still smarting from the fact that the Nobel Prize for Literature that year had gone to another Italian writer, the Sicilian poet, Salvatore Quasimodo. With him was Pier Paolo Pasolini who told me he was quite pleased with the film he had just written for Mauro Bolognini, called *La notte brava*, even if he said he'd had doubts about the casting of French actors, Jean-Claude Brialy and Laurent Terzieff, to play Roman boys. This would also be a candidate for our foreign press film award.

Sunday, November 22, 1959, was a day I underlined in my diary as an historic date in my Roman life. I finally saw *La Dolce Vita* at Cinecittà, a rough first cut without the musical score. Fellini told us it was being composed by Nino Rota but much of the 'original' music we heard on the temp track was more or less what we'd hear, cleaned up, in the finished film. Among the many spellbinding visuals I was particularly impressed by the opening shots of a statue of Christ being flown over the Roman rooftops by a helicopter, in which Mastroianni, as the journalist, is waving to girls sunbathing on a terrace. I was dazzled by the scenes in and around the Trevi fountain when Mastroianni wades in after Ekberg (what a fool I was to miss that night's shooting!). Dazzling too was the long erotic sequence in the castle north of Rome, once of the Odescalchi family, where the aristocrats mill around (the dialogue would be re-written for Fellini's dubbed final version). I was glad my friend, Audrey Macdonald, was sexily convincing in the memorable scene where she entices Marcello into a dark corner of the castle. I appreciated the scenes of the father's visit to Rome, and enjoyed Magali Noël's disarming contribution to them. They took us back to the mood of the fantasy Rimini of *I Vitelloni* and showed us that Marcello was still a good provincial at heart even if he has been contaminated by the 'dolce vita' of Rome. The one character in the film I thought unconvincing was Marcello's friend, Steiner, played glumly by Alain Cuny, who kills his children and then himself. Was Marcello's respect for him intended as ironical? The press conference scene in which I appear fleetingly was a triumph for Ekberg. In the rough cut we could often hear Federico bewitchingly giving directions from behind the camera, like a puppet master or magician, and she responded to his chides and direction with replies which were probably wittier than what a real star such as Anita's Sylvia would have been able to give. Though the finished film would probably be even more enthralling, I was sure that those of us who saw the rough cut would treasure the memory all our lives.

Audrey Macdonald in Fellini's *La Dolce Vita*.

Federico had apparently been organising these screenings for people whose opinions mattered to him. He took us to dinner afterwards to hear what we thought. I told Fellini that his film was far from being "just something to amuse" which he had said in the by-line piece I had 'written' for him. "It is much more important and is a devastating criticism of the hollowness of Rome today". He teased me: "So maybe now you'll prefer me to Luchino?".

I reminded him that I'd preferred *The Nights of Cabiria* to *The White Nights*. "Well you're making progress, Francescone!" he said affectionately. I told him I was sorry in a way that he hadn't after all made *Moraldo in città* (Moraldo in the City) the film he'd first proposed and the story of which would one day be published first in a film magazine. It would have shown what might have happened in Rome to his 'vitellone', Moraldo, after taking that train at the fade-out of the earlier film. In that story Moraldo would be seen sad and disillusioned after failing one feminine conquest after another. Federico interrupted me with his last tease: "You mean, Moraldo would have probably ended up becoming queer and you think that would have been more positive?" He left me blushing as he went on to ask opinions from the others who had seen the film.

Chapter 10

1959 was not only the year in which Federico Fellini made *La Dolce Vita*, and we privileged few had been shown its 'rough' cut, but it was also the centenary of the publication of Darwin's *The Origin of Species*. I had been prompted to dig out my Dent's Everyman edition of the book which I must have bought in the late 1940s. For the thinking world it was a book that had changed history or at least had challenged the Church's teaching on evolution. I wondered if Fellini's Steiner had read it? Not surprisingly the film had left me with more personal than philosophical doubts. It had a deep relevance to my own rather superficial Roman life. I too had chased across the city after royal princesses and movie stars. I too had attended a tea party very much like the one in the film where I'd heard Iris Tree herself reciting poetry for frivolous Roman intellectuals. After seeing that rough cut I wrote in my diary:

"This is a fantasy, a Rome that Federico has invented but which also manages to capture something of the Rome we all know and which we find irresistible in spite of its bad influence on those of us who have a lazy streak. His 'journalist' asks a lot of questions, but doesn't care enough to wait for the answers". But I also wrote that this film, more than any other since *Senso*, had made me feel I had been right to believe in the Italian cinema, and right to choose to live in this damned but beguiling city." It was up to me to try and find some of the answers that Fellini's Marcello hadn't the patience to wait for.

For the moment, however, that winter I had commitments as an actor. Audrey Macdonald had cast me as Doolittle in the *Pygmalion* she was directing (under a pseudonym) in a lovely small theatre called the Satiri in a curved building supposed to be on the site of the Pompeian theatre where the Senate was sitting when Caesar was killed on that fatal Ides of March. It seemed like a good omen all round. But when rehearsals were underway I was called to the

Titanus studios where veteran director, Mario Camerini, cast me for a role in his new film called *Via Margutta*. I prayed that the acting commitments were not going to clash but, indeed, I was called to start my scenes in the Camerini film the very same week as the last rehearsals of the Shaw play. Audrey was a bit upset because I badly needed more rehearsals especially with my Cockney accent.

On the very day of the opening, I had to go in the afternoon to do a scene in *Via Margutta* at the Titanus studios. It is something that often happens to actors who work in both films and theatre but for me it was doubly stressful as I doubted whether I was professionally experienced enough to be able to cope. But perhaps the challenge gave me stimulation and I managed very well on the opening night. Once I found I was getting laughs I enjoyed myself, and went a bit over the top as usual. Some of the Italian reviews would chastise me for this. The date of our Roman opening night was December 1st 1959, the day on which I began my 32nd year. I hardly remembered it was my birthday and hadn't the time or the energy to celebrate it with any of my lovers. The show was a success and was held over for a second week. Audrey was a wonderful Eliza and, though she is older than I am, I managed to make up quite well as her Dad, perhaps overdoing this too. I never felt that my Cockney accent was perfect but I heard no complaints, even from the English people in the audience.

In the same week I finished *Via Margutta*, which turned out to be quite a good part. I played the choreographer of a musical show playing at Rome's largest theatre, the Sistina. My girlfriend in the film (Marion Marshall) is a dancer in the show who is tempted to leave me for an artist, her ex-husband (Alex Nicol), who has been mixing with the Via Margutta crowd. But in the end, the artist is scared off by her American bossiness and she announces she is marrying me!

JFL on hearing the girl will marry him in Camerini's *Via Margutta*.

Not surprisingly I wasn't able to dedicate much time to the *News Chronicle* during these acting sprees. Fortunately, I wasn't being asked to cover the big event of the first week of December when President Eisenhower made an official visit to Rome, the first stop on a world tour which would take him to Karachi and New Delhi, and then back to Paris for a big summit meeting. A leading *NC* staff man was following the whole tour which had begun in Rome. He didn't need any help from me as it was all laid on by the PR people in Washington. However, on the day he was to leave, and he and his fellow travelers had to be at the airport to depart for Turkey, Eisenhower was calling first on the Pope and I was asked to cover this. It meant getting to the Vatican early in the morning though I'd been Doolittleing only a few hours before.

We newspaper men were obliged to wait in the Clementina Hall through which the President would walk, to be greeted by John XXIII at the entrance to his private library. I seem to remember that Eisenhower's son, John, and his wife, remained with us until they were summoned in to be presented to the Pope. We had to stand around for almost an hour without anywhere to sit. I looked at the frescoes but don't remember what they were. After a while I got the feeling that someone was staring at me. It was one of the two Swiss Guards standing at the entrance to the Pope's study.

I was a bit embarrassed when I realised he was even giving me an inviting smile. I didn't know what to do. I obviously couldn't chat him up. Finally the audience ended and the President and his party left. I got a final smile from the guard as I left.

Some days would pass before I had another occasion to go to the Vatican, for a press conference by the Secretary of State, Cardinal Tardini. And who should be one of the guards on duty at the entrance to the Cardinal's office but my seductive Swiss. This time I decided I had to do something about it and I scribbled my phone number on a piece of paper which I dropped discreetly at his feet on the way out. He must have picked it up for the next day I got a phone call and he immediately paid me a visit. It turned out that his interest was not mercenary. His 'problem' was that he had never been able to find anyone, woman or man, who could cope with the enormous Phallus with which Nature or, I think he said, the Almighty Lord, had blessed him. I did my best to oblige, but it wasn't easy.

I still had some romantic illusions but, at least, I had the satisfaction to end the 1950s with a casual partner whom I had first seen wearing the uniform designed by Michelangelo. The great artist may have felt guilty for letting, what he called in one of his sonnets, "lustful arrows", cross the Tiber in his direction, but I felt he shared our taste for masculine company. I had a copy of his sonnets in Italian, in an edition which contained sonnet XXXI, dedicated to his adored Tommaso Cavalieri, and usually cut from Italian school books. The sonnet contains the phrase "Resto prigioner d'un Cavalier armato". I was now more than certain that the 'weapon' with which his Chevalier was armed was the young man's Phallus. Maybe Symonds, who had translated the sonnets into English so splendidly, believed it too but, in Victorian England, he could hardly write it. The opening lines of his translation of sonnet XXXI do speak it clearly: "Why should I seek to ease intense desire/With still more tears and windy words of grief,/When heaven, or late or soon, sends no relief/To souls whom love hath robed around with fire?". The translator knew what he was talking about but, in his biography of the artist, he felt more at ease in expressing his conviction that Michelangelo's love for Vittoria Colonna was platonic.

Before Christmas I had to go to Cinecittà for a chore so I called on Fellini, and found him having a hard time persuading a famous light music conductor (and film composer), Armando Trovajoli and his orchestra, to play a Charleston badly for a scene in the film for which Federico was recording the sound. At lunch I told him about our Foreign Press Association's film prize and said he'd be a welcome guest if he'd honour us by his presence at the Excelsior for our gala. He was distressed when I told him that *La Dolce Vita* wouldn't be able to compete because the prize was only for films released during 1959. "But you've seen it", he said, before adding, "think how proud you would be if you and your colleagues would be the first in the world to give an award to my film!". He was teasing, of course, and certainly couldn't imagine yet how many awards his film would indeed receive. In the afternoon, I went back to Fellini's dubbing studio and recorded another off-screen line for the press conference sequence. Audrey Macdonald was there to redub one of hers for the scene in which she seduces Marcello. There was talk of touring our *Pygmalion* abroad in the New Year.

On Christmas Day the sun was shining and I had breakfast with my Trastevere lover on my double terrace. I phoned my mother who was spending her first Christmas with her new husband, Bertie. They were staying with her younger sister and his daughter and their respective families in Ramsgate. I would liked to have been with them and to have a good English yuletide dinner (and I would be with them the following year), but I spent my Roman Christmas dinner 1959 with a dear friend, Dick Watson, who played Pickering in our *Pygmalion*. We went to Meo Patacca for a strictly Italian yuletide feed.

My Swiss guard called me after getting back from Christmas leave and I let him pay me one more visit. There was no chance of a relationship with him and frankly he was becoming a bit too insistent. Before the year ended, I went to a matinée at the Goldoni Theatre, originally the court theatre of the Altemps Palace. The theatre was more than three-and-a-half centuries old and badly in need of repair. It was there I had made my first appearance on the stage in Rome, in Chekhov's *The Bear*, acting with Frances Reilly, the Irish actress, a widow of a hero of the Italian resistance. She managed the theatre with her somewhat eccentric minstrel son, Patrick Persichetti, and when they were not performing themselves they rented the theatre to Italian companies. This time, appropriately, to a company doing a Goldoni play, the Venetian dramatist's rarely performed *Il vecchio bizzarro* (The Odd Old Man). The Venetian dialect was not so difficult to understand as I had expected. The veteran Venetian actor, Cesco Baseggio, was on his last legs and needed help from the prompter, as had happened when I saw another of the great archeological relics of the traditional Italian theatre, Ruggero Ruggeri, giving one of his last performances of the Pirandello plays he had created in the early 1920s. Baseggio had such difficulty in hearing the prompter that when a horse carriage was scampering over the cobbled streets outside, he paused for a few moments apologetically but got a round of encouraging applause from the rather scarce audience when they understood the reason for his pause. In the last act, when Pantalone, the character he plays, has succeeded in reconciling the lovers, Goldoni gives him the wonderful line saying that the best remedy for lovers's quarrels and for old age is to: "Eat, drink and be merry". That got special applause too, coming as it did at the end of the year's holiday and so close to Piazza Navona where the Romans go wild between Christmas and the Epiphany.

The last book I read in 1959 was Roger Casement's sordid *Black Diaries*, with the unexpurgated chapter giving his 'list of expenses' for 1911 which the Irish accused Scotland Yard of having invented to discredit him. My own diaries at times came near to rivaling Casement's. I didn't think that they would ever incriminate me, even if the Italian armed forces might object to some of my exploits with their boys. My uniformed partners had taken more risks than me in letting me sometimes behave indiscreetly with them in public places. I decided to destroy the diaries after I had extracted what I considered printable. And I resolved to restrain myself in the new decade, at least in the recording of my adventures, out of respect for these lads who gave themselves to me, and who rarely, as on that occasion during the Spoleto Festival, expected exorbitant remuneration. Casement's diaries had also cost me a fortune. The 600 page tome was published in Paris by the Olympia Press in a limited edition of 1500 copies. Mine, which I had ordered from a Rome bookshop, was No184. It cost 5000 francs, more than I'd ever paid for a book, and more certainly than I'd paid for the favours of a carabiniere! At least my Swiss guard only cost me an occasional pizza!

I would begin the new decade by finally giving in to the modern age and installing a TV set in my flat, as much for the pleasure of my guests as for myself. It was becoming a bit of a bore having to go to the Foreign Press Club, or to eat in a nearby pizzeria, every time I wanted to see something special on the box. The last straw had come when one evening in a pizzeria in Trastevere while watching an Italian TV production of Oscar Wilde's *Lady Windermere's Fan*, the crowd around me, while munching their pizzas, were unusually silent. When I suddenly recognised a witty Wildeism translated (badly) into Italian I let out an appreciative guffaw only to find those at the next table shushing me. For them this was not a comedy, it was a melodrama about the suspected infidelities of ladies and gentlemen and was not to be laughed at!

The first TV set I installed was on hire and I had to put in a 100 lire coin every forty-five minutes. This soon became more tiresome than going outside to watch a whole programme. I changed it for a set of my own bought with the money from my first film cameo of the New Year, just in time to watch the San Remo Song Festival which would be a good excuse for a party. Domenico Modugno was present again at the 1960 festival, this time with a song called 'Libero' which was again of a standard above the other entries, though perhaps not as sensationally so as his winning songs in 1958 and 1959, 'Volare' and 'Piove' (which became known for its refrain: "Ciao Ciao Bambina"). The *Chronicle* had stupidly not wanted a story about 'Volare' the first year so I didn't offer it again, though 'Volare' had now become an international hit song. Instead, I wrote an article about the singer for *Films and Filming* (Jan60).

The film cameo of 1960 for which I'd been well paid was for *Risate di gioa* (Joyful Laughter) by Mario Monicelli, perhaps the most brilliant of the emerging Italian comedy directors. His scintillating comedy, *I soliti ignoti*, had been wittily retitled in America *Big Deal on Madonna Street*. Monicelli had great style and it was a pleasure watching him work on what promised to be a sophisticated comedy in the manner of Preston Sturges. The set at the Titanus Studios for the ballroom sequence in which I appeared as a waiter (wearing my own recently tailored suit of tails) seemed like a soirée in a real Roman palazzo because many of the extras were real aristocrats who had noble titles but who welcomed a few extra lire in their pockets. The honoured host of the off-screen soirée was the adorable Neapolitan comedian, Totò, who claimed to be descended from the last Emperor of Byzantium. He expected everyone to call him "Principe" (Prince). We did so, very respectfully, including Anna Magnani, his co-star in the film. She seemed in her element amongst the nobility and why shouldn't she? She lived in a palazzo. Totò and Magnani were playing two of a trio of shady thieves who were hoping to rob jewels and valuables from the party guests. An American actor, Ben Gazzara, was the third member of the trio. He seemed rather bewildered, clearly bemused at the reverence being paid to the 'supporting' cast.

Photo by G. B. Poletto

Risate di gioa. JFL, Ben Gazzara, Anna Magnani and Totò.

After that filmed party, I went to a real Rome party, given by a film producer, and I took my friend, Patricia. Antonioni was among the guests and he greeted me warmly as always. I asked him how he was getting on with the editing of *L'avventura*, the film which he had been shooting for most of the past year. I hadn't been able to pay a scheduled visit to the location on an island off the north coast of Sicily. He apologised for the production problems that had prevented my visit to the set. He told me that the film was almost ready and that he'd soon show it to me. I introduced him to Patricia and noticed that he seemed amused by her exuberance (she always gets quite camp after a few drinks). Later that evening, he beckoned me over and asked if I would like to come out to Cinecittà the next day, adding: "Dress up smartly and bring your lady friend with you. Find another young man who also has a 'befana' friend. I'll make it worth your while". I didn't of course tell Patricia that she'd been classified as a 'befana', the old witch of the Epiphany feast, an unkind word Italians use to describe an ageing or ugly woman. Patricia had been very good-looking when she was a young woman but her middle age was not being helped by excessive drinking.

She was thrilled at the idea and we had no difficulty in persuading an American friend of my age to join us and bring with him his 'befana', an Australian lady who, I think, was keeping him at the time. I was mystified as to what Michelangelo wanted us for, as I knew he had long ago finished shooting the film. It turned out that while cutting the last sequence in which Monica Vitti comes into the lounge of the San Domenico hotel in Taormina, he had discovered that when she looked to the left there had been a shot of other hotel guests but when she looked to the right there was nothing for her to see. That was where we came in, two ageing 'befane' with young men in attendance, all with a glass in their hand. We were standing in front of a back-projection blue-screen on which would be projected an image of a mantelpiece from the San Domenico. It was an amusing experience for which we were indeed paid "for our disturbance" and I felt pleased that I would be seen on the screen in another film that promised to be among the most important of 1960. Any day now *La Dolce Vita* would be getting its premiere and once again I'd be seen with a glass in my hand, looking rather tipsy and perhaps a bit silly. But I had better prospects in store, or so I thought.

John Francis Lane in Antonioni's *L'avventura.*

I had signed a contract to play a small role in the De Laurentiis production, *Under Ten Flags*, directed by veteran director, Duilio Coletti, the set of which I had visited in Syracuse in December. I had received a call for a costume fitting and thought I looked more glamorous in the uniform of a British naval officer than I had been in any of the cameos I had done so far. And there was the thrill of meeting and working with Charles Laughton who played the British Admiral. I hadn't yet received the script but, at the Press Club, I found in my mail box a communiqué issued by the press office which announced new additions to the cast: Ralph Truman, "who had appeared in *Henry V, Oliver Twist* and *Quo Vadis*"; Cecil Parker, "a distinguished stage and film actor who had made his first screen appearance in a silent film in 1928". The communiqué added that another new member of the cast was "John Francis Lane". It described me as: "a journalist in Rome since 1951, but also an actor". It went on to say that "like Charles Laughton, he studied at the Royal Academy of Dramatic Art". In reality, of course, I had only been at the Prep School of RADA. Nonetheless, I was a member of Equity so I had every right to call myself a professional. During a pause in the first day's shooting, 'Admiral' Laughton invited some of his 'fellow officers' to his dressing room to have a drink. He was in great form, telling jokes and camping it

John Francis Lane (top left), Charles Laughton (right)

up to see how we reacted. I think he was flirting with one of the company, certainly not with me. On the set he was rather awe-inspiring. He underplayed during the rehearsals but when the camera was shooting he would burst into action and round on the actor he was addressing with a viciously withering scowl. Of course this was good for the scene as it got the appropriate look of fright from the actor. But I wasn't invited again to Laughton's dressing room. Perhaps he had seen the press communiqué which mentioned I was a Rome-based journalist. My role ended up being little more than a glorified extra. At least I was better paid than an extra.

Not long afterwards I had another curious experience with the Dino De Laurentiis organization. In spite of the kudos attached to the making of *War and Peace* in 1956, Dino hadn't yet become the tycoon he was sure destiny had in store for him. The commercial and critical success of *La Grande Guerra* boosted his prestige and was one of the five candidates for our Foreign Press award for the best Italian film of 1959. We had rashly decided that the decision for the winner of the prize would be made at a meeting held in the Excelsior Hotel the same evening as the gala, but the Chairman, the Belgian film historian, Carl Vincent, warned us that in Italy it would be difficult to get stars and directors to come unless they knew they were going to get a prize. In addition to the two Venice winners, Rossellini and Monicelli, the other finalist candidates were Mauro Bolognini for *La Notte Brava*, Valerio Zurlini for *L'estate violenta*, and Pietro Germi for *Un maledetto imbroglio*. Rossellini and his star Vittorio De Sica were both out of town so I knew they couldn't come, which was a pity, but their film was unlikely to win. It was more important for us to secure the presence of the stars and director of *La Grande Guerra* and its producer. I rang Dino De Laurentiis to tell him he was invited along with Monicelli and the stars, Vittorio Gassman and Alberto Sordi. Obviously the presence of these popular actors was essential for the success of the event as a media attraction. Dino asked me immediately: "Have we won the prize?". I told him that the decision wouldn't be made until the night itself. He replied angrily that he had no intention of asking his actors and director to be present to see another film win. I knew that *La Grande Guerra* was probably the favourite but I couldn't promise him that it would win.

On the evening, we saw that both Bolognini and Zurlini were present without asking if their film had won. Peppino Amato, the producer of Germi's film, who lived in a suite of the Excelsior, told me Germi was sitting outside on the Via Veneto at Doney's café and would be available if we wanted him though he wasn't in evening dress (he was wearing a black tie which it said was requested on the invitation!). We objected strongly to Dino's refusal to come without knowing his film had won and, after some formal discussion over the Bolognini and Zurlini films which we admired, we ended up agreeing unanimously to give our award to Germi for his excellent adaptation of Gadda's contemporary classic novel written in Roman dialect. Germi had turned it into a very enjoyable thriller in which he himself had given a tongue-in-cheek performance in the leading role as the police inspector investigating what my friend Bill Weaver's excellent English translation of the novel had called *That Ugly Mess on Via Merulana*. I called Peppino Amato in his room to tell him that his film had won and asked him kindly to go out and fetch Germi to come in to pick up his award, even if his 'black tie' was on a lounge suit. Everyone was pleased with our choice. We would always be proud that the first of the Stampa Estera's film awards was given to Germi who wouldn't become famous internationally until he made *Divorce Italian Style* (1961) which won an Oscar for its screenplay. Nobody knew, neither my fellow jury members, nor probably even Germi or Amato remembered, that in a scene in the film, in a tavern in Trastevere, one of the merry guests in the background was JFL doing a cameo with a group of tourists singing: *Arrivederci, Roma*.

Chapter 11

Finally we were invited to see the finished *La Dolce Vita*. It had gained a lot from the polishing, and the editing of the sound, and of course, from the addition of Nino Rota's music but, like many who had been privileged to see the rough cut, I still treasured the impact of Fellini's work print with his own voice still giving directions off screen, while the actors and the non-actors were all acting with their original voices. He had almost completely rewritten the film in the dubbing. My enthusiasm for the film wasn't in any way diminished but I still felt a bit uneasy about the character of Marcello's friend, Steiner, sombrely played by Alain Cuny, who kills his children and himself. I could understand that Federico was using it to show the callousness of journalistic exploitation of every human tragedy, which was all very well in the miracle sequence, but in the case of Steiner, who was a close friend of Marcello's, his personal distress doesn't seem to have any particular influence on how Marcello behaves as a journalist. The ending of the film, on the beach at Fregene, when Marcello is drunk and doesn't recognise the girl who represented his only encounter with innocence, is perhaps Federico's reminder that Marcello, unlike Dante, couldn't recognise a Beatrice when he met her. As an honest Catholic at heart Fellini cheated a bit by ending his film with the moral downfall of his hero. As a newspaper man myself I remembered the way the press had behaved during the Montesi case in the 1950s. In my report in the *News Chronicle*, of the inconclusive verdict at the end of that trial in Venice, I concluded that nobody seemed to care anymore about what had happened to the poor girl whose dead body was washed up on a beach near Rome. In any case, it was clear that Fellini's film would be remembered not only in cinema history but also as a portrait of the superficiality of our times.

THE MOST TALKED ABOUT—THE MOST SHOCKED ABOUT FILM OF OUR YEARS

LA DOLCE VITA

AN ASTOR RELEASE
DIRECTED BY FEDERICO FELLINI

LA DOLCE VITA

FEDERICO FELLINI · MARCELLO MASTROIANNI · ANITA EKBERG · ANOUK AIMEE · YVONNE FURNEAUX · MAGALI NOEL · LEX BARKER · JACQUES SERNAS · ALAIN CUNY · WALTER SANTESSO · NADIA GRAY · Produced by GIUSEPPE AMATO and ANGELO RIZZOLI

Now that I'd seen the finished film I was less concerned with identifying myself with Marcello as a fellow chronicler of superficiality. I was proud to be associated with such a film. Henry Thody and I were both among those interviewed for our opinions by the Rome afternoon paper, *Paese Sera*. The uproar caused by the film at its premiere in Milan, and the angry editorial published in the Vatican newspaper, *Osservatore Romano*, which complained that the Church had been deeply offended by the way its Roman nobility were made fun of, might have been prompted by the wily publicist of the Rizzoli distribution company, but it certainly had the desired effect of provoking a scandal that boosted the film, attracting crowds clamouring to see it quickly for fear it would be banned. Afternoon screenings, which usually played to half-empty houses, were as crowded as the late night shows. The film immediately broke box office records. To his surprise, Federico found himself at the centre of attention in the world's media. I was asked by BBC radio to interview him and, though he spoke in his picturesque English, it went down well. I subsequently published the interview in *Films and Filming*.

My main concern at that point in 1960 was that the *News Chronicle* might fold before the Olympic Games started in August. I had turned down the invitation to be on the jury of the Venice Festival. Floris Ammannati, who had made the invitation, had been replaced by a more orthodox Catholic intellectual named Emilio Lonero. The leftists were campaigning against the new man so I was a bit relieved to be out of it even if at heart I had some regrets. I let my leftist friends believe I had turned down the invitation when Ammannati was replaced. I knew the *Chronicle*, if it did survive until August, would be sending out its sports reporters to cover the event for which Rome was getting keyed up. I love 'events', especially those in which many handsome males are involved as participants or spectators but my presence in Rome as a journalist was obviously not necessary.

In April, I felt a desperate need to get out of Rome for Easter even though my finances were quite low. It seemed a pity not to take advantage of an offer from BEA of a free return air ticket to Istanbul with the chance of a stop-over, on the way back, in Athens. I had been invited to visit the location of a film being made on the island of Rhodes but there had been no offer to pay the air fare. I was eager to finally see Greece, to which I had long been promising myself a visit. Those of us joining the flight in Rome were put in tourist class seats and given a measly box containing two dry rolls and a banana. An Irish journalist, whom I knew from the Foreign Press Club, had already discovered that the press party from London were installed in first class and insisted that we at least be served something decent to drink. The stewardess got the message and, after some consultation up front, told us we could transfer. While we were being served champagne there was some nervous staff scurrying back and forth which got us all a bit panicky. Suddenly it was announced we were landing at Athens which had not been scheduled on the way out. Evidently there was engine trouble and, as this was an inaugural flight, and representatives of most of the leading newspapers of Fleet Street were on board, obviously the pilot didn't want to take unnecessary risks.

In Athens, we were told that BEA was putting us up for the night in town and that the journey would continue the next day. I had nothing to complain about. I remembered the first time I had ever flown, at the age of seventeen, also on BEA. Then I was flying to Copenhagen on my way to southern Sweden but that BEA flight also had 'engine trouble' and we had to land in Amsterdam where BEA put us up for the night, thanks to which I was able to enjoy a feast of Van Gogh and Rembrandt, as well as other unscheduled pleasures, before proceeding to Scandinavia. On this occasion too the extra 24 hours were very welcome because it enabled me to have my first experience of ancient and modern Greece. I had been reading Henry Miller's *The Colossus of Maroussi* as an introduction to the trip. I knew immediately that he was right in saying, "there is no old or new, only Greece, a world conceived and created in perpetuity". The next morning, the Irishman and I visited the Acropolis which, the night before, we had only been able to glimpse from afar before its illumination was turned off. Seen close to in daylight it is one of those memorable 'firsts' that one treasures all one's life. After a first night in modern Athens, which seemed one of the ugliest cities I'd ever set eyes on, the 'first time' we climbed up through the Placa to see the Parthenon in all its splendour was something very special. It wetted my appetite for what was to come after my upcoming weekend in 'Constantinople' where BEA eventually succeeded in landing us, though too late to do the promised nocturnal boat trip on the Bosphorus.

We'd see the straits only from the air and from a hilltop when, on the second day, we went to the Hilton for a midday drink. My visit to Istanbul was not particularly exciting, even though it was stimulating to see what was left of the Byzantium over which 'our' Emperor Constantine had built the new capital of Christendom. I visited present-day Istanbul in the company of some of my fellow BEA travellers, the Irishman from Rome, a Turk from Cyprus and an Italian-Slovene timber merchant from Trieste, all unrepentant girl-chasers and drinkers. We explored the old city and the French quarter of the town. On the first day we ate caviar, lobster and a chateaubriand steak in an extravagant Franco-Turkish restaurant-night club whilst being entertained by belly dancers. The next day we explored some of the mosques and bazaars and the old cathedral of St. Sophia, which had been turned into a byzantine museum, though some of the original mosaics had not been uncovered. Istanbul was a confusing city, a mixture of Greek and Roman, Muslim and Hebrew as well as Byzantine, British and French.

I was not sorry to get back to Athens where I took it easy for two days before flying to Rhodes where I was to be guest of the film company making a spectacular war epic called *The Guns of Navarone*. My first meeting with the producer of the film, Carl Foreman, was in the afternoon after I had been comfortably installed in a beach bungalow in what seemed like a deluxe hotel. I was taken out in what I understood to be a T- boat (I knew about U-boats!) but which turned out to be the "tea-boat" taking beverages out to be served under precarious conditions to the English crew and actors shooting a scene on caïques in a not exactly calm Aegean sea. I spent a delightful week on the island, managing to find more pleasant company than I had enjoyed in Constantinople. The Greek sailors were more appealing than the Turks had seemed and I had no difficulties in fraternising with them. They were of course grateful for the few drachma I gave them after lovemaking which was much more spontaneous and passionate than most of their Italian conscript equivalents. In Rhodes, I also made some prestigious friends, John Schlesinger, who was filming commercials on the island, and Peter Yates, the assistant director to J. Lee Thompson who had taken over the direction of *Navarone* from Alexander Mackendrick, who evidently had not hit it off with the Big Boss, Foreman. I finally got a good interview with Foreman after I'd been the only one of the British columnists invited to a luncheon for the Greek press at which Foreman had nasty things to say about the British press. He said they had been ungrateful for the hospitality they'd been offered, complaining about the food in the hotel where we were all staying (the hotel belonged to a brother-in-law of Onassis). I think I would report faithfully and flatteringly in *Films and Filming* what Foreman had to say about his exile from Hollywood, as one on the blacklist, and his attempts to be an independent producer in England. I never really understood why he was making this film? For the money I presumed. He wanted to be a writer and was obviously an intellectual at heart.

But as a producer he certainly knew how to get his way. Rhodes, at the time, was a de-militarised area but Foreman had persuaded NATO to let Greek tanks and troops land on the island for scenes in the film. I didn't request interviews with the top stars, Gregory Peck and David Niven, but I had an amusing evening with Anthony Quinn, with whom I talked about food and Fellini. He made a personal appearance at the local cinema where they were showing Delannoy's dismal *Hunchback of Notre Dame* (1956), with a dubbed Quinn trying vainly to outpace the Quasimodo of Laughton (and the silent Lon Chaney) but he got a rapturous reception anyway from the audience. Afterwards, Quinn was happy to join in the revelries in a nearby tavern where we saw him performing, maybe for the first time, and quite spontaneously, the dance that was to make him even more popular in Greece a few years later, from *Zorba the Greek* (1964). I was a polite listener to Stanley Baker who complained at length about the bad reviews his recent films had received in *Films and Filming*. After all I didn't write the reviews. I got on well with the Mayor of Rhodes, probably because I didn't seem to be complaining, even about the food at the hotel (though the cook was changed during the week I was there and it certainly improved). He arranged for a charming Italian-speaking driver-guide to take me to the main archeological site of the island, Lindos, where I felt sorry for the donkey hired to carry me and my 95 kilos up to the local Acropolis which was well worth visiting. The driver told me that it was thanks to the Italians that the ruins had been dug and restored. It was the only time during my stay in Rhodes that I heard someone say good things about the Italian presence on Rhodes. I presumed these archeological good deeds had been done during the first Italian colonialisation on the island around 1910 and not during the more recent ill-fated attempt by Mussolini's armies which resulted in a humiliating defeat.

I went back to Athens in time for Easter, and found a decent inexpensive hotel in La Placa from where I organized, with some help from the tourist bureau, my excursions to some of the most famous ancient sites, first to Delphi and Olympus, then to the Peloponnese. I continued to have pleasing erotic adventures like those I'd had in Rhodes but the most romantic of them had a sad conclusion. It was a meeting with a young god named Demetrius, a magical encounter on a train taking me from Athens to Nauplion, an organised trip. There was an immediate attraction between us even though we only managed to speak in phrases I found in my Greek phrase book. He was a sailor going home on leave to Corinth. He made it clear he wanted me to get off the train with him and I was indeed very tempted, especially when, as the train was approaching his stop, he took me in his arms and kissed me on the mouth to the amusement of the other travelers who'd been following our 'conversation' with intense curiosity but who didn't seem at all shocked. But I didn't want to get involved. To this day I have always wondered what would have been the course of my life if I had gotten off that train in Corinth.

After that manqué romance I carried on exploring what there was to see, or rather imagine, of Mycenae after which I went to Epidaurus where I visited the theatre. It was a pity it was not the season for performances. Among the ruins at Epidauris I was particularly intrigued to find a temple dedicated to one of Apollo's sons, Aesculapius, who had links with 'our' Tiburtine island.

Once back in Trastevere, however, the reality of my life didn't allow for Hellenic dreams, only Roman uncertainties. I was angry with myself for having waited until I was over thirty to 'discover' Greece, but I had chosen the materialism of the Latin civilization. I had to come to terms with my Roman life. I appeared in only one film that Spring, and it wasn't well-paid, particularly not for the 'important' role I was playing, that of the British delegate to the UN assembly, at which the representative of the small country of Concordia runs into trouble with the Russians and Americans over a crucial vote. It was in *Romanoff and Juliet*, adapted and directed by Peter Ustinov from his own play. In the film, he repeats his stage performance in the lead role as a Condordian General who arranges for the children of the US and Russian ambassadors to fall in love. The children were played by John Gavin and Sandra Dee. When I complained that I was not being very well paid, the guy who hired me, and who knew of my double profession, replied "But as a journalist you should feel privileged to get a chance to interview Ustinov". It was true I had indeed hoped to interview Peter, for whom I had a great admiration but, of course, a director-writer-star is always too busy to give more than a cordial good morning and exchange a quip with such as me. Anyway, it was a pleasure to watch him at work.

Now that I had my own TV set I gave a 'dolce vita' party to watch the big event of the Spring, what the Italians were calling the "Windsor-Jones wedding". It would be a good show in the best British royal kitsch tradition even if I had my doubts that the photographer, Tony Armstrong-Jones, was going to upgrade Margaret's cultural life. Among my guests was Tamara Lees, a neighbour in Trastevere; an attractive English brunette who had become a movie star in Italian erotic melos and was living with a fellow American journalist friend.

When May arrived I soon felt my hay fever coming on, always an agony in stuffily hot Rome at that time of year. I had spent so much money in Greece that I couldn't think of going to the Cannes Festival where I knew the sea air was more adaptable to my seasonal ill. I had no professional commitment to go to the festival where both *La Dolce Vita* and *L'avventura* were showing in competition but I was not exactly a star player in either of those films. The chronicles from the Croisette seemed, for the moment, to be more interested in reporting on the new Jules Dassin film, *Never on Sunday*. In Greek, the film was called *Ilya* after the character played by Dassin's glamorous lady friend, Melina Mercouri. Before leaving Athens, I had bought the record of her singing the tantalising music for the film written by Manos Hadjidakis and had to console myself with listening to that.

In Rome, I was able to console myself professionally by showing a distinguished visitor around the city, the Czech director, Jiri Weiss. He was on holiday with his charming wife. He now seemed less ready to accept the negative aspects of the socialist regime in which he lived than he had been when I'd last seen him, when I'd interviewed him for a piece published as a by-line piece 'by' him for the March 1959 issue of *Films and Filming.* Jiri had taken refuge during the war in England and had worked with the Crown Film Unit, an experience which he treasured the memory of. He listed the advantages of working in a nationalised film industry, such as regular salary and not being at the mercy of producers, but he didn't hesitate to name the disadvantages, above all the red tape and the lack of a feeling of personal responsibility, even though the chief creative artists, the director, scriptwriter, cinematographer etc., got bonuses above their regular salaries. Weiss told me that "a socially structured society didn't mean that greed, meanness, slander, selfishness and petty provincialism had disappeared". In Rome, he told me sadly that things had gotten worse and that life for artists in Prague was getting grimmer.

I took him to visit the set of Visconti's new film *Rocco and his Brothers* for a scene being shot in a dilapidated Roman theatre, near Santa Maria Maggiore, where they had built what passed as a Milan boxing club. There were lots of half-naked young men lolling around the gymnasium. Luchino gave Jiri a cordial welcome even if he was too busy to have time for a chat. The following day, I went back alone to see Visconti shoot the boxing match with Alain Delon in the ring. Like Fellini he directed actors sometimes from behind the cameras, speaking in French more politely than when he spoke in Italian.

In Rome, the *Dolce Vita*, both the real thing and the film, were still the main topics of discussion. The news came from Cannes that Fellini had won the Golden Palm and that poor Antonioni, and a tearful Monica, had been subjected to the humiliation of hearing the festival audience whistle and jeer at *L'avventura*, though he would have the consolation of knowing that the more intelligent French, Italian and (some) British critics were acclaiming *L'avventura* as the revelation of the festival. I hadn't yet seen the film. After Cannes, Michelangelo went straight to Milan where he was shooting a new film, *La Notte*. I wrote him a letter (which I see from my carbon copy was dated May 26), in which I said I hoped he'd soon screen it for me. I told him that some stupid critic writing for *The Times* had written "the less said about *L'avventura* the better" but that *The Observer* had published an enthusiastic piece by an unsigned French critic (who I suspected was Louis Marcorelles) and that the editor of *Films and Filming* had written me to say he couldn't understand why the audience had been so hostile. Michelangelo kindly replied to my letter saying he would arrange a screening as soon as he got back to Rome. He said I'd be welcome to visit the set of his new film in Milan, on my own without waiting for an organised press visit. He wrote that Cannes had been "da infarto" ("enough to give you a heart attack"), and that *L'avventura* had won three prizes, to which he added: "thanks to your appearance!". He ended the letter by saying that: "Milan was an endless succession of parties which make Rome's 'dolce vita' a joke by comparison". Only when I'd eventually see *La Notte*, would I realise that he had not been going to parties in Milan for his own amusement but to discover material about this Milanese 'dolce vita' for his film.

I went to Milan in June and, taking refuge from the heat and bustle of the streets outside the Sforza Castle, I sat inside what was called the Axis Room, decorated with woodlike frescoes on its ceiling while on one wall was a fragment of a mural described as Leonardoesque, and I started a new diary. The chaos outside the castle was due to the building of a new metro station. On my first evening in Milan I went to the Piccolo Teatro to catch Giorgio Strehler's production of Goldoni's *Harlequin, Servant of Two Masters* which I had never been able to see before. Luckily for me it had been revived again in preparation for an overseas tour. In the coming decades it would travel from one end of the world to the other. I had thus managed to catch one of the last times that the Harlequin was played by Marcello Moretti, who had created the role when Strehler first staged it during the Piccolo's opening season in 1947. I had seen great comic performances in England, including Syd Field, and even Danny Kaye, but nothing to compare with the kind of improvised comic acting style which Strehler had re-created in his production of this 18th century play. The closest to it I had seen was the treasured memory of Barrault's Baptiste in *Les enfants du paradis* (1945). The average English theatergoer has little understanding of what Commedia dell'Arte was. For Italians it has always remained a raucous, popular and laughter-seeking entertainment with its broad comic antics like, one assumes, the comic performances of Shakespeare's actors on Elizabethan stages. I'd see Strehler's 'Arlecchino' many more times over a lifetime of theatre-going in Italy and, each time he revived it, he inserted new inventions to surprise his audiences without losing sight of the play's original traditions. The production would be kept alive thanks to the contribution made by the actor who took over the role after Moretti's death, the equally brilliant, Ferruccio Soleri, who would carry on playing Harlequin till in his eighties, training others to take over from him. Soleri played the part when London finally saw the production at Peter Daubeny's World Theatre Season in 1967.

I was in Milan, of course, to visit the set of Antonioni's *La Notte*. I found him shooting a scene in one of Milan's new skyscrapers chosen for the setting of a hospital scene where Mastroianni and Jeanne Moreau are visiting a sick friend. They were filming a helicopter flying by outside the windows, the pilot instructed by radio as to when he should fly past. Obviously this was the reason for shooting the scene from a height. The skyscraper was a very symbolic part of the new Milan society and the film would have a stunning opening shot of the first skyscraper to have been built there, the Pirelli HQ. That day, I observed how Antonioni managed to establish a background, like this helicopter passage, which wasn't intended as a dazzling special effect, but used as a simple distraction for the couple's mood. They are uneasy in the presence of a friend whose exuberance is a disguise for what they all know will probably be the last time they will see him alive.

Michelangelo invited me to dine with him in the evening, with Marcello and Jeanne Moreau. On the set, Moreau hadn't looked as sexy as she did in *Les Amants* (1959) but in the evening she was her bewitching self. Monica Vitti was also present of course. In the film, she was playing a supporting role to Moreau and had been obliged to turn brunette. It was a good meal with lively company. Also at the table were the set designer of the film, Piero Zuffi, and a leading Milan intellectual, Gaetano Baldacci, the former editor of what had been founded as a radical Milan daily, *Il Giorno* (financed by Enrico Mattei). We discussed the disturbing political situation in Rome and I realised I'd soon have to get back to follow what was going on.

On my way back to Rome, I couldn't resist stopping over in Spoleto for the Festival which was in full swing. There I saw Paul Taylor's New American Ballet Company in Taylor's latest creation, *Tablet*. Dancing with him was a stunning young German ballerina, Pina Bausch, destined to become one of the great icons of 20th century ballet. I was invited to lunch at Menotti's palazzo and found him as disarming as always and quite indifferent to the less enthusiastic reviews that this third Festival of Two Worlds had generated in the Italian papers. Among the interesting people I met at Menotti's was the Greek director, Michael Cacoyannis, whom I already knew from Cannes. He told me he was about to make a film for an Italian producer in Rome and that certainly there would be a part for me. Maybe this would keep my Hellenic dream alive for a while?

Before settling down to my work in Rome, I couldn't resist taking a trip, something of a postscript to my Greek travels, a consolation for not having been able to see a performance at Epidaurus. I took the fourteen-hour night train (second class) couchette journey to Syracuse and back again to see the fascinating Vittorio Gassman Company production of the whole of the Aeschylian Oresteian trilogy. The performance began at sunset and ended long after midnight. Because I was still young and eager, and didn't have access to the privileged press seats I'd have on future visits to this splendid theatre, I sat in (and with) the 'Gods', for more than six hours on stone steps, with only the cushion hired for a few lire, to soften my seat. It was an exhausting but rewarding experience.

When the performance started in the early evening it was a bit disturbing to have the sun still shining warmly on our faces, and lighting a distant view of the port of the not very attractive modern part of Syracuse but, once night descended and the stage was lit up, it was a spellbinding sight. I think there was some use of microphones because the leading players and chorus all made themselves heard without having to raise their voices in what was a very subtle production. I particularly appreciated Gassman's own performances (as Agamemnon in the first play and Orestes in the other two). The Italian translation was by Pier Paolo Pasolini, adapted from other translations he had compared. In the introduction to the published edition, Pasolini explained that he had worked "by instinct" as he didn't know Greek himself, but he had tried to give a "political" interpretation of the trilogy. He credited Athena with founding (in *The Eumenides*) the "first democratic assembly in history" against the tyrannical regime inherited from Agamemnon's time. This theory was consolidated by the correspondence between Gassman's communist intellectual co-director, Luciano Lucignani, with a British professor of classical philology at Birmingham University, George Thomson. For me it was the most memorable theatrical and educational experience I had so far had in an Italian theatre.

When I got back to Rome I had to cope with the gloomy Italian political situation which had worsened. The trouble was prompted by the decision of the former Minister of the Interior, the Christian Democrat politician, Fernando Tambroni, to agree to form a supposedly stand-by minority government. Opposed by the Left, and even by the small but influential centrist Social Democrat party, Tambroni was kept in power thanks to the votes of the neo-fascist MSI party which now wanted to hold its party congress in Genoa, a strictly leftist city with particular ties to the anti-fascist Resistance. Riots broke out in Genoa and in several other Italian cities, even in Rome, where the carabinieri on horseback charged at demonstrators near the gate of San Paolo, next door to the sheltered area of the protestant cemetery where not only Shelley's heart and Keats's bones were buried but also the urn containing the ashes of the founder of the Italian communist Party, Antonio Gramsci. The demonstration was organised by the partisans in honour of the martyrs of an uprising against the German occupation of Rome. The situation was getting very worrying and I wrote my first article about it. Almost immediately the NC sent Stephen Barber out to follow the developments. The Italians risked a coup d'etat which would be particularly inopportune with the city bracing itself for the Olympics, which were due to start in a few weeks time. Ten demonstrators had been killed during protests in different Italian cities from the 'Red' Reggio Emilia to the ultra-Christian Democrat and mafioso Palermo. I had become aware while following Italian politics during the past decade that, in Italy, there was still a lot of nostalgia for Mussolini and his regime. The so-called neo-fascist party MSI (Italian Social Movement) had deputies elected in parliament, even if it was considered "non-constitutional" and had riotous followers among the younger generation. I was convinced that Fascism like Nazism in Germany had been definitively defeated as an ideology but "fascism" (a word Italians had invented) was a 'state of mind' and described the mentality and behaviour of many states in our post-Second World War world. But it was clear that, during this summer of 1960, the riots in Italy were becoming a risk to its democracy.

By July, Tambroni had to resign and Fanfani was brought back again to form another minority coalition, this time, however, kept going by the abstention of the Nenni Socialists who seemed to be getting closer to reuniting with Giuseppe Saragat's breakaway Social Democrats. But, naturally, these hypothetical developments didn't really interest British readers. It would only have been a good 'story' if the Olympics had been threatened by a coup d'etat like the one that had just taken place in Turkey. When the Games did eventually take off I didn't have accreditation for the glamorous opening ceremony which I had to watch on TV. The only story I had in the *Chronicle*, the day after the inauguration, was about an Englishman who had committed suicide in Rome. I think to make it topical I suggested it might have been because he couldn't get a ticket for the Olympic Stadium!

It was time to escape from the Olympics in Rome, which had proved such a non-event for me, so I went to Venice anyway for the second week of the festival, curious to see how my substitute as juror, Peter Baker, was getting on. I couldn't help being envious when I found him basking in the generous hospitality of the Excelsior Hotel, its restaurants, bars and beaches. The films in competition so far that year were mostly duds, except perhaps for Billy Wilder's *The Apartment*, so his jury chore had not been giving him headaches... not yet anyway! The only Italian entry I had seen in advance was *The Long Night of '43*, an impressive first film about an episode in the Resistance in Ferrara, the home city of Giorgio Bassani, the author of the novella on which it was based, and the home city of the director, Florestano Vancini, who had made documentaries and been an assistant to, among others, Zurlini on *The Violent Summer*. Vancini's film was more about anti-fascist heroics than Zurlini's had been. Of course, in the summer of 1960 it was topical to talk about anti-fascism. Vancini's film also benefitted from the superb acting of two great Italian actors, Enrico Maria Salerno, as the pathetic invalid who witnesses a fascist massacre in the street below from his window, and the distinguished stage actor, Gino Cervi, who had dubbed Olivier's Hamlet into Italian, and who had played the communist mayor in the popular *Don Camillo* films. Here, Cervi was the nasty local fascist boss. I had no difficulty in convincing Peter to give it his vote for best first film.

None of us had yet seen the most eagerly awaited new Italian film of this year's festival, Visconti's *Rocco and his Brothers*. Little did any of us know then that Peter's decisive contrary vote would result in *Rocco* not getting the Golden Lion, which went instead to a soon to be forgotten film, André Cayatte's *Justice est faite*, so forgotten, in fact, that when I looked it up to remind me, in one

Renato Salvatori and Alain Delon in *Rocco and his Brothers*.

film dictionary it was mistakenly listed as being made in 1950 and in another, the director was named as Chabrol. Peter would later feel a bit guilty towards me as he knew I was a Visconti fan. After the festival he would write me a long letter saying why he had voted against *Rocco*, saying he felt Visconti had indulged too much in the violence of the rape and murder scene when Renato Salvatori stabs Annie Girardot six times. This scene was indeed over-violent but it didn't diminish the film's powerful impact. The scene would later be toned down when the film was released maybe more to please the censor than to appease Visconti's critics.

Renato Salvatori and Annie Girardot in *Rocco and his Brothers.*

I don't think Visconti ever knew that Baker was responsible or that I should have been in his place and he could have counted on my vote. Indirectly I felt responsible for that shameful verdict. I'd be very embarrassed a few weeks later when, at Cinecittà, Alain Delon saw me and came running after me to ask me to thank Peter for having supported their film! Maybe he remembered that *Films and Filming* had printed some very sexy photos of him and assumed that Peter had voted for the film.

I would meet Alain Delon again in September when Antonioni finally organised a screening of *L'avventura* to which I was invited. It was for a privileged few in a small screening room. I was sitting next to Alain while Luchino was on his other side. The young French actor, who seemed a very intelligent young man as well as being so sexy, was tremendously excited by the film, vibrating with enthusiasm from start to finish. I was vibrating too, not only from Alain's vicinity but because the film excited me too. The next time I'd see it I would really get the full impact of its content and what it represented in terms of style. But my first reaction is always what counts for me and I shared Delon's emotion at that first viewing. The fact that we never knew what had happened to the missing girl didn't worry me. It was not a Hitchcock after all. It was clear, however, and perhaps not surprisingly, that Luchino's reaction was much cooler. His courteous words to Michelangelo afterwards didn't compare to Alain's glowing praise.

In the autumn of 1960, after what had been such a barren summer, in terms of my own creativity, things began to pick up. I had several upcoming film cameos in the offing, the first of which was in a local detective flick, a spin-off from a popular TV series with Ubaldo Lay, the same actor who had created the role, a dick known as Inspector Sheridan. It was made by Giorgio Bianchi, a mediocre Grade-B director. I played a lawyer trying to defend a girl wrongly accused of murder. The best thing about the experience, apart from the money, was that we shot exteriors in one of the most enchanting hilltop towns south of Rome, Grottaferrata, where I espied a small villa I would have liked to rent.

I also did a day's work on a film called *Come September* with Rock Hudson and Lollobrigida, and managed to hide myself from being spotted by both stars who knew me. By now I was recognising that my presence on a set with big stars risked being misinterpreted. But I would have a profitable few days on the Michael Cacoyannis film, *The Wastrel* (Il relitto) with Van Heflin and the lovely Greek actress, Ellie Lambetti, neither of whom knew or cared who I was. I was just a bit-part actor in the film.

My best good news in September came from Fellini who wanted me to do the translation and the adaptation of the English dialogue for what was to be the dubbed version of *La Dolce Vita*. Columbia had bought the British rights and surprisingly wanted to release it dubbed, which I guessed (rightly as it would turn out!), an English audience wouldn't be particularly eager to see. But Columbia felt it was a film that was causing such a sensation round the world that its appeal would go beyond a purely arthouse audience. Who was I to object? It meant my going to London to follow the dubbing. Federico thought this was a good idea even though he knew I had no previous experience of dubbing. He felt he could trust me to keep an eye on his behalf on what they intended to do. It wasn't easy to fix a deal with his artful Neapolitan executive producer, Peppino Amato, whom I knew from our Foreign Press Film Award exploit when we'd given the prize to his Pietro Germi film. Federico insisted on them treating me well and I was set to work at the moviola on a first draft, trying to do the impossible task of finding dialogue that could be lip-synched into our prag- matic English language, substituting the twice as many lines that Federico's dubbing had put into the mouths of his Italian dubbing actors. Few of the voices had been those of the original players.

In early October, I was sent to London to meet the dubbing director hired by Columbia. To begin with I had to help him to find an actor to dub Mastroianni who had not yet learned to speak English. I was instructed to bring back tapes of our tests so that Fellini could choose the voice he thought sounded most suitable. I left for London on my first flight from the new airport at Fiumicino named after Leonardo da Vinci. Also waiting for the plane was Dino De Laurentiis with whom I chatted amiably. He was still feeling rather sore that he had refused to produce Federico's film which was already becoming a top moneymaker of the year at home and abroad. I was embarrassed when the flight was called and we separated, as he, at his own expense, was flying economy class, while Columbia had treated me to a first class ticket. It seemed like a good omen for my return to the London where I had not worked professionally for a decade.

At first I felt pleased with myself. I was working in Wardour Street with my expenses being paid handsomely by an American movie major and the promise of a weekly salary paid into my Rome bank. If all went well I'd have money enough to carry me through much of the winter. I knew from recent visits that London was a very different city from the one I fled in 1947. On October 17th, I wrote in my diary that while feeling 'at home' in many ways, I couldn't fit into the pattern of such a different lifestyle from that which I had become accustomed to in Rome.

That evening I had phoned the home of Stephen Barber to find out how things were going at the *Chronicle* and if the 'eager beaver' who'd taken over from me was doing all right. Steve was not there. His wife, Deidre, told me glumly that he was at the paper, putting to bed what would be the last issue. It was closing down the next day. It was sad news, of course, but I did feel a bit relieved that I had quit before the catastrophe happened. She said that if I was staying on I'd be invited to the wake in a few weeks time.

Meanwhile in Wardour Street, all was going well, even if, as I had suspected, I was already becoming aware that it was not going to be easy for me to satisfy my two masters, Federico, who wanted his original style to be respected, and I was the uneasy custodian of this, and the Columbia bosses who expected things to be done their way. They had bullied the director they'd hired, an Ealing Studios chap called Michael Truman, into obeying their wishes. Fortunately, Michael adored Fellini's work and kept reassuring me he would do his best to respect the original. For the moment we were interviewing actors and found that the agents were not very happy to send their actors round as it was considered rather degrading in the profession for an actor to do dubbing. It meant that the actor had nothing better to do. We taped a few voices of young actors who didn't even know who Fellini was. Then one day who should turn up but Kenneth Haigh, the actor who created the part of Jimmy Porter in the first production of John Osborne's *Look Back in Anger*. He was a bit haughty at first because his agent was not enthusiastic about him coming to this audition but, seeing he was out of work, he had agreed to give it a try. A first point in his favour with us was that he did indeed know who Fellini was. He had seen *La Strada* and had heard about the success of *La Dolce Vita* and, I think, he had seen Marcello on the screen in Paris. For his audition we chose the scene of Marcello and Steiner in the church. Michael and I agreed that his reading was excellent.

I flew back to Rome with the tapes of the most promising five actors we had tested and let Federico hear them without me making any comment. He listened several times to the tapes and in the end asked me about Ken, whose voice obviously appealed to him. I then told him who Ken was and said that we liked his voice too, and that the actor was an admirer of Federico's work. He was happy to give his consent. He wrote a nice letter to Michael saying that he liked Haigh's voice. The Columbia people came to an agreement with Ken's agent who made only one condition, that Ken's name should not appear on the credit titles or in any of the publicity as "Mastroianni's voice".

I had a few days before I had to be back in London, as the loops would not yet be ready for us to start the dubbing, so I spent my time finishing articles for a new Italian special issue of *Films and Filming*. The most difficult article to write was one on Antonioni. *L'avventura* was about to open in London and I knew that many critics would be writing think-pieces. I had by now seen the film several times, most recently a week ago in Rome with a second run audience. I had been rather dismayed to see the audience become restless and, like the audience at Cannes who should have known better, unwilling to accept Antonioni's new kind of storytelling. The stupid reaction of the audience made me like the film even more. So I concentrated all my attention to writing the article in the last weekend of 'freedom' before I knew I would be closed up all day in the depths of the Soho Square dubbing studios.

I hadn't yet finished this chore when I was summoned back to London. I sat at my typewriter in a rather uninspiring hotel room in Queen's Gate, where I was staying until I knew exactly how much I was going to be earning during the coming winter. I still had no contract with Amato in Rome and the Columbia people were only paying me expenses week by week. But I was quite pleased with what I wrote about Antonioni. I began by quoting Alberto Moravia on the subject of his most recent novel, *La Noia* (Boredom), which had a lot in common with Antonioni's film. He wrote "I am convinced, and Dostoevsky proves it to us, that the psychology of any character, if it is deeply and studiously examined, will eventually reveal ideas with universal values". I went on to say that even if Antonioni seems to be outside the social current of the Italian realist cinema, it seemed clear to me that he was the contemporary director most concerned with the changing values of our society. In writing the article I had to be careful to not contradict other articles I had either written myself or adapted as by-line pieces from interviews I'd done with other directors. I hadn't time to go to Hansom Books, the publishers of *Films and Filming*, to find out what was going into print. I was waiting for the proofs. I knew anyway that we had received permission to publish my translation of the Steiner literary party in *La Dolce Vita*. So I mailed my Antonioni piece to Baker on the Sunday evening, getting rather angry because I couldn't buy postage stamps from a tobacconist's. Somebody kindly reminded me that I could get them from a machine outside a post office and it took me some time to find one which was not empty. I didn't feel like a Londoner. I was a 'bloody foreigner'. I went to a cinema in the afternoon and saw a wonderful new British film, *Saturday Night and Sunday Morning* with the superb newcomer, Albert Finney, who acted like a real English working class boy without one thinking he was acting. Finney was the only current British actor I found attractive.

Albert Finney in *Saturday Night and Sunday Morning* (© British Lion)

The film made me want to misbehave with that kind of English working class lad but I didn't speak their language and didn't dare venture into the East End. I was resigned to the fact that celebrating 'on the town' in London on a Sunday evening wasn't quite the same as in Rome. So I went to a fish and chip shop, where you couldn't even order a beer, and by the time I got to a pub it was closing time. I went to bed early so I could face the ordeal awaiting me in Soho Square on the Monday morning.

We had already seen the subtitled print of *La Dolce Vita* and I thought the titles were pretty weak. Fellini had given me a copy of them to check and I had made a few corrections, such as a line said by the airport mechanic after setting eyes on Anita Ekberg. In Italian he had exclaimed: "I'll kill my wife tonight", whereas the title read: "My wife will kill me". My corrected line got a big laugh at our screening and one of the Columbia boys murmured: "The titles are good!". But inevitably the titles didn't have the space to convey the cynical bite in most of Fellini's language. I wondered if we'd be able to squeeze it into the dubbed dialogue? The Columbia people were already complaining that my dialogue was: "Too British". I told them frankly that they'd have to do an American version if they wanted to show it in English in the U.S. but I discovered that Columbia had so far only bought the U.K. rights. Amato was still in the process of doing an American deal. I discussed this with Truman and we agreed that where possible we could try to get what was called a 'mid-Atlantic accent' like that adopted by many British actors when they go to California. But I had been hired (even if not yet officially contracted!) to write an English-language version. There was still time of course for them to throw me out so I had to be careful what I said.

At the first morning's dubbing session with Haigh, I was relieved to find that in spite of his haughtiness he seemed comfortable with the first lines we gave him. It was clear, however, that our main problem was not so much in deciding what they were saying in the dubbed version but in getting the lines to synch. Of course my inexperience made the job more difficult. It was a hopeless task. I had to bluff a lot. Often I had to reduce the number of words but I would put my foot down when it was a question of content. The first big row came over the line that Marcello speaks when he wades into the Trevi fountain after Anitona-Sylvia. My literal translation of Marcello's line was perhaps a bit colourless: "She's right. I have been wrong in everything. We are all so wrong". But that was what Federico wanted him to say. It was a confession of helplessness. But Truman had evidently been told by the Columbia crowd to make it sound more lecherous and Haigh agreed. It was evidently felt that this touch of Latin lover sensuality would get a big laugh when the water of the fountain was suddenly turned off. I suggested instead that Marcello should say: "She must be a goddess. Perhaps I am unworthy of her. Perhaps everybody is!". This gives more point to his subsequent line: "Sylvia, who are you?". I insisted on telephoning Federico to ask him what we should do. He agreed that Marcello should not be playing the Latin lover. "Tell them this isn't a sequel to *Three Coins in the Fountain*," he said, adding "Go ahead, Francescone, and tell them to do as you say. On my orders". It was a victory for me and we reached a compromise over the lines. The lecherous tone was played down. So I ended the first week in the Soho cellar feeling a bit more confident that I was doing what I was sent to London to do and was hopefully being paid to do it. On the phone to Federico I had reminded him to give Amato a nudge about my contract. They were coming to London for the premiere and that would be the occasion to insist, hoping I hadn't been kicked out by then.

On the next Saturday I treated myself to an expensive theatre outing, paying £3 for a black market ticket to a charity matinee of *Romeo and Juliet*, at the Old Vic, attended by the Queen Mother; the much-acclaimed production by Visconti's former assistant and designer, Franco Zeffirelli, who had already been acclaimed for his

Covent Garden productions of *Cav and Pag* (the former, in particular, staged with stunning realism). I was very impressed by
the way Franco, who I had not yet met, succeeded in getting the
English actors to behave like Italians, something that Peter Brook
had tried to achieve without the same success in his Stratford
production of the same play I had seen a few years before. This
obviously talented Italian director had succeeded in bringing
out some of the incredibly saucy meanings in many of the lines
that were often missed in English productions. This was above
all true of the lines spoken by the Nurse and Mercutio, the two
most bawdily written characters in the play. Juliet was played by
a young actress called Judy Dench. I'm glad I noted in my diary
that she was "very promising". The Romeo was John Stride. Like
the other young males in the cast, he had been obliged by the
Italian director to grow his own hair long like a Renaissance boy.
In the England of 1960, young men still sported crew cuts. The
Capulets and Montagues were, of course, from the Middle Ages
but it was fair enough for Zeffirelli to give a Renaissance painting
feel to the play, especially since the director was a Florentine. I
could see that the Queen Mum was having a good time and this
encouraged the audience to react in the same way. It made me wish
that I could borrow some of Shakespeare's racy Elizabethan
language for Fellini's Roma of today. It's amazing how well our
Bard had understood the Italian mentality. Was it true, as some
have suggested in Italy, that he was an immigrant who had really
been born in Sicily and was named Crollalanza?

That weekend, I went to visit my mother and her jovial husband
in his cottage on the Sussex downs to which they had now moved.
It was the first time I had been able to visit their home. Bertie
brought me a cup of tea on Sunday morning and gave me a book
of stories, about the adventurous life of merchant sea captains,
one of which was written by him. I was delighted to find that
mother and her new mate seemed to have created a happy ménage.

They even seemed to be sleeping in the same bed which she had sworn they would never do. I spent most of the weekend reading and correcting the proofs of the Italian issue of *Films and Filming*. Before leaving for some film event in Mexico City (lucky him!) Peter Baker had told me he was very pleased with my Antonioni article. I had been asked by a Scottish publisher to translate the day-by-day diary of the making of *La Dolce Vita* by Tullio Kezich and I had rashly accepted, even though I thought it unlikely that I would find the time or the energy to deliver it by January. I should have been writing my own book about Fellini. Once the film opened I was sure every publisher in the English-speaking world would be eager to commission one.

In our Soho studio, the next Monday morning, it was scheduled that we were to do Marcello's dialogue in the scenes with Steiner but, as we hadn't yet found an actor to dub Alain Cluny, we thankfully put them off. Steiner was a caricature of a man in a spiritual crisis but Federico seemed to want us to take the man seriously. Or was the scene included to show the shallowness of Marcello's own life? Could I dare to give the scene a sort of Wildean flavour? I'd have to wait to discuss it with Federico when he came for the imminent British premiere.

Alain Cuny and Marcello Mastroianni
in Fellini's *La Dolce Vita*.

Chapter 13

I went to the wake for the *News Chronicle* and had a merry evening even though it was a rather sad occasion. The paper was selling a million copies but, in those days, when television had a monopoly on advertising, and only the gutter press, or the big conservative papers like *The Times* and *The Telegraph*, which had powerful support from the Establishment, could count on getting the ads which a daily paper needed to survive. It was a bad time for Fleet Street. Deidre Barber was crowing about the fact that Steve had been taken on by the *Telegraph* and was going to Delhi as their correspondent. I could see her enjoying her role as a Memsaab. The 'wake' was in an expensive restaurant and Steve told me they were all going dutch but that I was his guest.

A few nights later I'd go to what was becoming my favourite English restaurant, Wheeler's, invited by Antonioni and Monica who had arrived in London for the opening of *L'avventura*. Monica told me that at the conference after the press screening she had been asked whether she and Michelangelo were intending to get married. She told them she was there to talk about the film. I told her that if they showed interest in her private life it meant she was obviously on the way to becoming a big star and this consoled her a bit. In London, everyone was enchanted by her lively personality, and the reviews for the film were mostly excellent. Antonioni was particularly gratified that *The Times* had published an enthusiastic review saying the film was "a masterpiece". This compensated for the nasty remark written by their reporter at Cannes. Before they returned to Rome, I found them seats for, and joined them to see at Her Majesty's Theatre, the musical hit *West Side Story*, which Monica and I enjoyed immensely. Michelangelo dozed a bit.

I continued to find time for the theatre to cheer me up after a day of dubbing depressions. I saw Paul Scofield in Robert Bolt's *A Man For All Seasons* about Thomas More and his conflict with

Henry VIII for which he was executed. More is remembered as a saint for Italians, San Tommaso Moro. I also saw a sensational play, *The Caretaker* by the new dramatist, Harold Pinter, which quite stunned me for its unconventional wordplay, used not just to amuse but also to express feelings. This was a 'new' thing for the British stage. The matinée audience loved it and laughed a lot, though I felt the play was not just for the pleasure of a West End public, it had a great deal of philosophical meaning. It was a great step forward from the 'angry' writers of the so-called 'kitchen sink theatre'. When I returned to the dubbing studio the day after, I felt some of Pinter's double-edged humour would be appropriate for our film. I wished I had taken Michelangelo to see it as I am sure he would have appreciated it more than the Bernstein musical.

December 1st, I spent my 32nd birthday working and gave my colleagues a cup of champagne. They all seem surprised to hear that I was still under forty. Maybe it was London that was making me look and feel older? But I was gaining more confidence in myself as I felt that I was becoming rather essential to the pretty hopeless job we were engaged in. On the eve of Federico's arrival, the BBC transmitted the TV interview he had done in Rome sometime before. He had asked me to check it with a view to telling them not to broadcast it. I told him not to worry. It wasn't as disastrous as he feared. He was self-conscious about his English which indeed was, at times, not always easy to understand. But I took the responsibility of letting them broadcast it. His English was picturesque but it was disarming and conveyed his personality. He hadn't wanted to come to London. He was still not adapting himself to the international role he was now expected to play. All the papers were getting worked up about his arrival. They realised that this was the first newsworthy film of the 1960s. I was asked by the *Mail* to tell them Federico's life story which I did over the phone. The article appeared the next day without, of course, mentioning me. *The Daily Herald* who had commissioned me to write a paid piece then called back telling me not to bother. I was being treated as if I were his PR man but nobody at Columbia thought of asking me to go to the airport to meet him. All the bigwigs went themselves. I only caught up with the circus at Claridge's where poor Federico already looked harassed. He seemed relieved to see me. His pest of an assistant, Guidarino Guidi, had come with him and, as he and I didn't get along too well, I left him to look after Federico's first day in London.

At Claridge's, I had run into an old friend, Gavin Lambert, who had been flown in from LA, where he now lived, to work on the script of a film being made in London, an adaptation of Tennessee Williams's novel *The Roman Spring of Mrs. Stone.* He invited me to a party given by José Quintero, a Broadway theatre director who was directing the film. I went to the party with Gavin and found that it was in honour of none other than Lotte Lenya, Kurt Weill's widow, who played a role in the film. My adored Vivien Leigh, who played Mrs. Stone, was there and I exchanged a few words mentioning our mutual friend, Ian Dallas. When she heard that I lived in Rome she asked me why the Italians were being so sensitive about the film being shot there. "They say it's about an immoral woman and would be bad for Rome's image," she told me. I explained that the Church interfered in everything in Italy. But I suggested that maybe they also felt that the film, like the book, would give too much importance to young Italians being shown as gigolos. Latin Lovers were all very well if they were mature like Rossano Brazzi. "But aren't the young men on the make?" she asked. "Of course", I said, obviously without adding that I (like Tennessee!) knew that from personal experience. I explained that "the government doesn't like it to be shown that it is unemployment which drives the young men to this extreme". Vivien still seemed perplexed and was distracted by her current boyfriend, a Canadian, who wanted to leave the party. I had heard that she had resigned herself to the divorce from Sir Larry.

Quintero's assistant was Peter Yates whom I'd met during the filming of *Navarone* in Rhodes. When he saw me he greeted me warmly. Both he and his wife, who had been the publicist on the Foreman film, told me how much they'd enjoyed my *Films and Filming* article from the Rhodes location. They told me laughingly that only Stanley Baker and James Darren hadn't liked it.

The press screening of *La Dolce Vita* was held the next morning. Fellini, and those looking after him, arrived for the end of it. He was upset there was no applause but I explained that the press here rarely applauded. The critics left before the press conference started. The conference had been arranged for the columnists. The questions were mostly fatuous. Federico gave complex replies which the team of interpreters had difficulty in translating. In any case, I'd prepared him with a few answers in English, quoted from the article 'by him' that we were about to publish in *Films and Filming*, and this helped him out. There was much excitement at the Columbia office as everyone who was anyone in London was begging for tickets for the premiere. While I was there getting two for myself, I heard a secretary take a call from Lord Beaverbrook who wanted seats for himself and for Lady Churchill.

It was a memorable evening. The film was received with respectful silence and only a few laughs (those subtitles!) but at the end there was much applause, cut short by God Save the Queen. Fellini was again bewildered. We explained that, as it was a long film, the cinema employees were in a hurry to close down for the night. There was a big party afterwards at the Orchid Room of the Dorchester to which I took Ian Dallas who, having arrived that morning, had come with me to see the film and was quite overwhelmed by it. At the party we were sitting at a table with Lord Hambleden and his Italian wife. When I was a 'dolce vita' journalist like Marcello I had covered their glamorous wedding in Rome. I didn't remind them of this because I couldn't remember whether I'd written my usual sarcastic report on glamorous weddings.

I found a moment to introduce Ian to Federico who seemed intrigued by him. At another party during his London visit they met again and I could see that they got along very well. Federico would tell me that Ian reminded him of a magician he'd known during his early years in Rimini. We'd find out more about this when Federico would cast Ian in his subsequent film, *8 1/2*.

The gloomy atmosphere of our dubbing studio had been brightened by the presence of an adorable Italian actress, Lisa Gastoni, who lived in London and spoke English with a sexy accent which was very suitable for the dubbing of Anouk Aimée. Michael Truman and I had arranged that she should be there the morning when Federico and Marcello came to watch us at work. We were all delighted with the way Lisa dubbed the long sensual off-screen speech where Maddalena describes the ancestral pedigrees of the castle inhabitants. I felt that my dialogue while not quite worthy of Pinter did at least have an appropriate touch of Noel Coward. Naturally our visitors were enchanted by Lisa. I think the lunch we all had together in Soho was the event of their week in London that Federico and Marcello enjoyed the most. But I was pleased that Federico also enjoyed the visit we made to the National Film Theatre, where it had been arranged for him to meet the representatives of fifty British film societies. It was an occasion when translating for Federico was truly a pleasure. Though most of the film buffs had only seen his early films, he was stimulated by them into being a little less mystical than he had been with the press, probably because he could tell they had a genuine love for cinema. I felt on that occasion that 'our' Federico was now truly one of the cinema 'Greats' and not just a subject for the scandalmongers.

A luncheon with Britain's leading film critic, Dilys Powell, was also rewarding because she clearly had understood what *La Dolce Vita* was all about and what it meant for world cinema. I was so taken up by these more interesting aspects of Federico's visit that only after he had left did I remember that I had forgotten to urge him to put pressure on Amato (who had left before he did) to reassure me that my contract problem was being looked after.

John Francis Lane with Federico Fellini (photograph by Roloff Beny)

With Fellini's departure, life for me in London returned to normal which meant eight hours a day closed up in a cellar in Soho Square. So instead of spending my evenings and weekends translating Kezich's *La Dolce Vita* diary for the Scottish publishers, which I had decided I would not be able to finish by the deadline they had set me, I went in search of cultural events. I attended a Sunday night try-out of *On the Wall*, a new play at the Royal Court by a dramatist called Henry Chapman. The play, set on a building site, intrigued me even though the idea of making drama out of men at work seemed more suited to a strictly agitprop theatrical site or to more theatrically inventive dramatists (as David Storey would become). Still, these were days when being politically committed was a way of life. I went backstage afterwards to greet one of the actors I knew, Norman Rossington, and we went out to eat at the pub nearby. We were joined by my old *Sequence* friends, Lindsay Anderson and Karel Reisz. When I told them why I was in London, they told me they'd seen *La Dolce Vita* but they didn't seem wildly enthusiastic. "Maybe it wasn't 'politically committed' enough?", I asked sarcastically. Lindsay spluttered his indignation about the film. Karel also had reservations but at least he was full of admiration for Fellini as a director. Karel was a European, born of Czech parents, who had taken refuge in England after the Munich pact with Hitler. Lindsay was born in India of a colonialist military family and had been 'angry' since childhood against the 'dolce vita' of the Britons in Delhi. He recounted that he'd gotten into trouble with the fellow officers of his high ranking military father when he and his friends put up a red flag on the garrison wall after the Labour Party victory at the elections in 1945.

I was just beginning to get into a heated argument with them when who should join us but Albert Finney! I had been on the point of reproaching Lindsay for what I considered his banal applause-catching direction of *Billy Liar* but now that Billy himself was with us I could only gape at him and guffaw at their jokes which seemed on the level of the play. I limited myself to saying that I had found the humour of the play too dependent for laughs on the clichés which Billy and his fellow Yorkshire pals were expounding, and when I told Albie [Finney] that I'd probably been put off by sitting in the cheap seats at the back of the stalls, he said he'd fix me better seats, if I let him know in advance, preferably for an evening performance (I'd seen it at a matinée with the tea-tray ladies). He added, "Come back and tell me afterwards what you think and we'll have a bite together". The thought of a 'bite' with the most sexy British actor I'd ever set eyes on left me quivering with excitement. I had difficulty sleeping that night. To be truthful, it was getting more and more difficult for me to sleep anyway in the small bed in my cramped room at Queen's Gate so I got Ian to find me something more comfortable, even if more expensive, in the West End. He came up with a lovely old-fashioned hotel in Jermyn Street called The Cavendish (long since demolished). I moved in just before Christmas and, as I noted in my diary, I had my first good night's sleep since I came to London six weeks ago. It was a large room with a hopelessly inadequate gas fire that was difficult to light and turn off, and which left a nasty smell. In my dreary Queen's Gate hotel I had been suffering from over-heating. I felt I was in Baron Corvo territory but I was happier. They told me they'd find me a better room after Christmas. It was gratifying anyway to know I staying was just across the street from the Royal Academy and that there were a dozen first-run cinemas and many large theatres within walking distance.

I was glad to get away for Christmas. My mother had arranged for me to spend it with her family in Ramsgate. It was to be a trip into my past, beginning with the train out from Victoria Station during which my feelings were very mixed, grim at first as I passed down through the Orpington area, more nostalgic and sentimental as we came closer to East Kent where, after all, I couldn't complain that I'd had an unhappy childhood. My mother's younger sister,

Muriel, whom I'd always called Auntie Moo and been very fond of, now ran a boarding house in Ramsgate and made sure I was comfortable. Mum and Bertie stayed in a holidaymakers hotel re-opened for the festive season and that's where we ate our Christmas dinner, and where the whole family attended a grotesque fancy dress ball at which everyone tried to get me off with a quite intelligent but wallflowerish local young woman. At the party, however, her younger brother turned up, surprisingly in drag, and showing off a very appealing masculine figure. I came quite near to making a match with him instead of his sister. But he was too shy to oblige when we met in the loo and I asked him to show me what he had under his skirt. That was the closest I came to offbeat entertainment during what was to prove rather uninspiring English festive days, but I suppose the protracted 'normalcy' of it all was good for me, especially as in England there are always two sides to what passes for 'normal'.

On Boxing Day, we went to see a pantomime, an entertaining 'English' experience I had long forgotten. The booing and hissing of the villain, in this improbable version of *Robin Hood*, was great fun and the Dame was another young man in drag. This one however looked a bit like Tommy Steele. That evening in the local nightclub I ran into him, still with his make-up on and he invited me to come for a walk with him to the beach but I declined politely. This Kentish Tommy Steele belonged to the category of those camp characters at Fellini's 'dolce vita' parties. I preferred the Albert Finneys to the Tommy Steeles of England 1960.

Back in the Soho Square cellar after Christmas, it so happened that one of the first characters we had to dub was indeed the queer Pierone who feeds Marcello gossip at the nightclub, and is on the beach at the end peering at the monster fish. Federico was inclined to exaggerate in his send-up of queers. This attitude was typical of many Italian hearty heterosexuals who only let their own hair down with the excuse of carnival, where even those who spend the rest of the year boasting of their virility and teasing the queers, can go out in drag. In *I Vitelloni*, Federico had already parodied the aged homo actor (on that wind-swept wintry beach not so very different from that of Ramsgate where I would probably have ended up with my Kentish Tommy Steele). In *La Dolce Vita*, the younger queers were the object of his tease. Pierone, played in the film by Giò Staiano, was being dubbed by a dancer-actor called Harold Lang, whom I had met in Athens and was glad to see again and we had a camp lunch together. The lines I had written for him were okay. Less convincing were the bitchy remarks I had written for the character played by Laura Betti at the final orgy. To dub her lines, Truman had picked a bright actress of mixed Scottish-Italian blood, Adrienne Corri, who made intelligent suggestions. Together we found just the right words for both meaning and synch.

By New Year's Eve, the Cavendish management had moved me into a more comfortable room, almost a suite, with a view of a rather sinister Victorian courtyard of the St James area, where I'd already discovered there was a strip club called The Keyhole. The hotel management told me I could have a key to a back entrance from the courtyard and added with a twinkle that if I wanted to bring friends in I could do so. Maybe they had seen me fraternising with a girl from The Keyhole and her drunken Irish husband? However, with my current luck, I doubted I'd find someone to share the splendid double bed with me. I even had a bathroom to myself, though the hot water wasn't always available.

I had received courteous invitations to various New Year's Eve parties in the Wardour Street world, dress up affairs, but none appealed to me. Silly of me not to be social in a world where profitable professional and private contacts were often made at parties. I ended up seeing the New Year in by myself; repeating exactly the experience I had had in London on V. J. Night in 1945. Then only sixteen years old and a virgin, I had hoped vainly to be ravished amongst the crowds in Trafalgar Square. This time I wanted to do the ravishing but again had no luck.

On New Year's Day 1961, I went for lunch at Otello's, the Italian restaurant in Soho, where I now ate regularly and found, as always, a warm welcome, even if the waiters looked as if they had been up most of the night. I ate a very good meal and was rewarded with a delightful encounter with a young architecture student from Milan, who was holidaying in London and feeling lonely too. At least I was able to start the New Year talking intelligently to someone who knew who Fellini and Antonioni were and who had seen their films. To my surprise he didn't seem surprised when I asked him if he'd like to come back to my place. He was delighted to help me inaugurate my now accessible rooms at The Cavendish. He wasn't exactly a proletarian type but I was happy to inaugurate the year with a young Italian. I think he saw me as a sort of Oscar Wilde. The setting was appropriately Victorian. It consoled me for the fact that I probably would have to spend at least the first month of 1961 trapped in London.

As it turned out, I'd be in London till early March. The work on the dubbing proceeded more smoothly, both Michael and I were eager to get it finished. We were resigned to the idea that it was a doomed mission but we were determined to do as good a job as possible under the circumstances. We didn't fight anymore because I realized it had been wrong of me to upset him when I had sometimes criticised him in the presence of the others in the crew. We were both aware that, although we disagreed on a lot of points, we needed each other. Anyway, the film was doing very well in the original version in selected first-run cinemas, and the Columbia people didn't seem in a hurry to get our English version out on general release. There had been some discussion over whether the final dubbing mix should be done in Rome, as Federico preferred, or in London as they wanted. In the end, Federico agreed to come to London for two weeks in February. It meant I'd pick up some more cash, and I got a nice letter from Federico reassuring me that I would get the extra money I'd asked for from Amato when I got back to Rome. But there was still the problem of Michael. He wanted everything to be logical in a pedantic English way when there was nothing logical about Federico's dialogue or the way he had dubbed it into Italian. For example, the scene when Marcello and Maddalena come out of the nightclub is quite magical. It doesn't really matter what the boys are shouting to them. In dubbing the photographers, Michael insisted we had to hear every line and see who was speaking, but that was not Federico's style. I let Michael have his way on that but when we dubbed Sylvia's press conference I insisted we did things my way. The question in Italian "Do you believe in the friendship of peoples?" sounded silly when translated into English, but I found a solution to the problem of synching on the 'p' of 'peoples', with: "Are you worried by the increase in population?". For the question: "Do you believe in the Italian neo-realist cinema?", a send-up by Federico of magazines like Guido Aristarco's *Cinema Nuovo*, which wouldn't mean anything to an English audience, I changed it to: "Do you believe realism is alive or dead". The dubbing of the miracle sequence went quite well, as Michael had found some excellent character actors to play peasants and reporters. When Yvonne Furneaux's ingenuous Emma is told by the Russian-accented woman it doesn't matter whether it was really a miracle or not, what counts, she says, is that you have Faith. For a Catholic this seems obvious. But Michael wanted to be empirical about it, something again quite far from the Fellini world. As one who doesn't believe in miracles, I couldn't offer a logical alternative so in the end we translated the line literally without trying to explain it. I don't think Federico believed in miracles either but he was very attached to people who did. In spite of her French name, Furneaux was English and we had her original soundtrack. When the English version was released, I wrote an article for *Films and Filming* about my dubbing experiences. A reader complained that, when watching the scene of Marcello and his girlfriend having a fight in a country road, she wanted to hear Mastroianni's own voice. I replied that if she'd seen the Italian 'original' she wouldn't have heard the real voice of the English actress! Furneaux appeared in another of 'my films' that year, *Via Margutta*.

When Norman Rossington came in to do a morning's dubbing for us, of Paparazzo, he asked me whether I'd been back to see *Billy Liar* again as I had promised Albie Finney. I said I hadn't had time. Over lunch we called Albie who said he'd leave seats for me the next night. Everyone in London was raving about the play which was the hit of the moment. So I went again and had to admit that I had been unfair. Thanks to the good seat upfront I realised that in the back stalls at that matinée I had been irritated by the laughter which came between where I was sitting and the actors on the stage. I still didn't think much of the play itself which seemed to be a superficial look at the fantasies of a working-class English boy, but certainly Albie gave every line it's full worth and managed to give some depth to the character. I went back afterwards to thank him for the ticket and told him why I had been put off the first time. He told me he didn't think he'd accept the offer to star in the film version because the producers didn't want Lindsay to direct it. The writers had objected to the way Lindsay had behaved towards them at the previews in Brighton, and subsequently rejected an offer of the film rights from Tony Richardson's Woodfall Films who wanted to buy it for Lindsay to direct. They had sold them instead to the producer, Joseph Janni, who bought it for John Schlesinger. I bought Keith Waterhouse's original novel and it seemed to me to be better than the play.

As our dubbing chores moved towards the final week we had re-takes to do with Ken Haigh, who had just come back from doing a TV play in Hollywood, and who reluctantly graced us some of his time whilst wondering why the re-takes were necessary. They were but it wasn't his fault. He did in fact help us to improve the earlier dub. And he still had the Steiner scenes to do, which

Michael and I had re-written. Neither of us believed in the Steiner character but fortunately Michael had found a wonderful actor, John Le Mesurier, to dub Alain Cuny. Le Mesurier succeeded in giving the lines conviction without us having to resort to the kind of irony that I had at one point envisaged and which would have been inappropriate in the context. The English actor gave more sense to the part than perhaps had been conveyed in Romolo Valli's dubbing of the original Italian track. We were deeply moved when Mesurier said the line about Morandi's paintings, and when he described his children's talents. I still wasn't sure that Federico had expected the part to be taken seriously but, in order to believe in the man's subsequent tragic act, it was necessary to believe in what he was saying. I insisted on him saying the last enigmatic words exactly as I'd translated them. They do explain something of his desperate gesture:

"We must succeed in loving so intensely that we live outside of time... detached".

The word 'detached' which fitted into synch seemed very relevant not only to the existentialist feel of the character (which maybe Federico was digging at) but also to the ideas that were emerging from the best of the 'new British theatre' led by Pinter.

Chapter 14

Michael and I celebrated the end of the practical dubbing chores by hosting a lunch, with much Italian wine, at Otello's, for our valiant technicians. Michael passed the bill on to Columbia. There was still a lot of work to do, mostly technical, before we would be ready to summon Federico to London. So I was free to take two weeks off for what was not exactly a holiday. In Eastbourne, my Mother had laid on a rather delicate but essential dental visit for me. But before that I had a few extra professional commitments in London. I had been asked to go to Broadcasting House to record introductions to the interviews I'd done with Fellini and Antonioni for BBC Talks. They seemed pleased with my efforts. At a social event, I ran into Peter Yates again. Seeing I was still in London, he had begged me to come to Shepperton where they were going to shoot interiors for *The Roman Spring of Mrs. Stone*. Peter wanted me to appear in a party scene which was supposed to be taking place in a villa on the Appian Way. Peter said enthusiastically: "If people see you in the scene they'll think we shot it in Rome!" I was delighted of course, and enjoyed the chore even if Quintero didn't give me any lines. I became friendly with a young Italian who was playing a bit part but I also got on well with the young male star who was playing Mrs. Stone's Italian gigolo, Warren Beatty. He told me he was looking forward to coming to Rome where they going to shoot some locations after all. He made me promise to show him round some of the 'dolce vita' sites. I said I'd be only too pleased to oblige.

The dental visit to Eastbourne resulted in me having all my decaying teeth removed in one go, a rather painful but successful operation even though it would take me some time to toughen my gums and get used to the splendid dentures which had been prepared for me. I had to stay the whole two weeks shut up under the care of mother and my stepfather who was a helpful teacher in adapting to the new teeth, something he had a long experience with. It was pleasant to be in the isolation of the Sussex Downs and I managed to avoid being seen by visitors to the house. To my amazement, my mother had fixed the whole medical junket, dentures included, on the Health Service. So it only cost me the minimum charge of £5 (in Italy it would have cost me 5 million lire). It was the British contribution to my well-being for which I would be most eternally grateful. It would have been worth coming to England this winter for that alone. My new condition promised to give a new impulse to my erotic life when I got back to Rome.

I had to return to London for Fellini's arrival and for the tedious task of the final sound mix, a technical chore for which I was necessary only as an interpreter. I no longer kept a daily diary but I remember it wasn't an easy task. There were often moments when I could tell that Federico wasn't too pleased with the sound in English. I soon gave up trying to make excuses and blamed everything on the necessity for synch. Federico and I had few occasions to be alone, but occasionally we'd eat together. I had been on an almost liquid diet for the whole period of the dental operation but, back in London, I was beginning to eat normally. I remember the first time I bit my way into a good fillet steak was when Federico took me to lunch. I told him what I had been through in the past fortnight and he complimented me on my courage. We then had a long and rather intimate discussion about sexual habits. When I told him about my Swiss guard and my regrets that I had lost contact with him and so couldn't exercise my new potential oral gifts on him, Federico was amused and asked me a very curious question. Did I think that women were particularly anxious about penis sizes? I replied that I was hardly the right person to be able to judge what women preferred but said that my Swiss friend had told me that his extra-large weapon had often frightened off the girls. Walking back to Soho Square, I asked Federico why he put so many freaks into his films. He told me to look around me in Soho and I saw what he meant. I suppose I should have felt grateful he didn't tell me to look in a mirror.

Soon afterwards, with our chores in Soho Square now concluded, after four months of winter, the longest period I had spent on British soil since I quit my homeland in 1947, I was ready to leave London. On March 10th 1961, I finally left for Rome, stopping over in Paris for a long weekend to re-acclimatise myself to the 'continent'. Eleven years had passed since I lived in Paris as a student. The city seemed much more frenetic. At the Gare du Nord I had to queue for twenty-five minutes for a taxi and the (woman) driver refused to help me with my voluminous luggage. Ian Dallas was in town and had found me a nice hotel next door to where Jean Cocteau and Colette had lived. It was surprisingly cheap considering that the arched window of my room looked out over the Palais Royal. The main reason for the stop over in Paris was to see Luchino Visconti's much acclaimed French production of '*Tis Pity She's a Whore* with Alain Delon and Romy Schneider. Unfortunately Schneider had appendicitis and the performances were suspended. However, I was able to see a new Jean Vilar production of Brechts *La résistible ascension d'Arturo Ui*, not alas in the Banlieu theatre where I'd seen his *Mère Courage* years before, but now in the institutional, vast and non-air-conditioned space of the Palais de Chaillot. In spite of the discomfort in the auditorium, the production was exciting. Thousands of spectators roared their approval for Vilar's splendid company and the scintillating interpretation of the ironical and always topical parable of the Hitler of the Chicago cauliflower market.

But the most memorable experience of this Paris visit was arranged by Ian who took me to see his friend, Edith Piaf, in whose home he was staying (he was translating songs for her into English for a forthcoming American tour). I hadn't seen her on a stage for many years and naturally it was distressing for me to see how frail she had become. Yet when she started to sing she was still the great Piaf of always. We saw her two nights running. On the second, Ian took me backstage to meet her. She was tired from the performance, and looked even frailer in person than she had done on the stage, but she lit up when we complimented her, and smirked: "Oui, I did sing well tonight, I know. Glad you appreciated it". She could tell we were sincere and gave us a warm welcome. When Ian told her I was a friend of Fellini's she shouted with joy "Federicooo? But when is he coming to visit me again? He's the only director who could make a film of my life. I have seen *La Strada* fifty times! I should have played Gelsomina". Pity she hadn't, I thought! When she was changed and was ready to leave she looked smaller still, a real 'gamine'. Outside the stage door there were a few fans waiting to get record sleeves autographed. She waved them a kiss as she got into a taxi with Ian, and she waved one to me, saying "Un baiser pour Federicoo!". The next day, Ian told me she had insisted on rehearsing the songs until 3 a.m.

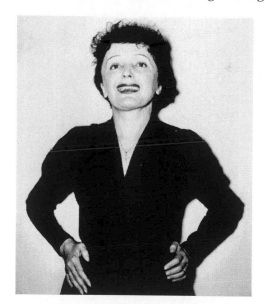

Edith Piaf

I had arranged it that I should arrive back in Rome on the Ides of March, my tenth anniversary as a Roman resident even if I had still not yet officially signed up at the city's registry office. I felt a bit weepy when I arrived at the Stazione Termini where this time Enzo was there to meet me. But as the days went by I was soon back into my Roman 'rut', the materialistic life-style I had chosen. Ian's arrival a few days later gave me only a temporary boost. He was on his way to Greece where he said he was going to finish a new play. He had a new lover whom he said would help him to concentrate. I was envious that his lovers were useful to him creatively. Mine only distracted me from my work.

I told Fellini that Ian was in town and he invited us to lunch at a wonderful restaurant on the Appian Way called L'escargot. We gave him Edith Piaf's message and he told us he had wanted Edith for a part in *La Dolce Vita* but she had other commitments. Federico questioned Ian about Laurence Olivier whom, it seemed, had been proposed for the lead in his new film, but Ian was so enthusiastic about Larry's greatness that Federico was awed. I think he'd decided anyway that Marcello would again be his leading man.

Among the new Italian films I saw in the Spring of 1961 the most interesting was undoubtedly De Sica's adaptation of Moravia's novel *La Ciociara* (Two Women), an emotional war-time melodrama with the great performance from Sophia Loren that those of us who had always adored her were convinced she would give when she got the right part. It was incredible to think that the producer, Carlo Ponti, who was taking such a personal interest in Sophia's career, should have thought of asking Sophia to play the daughter who gets raped and asking Magnani to play the role of mother! Naturally, Magnani laughed in his face. De Sica was intelligent enough to insist that Sophia play the mother, and that the daughter should be played by an adolescent. Though Italians generally know the history of the liberation of Italy from the German occupation, and they know a lot about the progress of the liberating army up the peninsula, not many of us knew until we read the novel, or saw the film, of the sordid details of the Moroccan soldiers' behaviour as part of the 'liberating' army. Moravia, an anti-fascist who had fled Rome during the German occupation, and who had hid in the area between Naples and Rome, had seen at first hand events similar to what he described in his novel.

Sophia Loren in *La Ciociara* (Two Women).

JFL accompanying Alberto Moravia to Capri
for a South Bank Show interview in 1983.

Another new Italian film I saw during that spring was a somewhat more modest work with the title *Call 22.22 for Lieutenant
Sheridan*. In my diary, I wrote that its "highlight was one of the
more outrageously over the top performances by a secondary character that will probably be seen for a long time on Italian screens".
That actor, of course, was JFL. I wrote that I belonged "to the
school of Charles Laughton but having had the privilege to act
with that great actor I ought to have learned how to ham with
grace and wit". I added that I hoped after seeing my 'performance'
on the screen as a lawyer I would recognise my faults and hopefully,
if given better direction than I was on this film, I might improve.

In April, I went to see José Quintero and the *Roman Spring* crowd
filming in the Piazza di Spagna. During the weeks they were shooting in Rome I wasted some time courting the young Italian actor
I had met during the filming of the party scene in London. On the
set I preferred to dedicate my attention to the much more interesting and promising member of the cast, Warren Beatty. At least
with him I had no illusions! One afternoon, when he had finished
shooting, he reminded me that in London I had promised to take
him on a tour of the dolce vita sites. It was obvious that the ones
he was interested in were those that Fellini had invented. We drove
off in his flashy Alfa Romeo and, after pointing out the ruins of
the Caracalla Baths, where Federico had shot the open-air night
club sequence with Ekberg and Lex Barker, we arrived at the city
walls where, in the film we see Fellini whores promoting their
wares, but there was nobody around so early in the evening. I
didn't know where to take him next. We reached the Appian Way
and I started pointing out historical sites. Then suddenly I saw a
sign indicating the way to the Fosse Ardeatine. I knew the tragic
story behind the place. I told Beatty to drive there and I'd explain.
I'd suddenly felt a bit moralistic and wanted to show the handsome
young movie star that Italy was not only the 'dolce vita'. I told him
what had happened there. Hitler had ordered the execution of

hostages in reprisal for partisans killing German soldiers in a street of the then German-occupied Rome. I could see that this was not the sort of 'site' that Warren had expected me to take him to see. But he was game to come along. We went inside the mausoleum built on the site where the pitiful remains of the corpses of three hundred and thirty-five Italians had been dug up. The Nazis had flung the corpses into a pit, the 'fosse', off the Via Ardeatine. I had been there once before for an official ceremony and had perhaps been put off by the array of priests (Jewish as well as Catholic) and by the rhetoric of the politicians. This time, however, as we walked along the rows of simple tombs written with the name and the age and profession of the victims who were known to have died there, few of whom had been actually identified, I felt a rare upsurge of emotion. I could see that Warren was also deeply moved. We said nothing and drove back to Rome in silence, forgetting about the 'dolce vita'.

Vivien Leigh, Warren Beatty and Lotte Lenya
in *The Roman Spring of Miss Stone*.

Many years later, when Warren had become a top Hollywood star, he came to Venice for the presentation of *Reds* (1981), a film he had directed (and for which he would win the Academy Award). At his press conference I stood up to ask a question. He looked at me and exclaimed, "I think I know you don't I?". Later, I went to his room at the Excelsior and I reminded him where we had last seen each other. "I remember that day" he said, "I've never forgotten what you took me to see. It was a very moving experience". I felt he was sincere.

I was glad to be freed of the responsibility of the *News Chronicle* but my London experiences had not brought any significant follow-ups. I had finally received the promised cash for what was still owed to me by Peppino Amato's office for the Italian part of my fee for my *La Dolce Vita* chore, and had been able to pay the domestic debts that had accumulated in my absence. But money was running short. I had committed myself to go to Cannes to write a report for *Films and Filming*, but the festival was paying only for one week's hospitality. To save money, I was obliged to travel up by train in a second class couchette. In any case, I was very glad to be there because I was making my festival debut as an actor in a competition film, Cacoyannis's *The Wastrel*. I was embarrassed to find myself duly listed among the actors of the film, and to find that they'd put me in the seats of honour not far from the director and the stars, Van Heflin, Ellie Lambetti and her husband, Frederick Wakeman, author of the novel, *The Hucksters*, on which the film was based. I ended my report on this Cannes Festival, which appeared in the July edition, with the following paragraph: "Michael Cacoyannis reverted to his native Cyprus in order to give a nationality to *The Wastrel* which was made by an Italian producer and shot in English. As my name was on the acting credits of this film it would not perhaps be tactful to attempt a critical assessment of it. The film was very warmly received by the Sunday afternoon public and more coolly by the critics at the press screening."

The only comment I added was: "Let us hope that after two films in English, Cacoyannis will soon find the way to return to Greece and shoot a film in his own language and about his own people. He has it in him to give us a great film yet". Michael Cacoyannis would, in fact, return to Greece to make *Zorba the Greek* (1964).

In Cannes, someone at Columbia told me that our English version of *La Dolce Vita* had opened in Manchester simultaneously with the subtitled Italian version which did the big business so ours was soon pulled. Must I admit to complete failure, I wondered? I knew from the start that it was a doomed chore. Michael Truman and I had done what we could. Federico knew this and would one day call me in to go to London again on a similarly doomed post-synchronisation chore so he obviously didn't blame me. But on that occasion (for *Satyricon*) I'd give up after a couple of weeks because the distributors had employed Charles Wood, who had written the second Beatles film, *Help!* (and who must have cost them a fortune) to write a literate English version (after all the film was based on

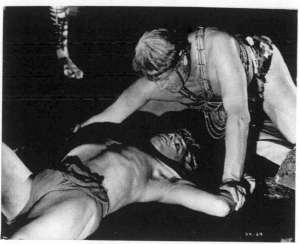

Fellini's *Satyricon* (1969)

a Latin classic!) and everyone soon became aware that, although in his contract he had committed himself to filming in English, Fellini had, of course, shot some of his actors speaking in Italian. I think *La Dolce Vita* was dubbed again into American English when the picture was bought by another company for its American release, I don't know with what results. At this point, I chose to remember *La Dolce Vita* only for its original version.

Meanwhile in Rome, 'Hollywood-on-the-Tiber' was becoming an Italian rather than an American phenomenon and not surprisingly it was Dino De Laurentiis who was becoming its Selznick. On a rainy day, some years before I had visited the site of the new studios which De Laurentiis was building on the Via Pontina, and I saw the Italian premier, Amintore Fanfani lay the foundation stone. Dino had succeeded in persuading the powers-that-be to move the boundaries of the Italian South (the Mezzogiorno) a few kilometers north so that he could qualify for state funding for the project, a new Cinecittà, which wouldn't be inaugurated till 1963 and would become known as Dinocittà. It was there that Dino planned to film the whole of The Bible with several famous directors but only the first part, directed by John Huston and written by Christopher Fry, was ever finished. In 1961, Dino made another biblical film scripted by Fry, *Barabbas*, based on a novel by Nobel prize winning Swedish author, Pär Lagerkvist. Richard Fleischer directed. Anthony Quinn played the title role. I visited the set of Jerusalem where Pilate (Arthur Kennedy) asks the Jews if they want him to release Jesus or Barabbas. Beside me, standing behind the cameras was Jesus himself, played by Silvana Mangano's brother, Roy. I remembered having seen him, a promisingly handsome youth in blue jeans, in another production by his brother-in-law. He looked a convincing J.C. even when smoking a cigarette off-screen. But there was something very unconvincing about the film. Fleischer didn't seem the right director for such a subject unless of course this 'Save Barabbas' tale was going to be just another dose of religious peplum. I was told that in this script, when Jesus is being crucified, the film would cut to Barabbas having sex with a woman played by this Jesus's real life sister, i.e. Silvana.

In June, my mother and her husband paid a brief visit to Rome while on a Mediterranean cruise. I took them to dinner at the amusing Meo Patacca tavern in Trastevere which was now so crowded with local and foreign tourists that it was losing the appeal it once had for us 'across the Tiber' residents. But, of course, Mum and Bertie loved it and they got rather tipsy on the vernaccia wine so I had to take them back to their hotel in a taxi. I managed to hide from them that I was in a precarious financial state with no promise of work that summer. Fortunately, she had told me that a small sum was on the way to me, left by my stepsister, Olive, the daughter of my father's first wife who, like her mother, had been involved in spiritualism. She had been rather less professionally competent than her mum who, in other centuries, would probably have been burned as a witch. Olive Lane had died while I was in London, the previous winter, and I had attended her rather macabre funeral, a cremation ceremony in Sidcup where my father had set her up in business when we moved to nearby Orpington. My mother had always refused to go to their séances but she told me that Olive had claimed that my father's spirit had turned up at one of them and said he was sorry he had left most of his money to me as he had been observing how rashly I was squandering it. My mother said she had been indignant at what Olive had told her but couldn't help adding, at that evening at Meo Petacca's over the umpteenth glass of vernaccia wine, that IF my father HAD made an appearance he would certainly have said just that. Both Bertie and I had a good laugh. I was grateful however that Olive remembered me in her will. That small inheritance would help me to get through the summer of 1961.

I even managed to get to the sea a few times during the June heatwave. I went with Enzo who began to turn into a negro. I was already aware that I had to take it easy in the Italian sun even though a tan made one feel good. I was to pay for excesses in my later years when the damage done by all that exposure to Apollo's rays proved to have disastrous results on my Nordic skin.

I couldn't resist at least one visit to that year's Spoleto Festival where I saw Visconti's production of the Wilde-Strauss *Salomé*. It struck me as the most sublime achievement so far of the director I had described in an article for *Films and Filming* as 'The Last Decadent' (July 1956). I managed to tell him how much I had enjoyed it and, this time, he seemed to appreciate my enthusiasm. Spoleto that year also hosted the very first comprehensive festival of 'New American Cinema'. Midnight screenings of all that the American avant-garde had to offer, from the bewilderingly absurd, Jonas Mekas's *Guns in the Trees*, to the futile and the pretentious, Gregory Markopoulis's *Serenity*, to the genuinely poetic, Curtis Harrington's *Night Tide* with Dennis Hopper as a sailor in love with a mermaid.

Back in Rome, after a luncheon for Zavattini, and the directors hired to make a portmanteau film he was preparing about "Italian women and love", *Le italiane e l'amore*, I was inspired to write a short script inspired by Curtis Harrington's mermaid, about an Italian girl who meets a young English sailor in a port like Pisa but, because both were virgins, they end up being too shy to make love. I called it *Pudore* (Modesty), and sent it to Zavattini who said he liked the idea but he already had all the stories he needed for the film.

I now had an agent who thought I had a good chance of a part in a French film, *Vie privée*, with Marcello Mastroianni and Brigitte Bardot which Louis Malle would be shooting in, of all places, Spoleto. I was also up for a part in *Cleopatra* which was due to start shooting in Rome in September.

Antonioni was preparing to shoot his new film, *The Eclipse*. Thanks to him, I had been commissioned by the publisher Cappelli in Bologna to edit the book of the film. I visited the first day's shoot, out in the modern EUR district where Mussolini had planned to hold a Rome Universal Exhibition in 1942. It is one of the few parts of Rome where you don't feel a prisoner of the distant past. Sergio Leone and Pier Paolo Pasolini would be among the film people who'd choose to live there. And it was here, in a street called the Avenue of Humanism, that Antonioni had set the home of the leading character, Vittoria, played by Monica Vitti. On this first night's shoot, we saw the filming of the scene in which Alain Delon arrives in the glamorous new Giulietta Spyder Sprint, which the producer, Robert Hakim, had bought for the film and would keep for himself afterwards. Alain had arrived at the location in his own Ferrari. For the first take, Alain had to drive up looking for Vittoria's house. After eight takes, with Alain pulling up with a screech of Spyder Sprint brakes, Hakim began to look worried. The car was new, bought that very morning, and hadn't yet been run in. A member of the crew was entrusted with driving it off when it is seen being stolen by a drunken passerby while Alain is distractedly calling up to Vittoria's window. The drunk was played by a Greek-American friend of mine, Cyrus Elias, who had acted in our *Millionairess* in Naples. Monica was not doing the reverse shot that night but she was there to join us all in a glass of champagne after the first take wrapped.

Antonioni told me it wouldn't be necessary to keep a day-to-day diary of the shooting for the book, as had been done with others in the Cappelli series, but I'd be welcome on the set whenever I wanted to come. I had decided anyway that I would keep a diary of the days I visited the set and publish it in *Films and Filming* (March 1962). After that first day's shoot, Monica Vitti had to go to Saint Vincent in the Aosta region to collect an award, a Grolla d'Oro, for her performance in *L'avventura*. When she got back, I went to the EUR district to watch the filming of the scene when the firemen lift Piero's wonderful white Giulietta Spyder out of the lake into which a drunken passerby had driven it. Of course Robert Hakim's new Spyder wasn't used. The production people had managed to find a substitute car body. It was a terrifyingly hot day. The only people who seemed to be enjoying themselves were the crew members obliged to do what we were all longing to do, which was wade into the lake to where Pasqualino De Santis's camera was positioned. The camera was on a platform so as to frame in the background, a shot of the oblong skyscraper of the Roman HQ of the ENI petroleum agency. Michelangelo wanted us to see the skyscraper when the car is hauled out of the lake. The scene had to be shot exactly with the light of sunset to get a particular lighting effect when we see the dead driver's hand hanging over the door of the driver's seat. But when they were finally ready to shoot the scene, and the director of photography, Gianni di Venanzo, had given the OK, the firemen's wires broke as the car was being lifted and it fell back into the lake. Michelangelo was furious. The scene had to be put off until the next day's sunset.

Filming the Spyder in the lake for Antonioni's *The Eclipse*.

The whole effort and the technical complications were necessary in order to show Monica-Vittoria's reaction to seeing the dead hand which, those of us who had read the script knew, would have an effect on her restless mood in the follow-up scene when Delon-Piero is making another attempt to seduce her. A writer can describe a sequence like this in words but a filmmaker has to tell it through images which depend on a score of technical and unpredictable circumstances.

Delon's first dialogue scene was filmed on July 22nd, when Monica was away collecting her award. Franco Indovina stood in for her and played the 'balcony scene' with Delon. Franco was the stand-in for everyone. He was still being teased about the brilliant way he stood-in for Lea Massari when she had to dive into the icy and shark-ridden waters of the Aeolian Sea during *L'avventura*. A photograph of Franco looking very becoming in a bikini was published in an Italian weekly! Tonight he acted Monica's line with great feeling. Nobody was the least bit embarrassed. The next set I visited on *The Eclipse* was at the Rome Stock Exchange where they were shooting during the mid-August bank holiday when it was closed. Michelangelo told me: "The Rome Borsa is unlike any other Stock Exchange. Unlike Milan, London and New York, where High Finance reigns supreme, here in Rome it's more middle-class with small-time gamblers like Vittoria's mother in the film who loses ten million lire in one day's market crash." Antonioni's technical advisor was a young man called Paolo, a prototype for Delon's Piero, who told me he was delighted to be able to spend these two weeks dressed sportively when normally he worked in a suit and tie. Brokers may dress like gentlemen but when there's panic they shout like farmers selling cattle in the market place. I could see that Michelangelo would not only be dealing with the crisis in feelings in this film.

Chapter 15

It was a pity I was unable to get to the Venice Film Festival in 1961 because I had, again, done the translations for the catalogue and would have been able to benefit from full hospitality, even though Peter Baker had the accreditation for *Films and Filming*. The Golden Lion went to Alain Resnais's dazzling *L'année dernière à Marienbad* but the festival, now run by a veteran Italian film critic, Domenico Meccoli, would go down in history for showing the exceptional debut features of three new Italian directors: Pier Paolo Pasolini's *Accattone*, Ermanno Olmi's *Il Posto*, both out of competition, and Vittorio De Seta's *Bandits of Orgosolo* in competition. De Seta won the award for best first feature. He had made some of the most beautiful shorts seen in recent years mostly about people at work on the sea or land. The eagerly awaited De Sica-Zavattini *The Last Judgement*, with its starry cast and ambitious premise, the voice of God sounds in the sky over Naples to announce the start of Judgement Day, was coolly received. I'd soon see these films in Rome.

I stayed in Rome because I had too many problems to resolve. I was working on the book of *The Eclipse* and had obtained personal reports from some of Michelangelo's closest collaborators, including Monica and Alain, and a piece entitled 'Words' by scriptwriter, Tonino Guerra. But my main concern was my immediate future as a film actor. I was hoping for better cameos than those I'd had to date. I had signed a contract for a part in a film called *Lovers Must Learn* (later retitled *Rome Adventure*) which was to take me to various locations in central Italy, an appealing prospect. Of my promised part in *Cleopatra* there was still no news but the film was finally taking off amid much bustle and gossip in and around Cinecittà. Kenneth Haigh came to Rome to do a test for the part of Brutus and seemed to think he would get the part (and he did). I told Fellini that Ken was in town and we had lunch together, at which we managed to avoid talking about the flop of our English dubbed version of *La Dolce Vita*, except to joke about Ken's more erotic interpretation of the scene when Marcello follows Anita into the fountain. Fellini conceded that with hindsight maybe it wouldn't have been such a bad idea to make it sound more sensual. We got into an intimate discussion with Ken about Anita's erotic powers of which Federico claimed to have had first hand experience. I wondered whether what he told us was true or if he had only dreamed about it?

Early in September, I started work on *Lovers Must Learn*. The director was Delmer Daves, a Hollywood professional whose work I was not familiar with. His wife, Mary Lawrence, was great fun. Talking with her, I realized I had seen at least one of her husband's films, *Demetrius and the Gladiators* (1954), a campy story about Caligula which starred Victor Mature as a Centurion Christian and was one of the first CinemaScope spectaculars. I remembered that Daves had succeeded in filling out the widescreen much better than any of the other directors of these epics, using the new system inaugurated by the dismal *The Robe* (1953) with Richard Burton. Our first location was in one of the marble quarries near Carrara in Tuscany where my adored Michelangelo Buonarroti had picked the blocks from which he would carve many of his statues (but not the one for David which he had found already in Florence). I was playing a tourist in a group which included the young stars of the film, Troy Donahue and Suzanne Pleshette, both very attractive but not particularly interesting as actors or people. Daves didn't seem to care much about the film and gave us very little direction, always trying to make do with one take. Next, we went to Siena where we were filmed on a raised platform in the magical Piazza del Campo from where we were supposed to be watching the Palio. I was the only person among those 'watching' the race who had actually seen it for real but I don't think this gave me any advantage over my fellow players. We all felt rather silly and, unsurprisingly, the locals thought so too. Fortunately, while in

Siena, I found time to see some of the most famous paintings of the Siennese school, including the Maestà by Duccio, which was being restored when I had previously visited the museum. I had another day's filming at an interesting artistic site I had not yet visited, the park of Bomarzo just north of Rome. It seemed like something from a Cocteau film, full of grotesque statues of animals and monsters. Daves seemed to liven up at this location, perhaps because he felt he was at last filming less conventional touristy backgrounds. Indeed he had great fun obliging me to disappear under a monster's belly, shouting silly lines of excitement, only to emerge from the other side staring up in amazement at the beast's

John Francis Lane in 'Rome Adventure'.

testicles. Everyone was roaring with laughter. The crew said it was the funniest moment of the whole film. I never saw the film until it turned up (in Italian of course) on a satellite TV channel many decades later when I saw that, in Italy at least, it wasn't clear what I was getting excited about. When she was back in California, Mrs. Daves wrote me a sweet letter saying that my scenes had gone down very well, particularly the one in Bomarzo!

Back in Rome I had been worried about missing my *Cleopatra* call, but I was informed that Mankiewicz had written out my part of the drunken senator. My bursting into the crowds watching the procession of the arrival into Rome of Cleopatra would have risked upsetting the carefully plotted choreography which had been under rehearsal for weeks. However, the casting director promised me that I was up for a part in the banquet scene when Cleopatra entertains Mark Antony to dinner. There was much talk in Rome of a romance blossoming between Liz Taylor and Richard Burton but, because I was now more an actor than a newspaper man, I wasn't interested in following the gossip too closely.

I was still trying to follow the serious events of the Italian cinema closely. I finally had the chance to see Olmi's film *Il posto* which had got a warm reception in Venice even though the leftist critics were being a bit snooty because it was considered too much a Catholic intellectual's film. The film certainly was in the neo-realist tradition but it dealt with, even if somewhat whimsically, the problem of a provincial youngster's search for a job in contemporary Milan and the humiliating tests he had to submit to for the big Milan firm who would employ him. Though there was a rather parochial feel about the film, Olmi clearly was a natural filmmaker, displaying something of the mood of recent Russian films like *Ballad of a Soldier*. The boy was played by a non-professional and you never felt he was acting. I predicted a great future for it abroad starting with the London Festival to which I was told it had already been invited (it did indeed win the LFF's only award).

In October, I had two articles published in *The Times* as 'a special correspondent'. One was on Antonioni and *The Eclipse*, the other was on Pasolini which was entitled 'Italy Has New Controversial Figure'. I described him as an "exotic and prolific genius" and compared him to Gabriele D'Annunzio, another Italian poet who displayed "charlatanesque flamboyance", and whose private life could be identified with his fiction even if from opposite political and sexual viewpoints. PPP's *Accattone* had run into trouble with the censor before it opened in Rome and Pasolini was being attacked by neo-fascists and the conformists. I was very impressed by the film. One could see in it a poet discovering film language rather like an illiterate might discover the use of words. Pasolini had learned a lesson or two from his peers (from Bergman and Bunuel, for example) but he still succeeded in crafting an individual style. Franco Citti, the brother of Sergio, Pier Paolo's consultant on the dialect and customs of the Roman sub-proletariat, the local 'teddy boys', played the lead. The Citti brothers came from that world. Franco had an extraordinarily photogenic face, perhaps on a level with the young Gary Cooper or Marlon Brando. But Citti was not an actor. He had been dubbed by a professional actor who succeeded in mastering the Roman accent and added that necessary vocal conviction to a performance that was visually strong in itself.

Pier Paolo Pasolini

Franco Citti

I didn't feel much sympathy for Pasolini's louts from the Roman 'borgate', the city's suburban slums, but he succeeded in making the viewer feel that they were victims of a cruel reality. Like Bunuel in the slums of Mexico City in *Los Olvidados*, here was a poet using the film medium to describe a sordid reality but without resorting to preaching (as De Santis was inclined to do in his communist-messaged melodramas). In 1950, in Mexico, Bunuel added some of the surrealist touches of his twenties films to the realism of his story of hopeless delinquents. Pasolini also included an effective surrealistic dream sequence. After seeing *Accattone* I'd feel less inclined to call my current lover, Enzo, a 'delinquent'. I felt I knew how to deal with him and his friends even when they were getting themselves into trouble. Though 'my' boys in Trastevere looked and spoke like the louts in Pasolini's film, and they too could steal and dabble in prostitution (more often with their own bodies than with those of their girlfriends as in *Accattone!*), they had hearts and a more pleasing sense of humour. My lads were the 'children' of the Roman dialect poets Belli and Trilussa, and had an instinctive moral code of loyalty.

The December 1961 issue of *Films and Filming* carried an article of mine with the rather pretentious title 'The Triumph of Italy's Realism'. In it I discussed the films of De Seta, Olmi and Pasolini, enthusing first about the Sicilian-born De Seta's poetic documentaries: "mostly in colour using to great effect the wide screen, the natural sound effects and (local) music". De Seta's feature film, *Bandits of Orgosolo*, is about a young Sardinian shepherd who is unwittingly involved in the killing of a carabiniere and flees to the mountains, taking with him his kid brother and their flock. But the sheep cannot survive on the rocky mountains and, in desperation, the two boys procure a gun and steal other people's sheep. De Seta was thus telling how a new bandit is born. I quoted Danilo Dolci, who said that for an un-educated Sicilian there are only two choices, either to die of hunger or become a bandit.

In reality they had three other choices, to become a priest or a policeman or to emigrate. In Sardinia it was the same. The only flaw I could see in De Seta's moving film was that it had been considered necessary to dub the non-professional actors into an Italian more comprehensible to Italian audiences. Since it wasn't likely to be a commercial success it seemed a pity not to have shown it with subtitles as Visconti had done for *La terra trema*, which was first released with the original Sicilian dialect track subtitled (later he too had to consent to it being dubbed by actors who spoke with a more accessible Sicilian accent). Pasolini would say that he always regretted giving in to his producer who wanted Franco Citti to be dubbed. Often it was an economic problem of non-professionals requiring more time in post-production to dub themselves than professional dubbers. But, in any case, Italian audiences would never accept subtitled films especially if they were Italian. Eduardo De Filippo would one day tell me that he had to speak a little less in dialect outside Naples on the stage and always in films. As I had learned from my experience in London, nobody cared that most of the players in Fellini's original versions had been dubbed by actors different from those seen on the screen.

I learned that Angelo Rizzoli, the producer who had made a fortune out of *La Dolce Vita*, had set up a production company called 'Federiz', to produce Federico's next film and to support young directors. But the company had turned down the Pasolini film when it was still only a proposal, and also the films by Olmi and De Seta when their producers had asked for support in post-production. Thus Federico missed the chance to become the godfather to the three most important post-neorealist filmmakers of the new decade. Obviously, Fellini didn't care much about other people's films, but I'm sure the rejection could be attributed more to Federico's production partner who was concentrating the company's attention on the new film that Federico was preparing. We were all getting more and more curious to find out what this new film would be. It was still mostly in Federico's head.

Towards the end of October, I stupidly got myself involved in a political demonstration at a meeting of the Socialist International. In addition to the French and Italian social democrat leaders, Guy Mollet and Giuseppe Saragat, the British Labour Party leader, Hugh Gaitskell, was among the speakers. It was the time of the Algerian crisis. I evidently shouted an angry comment in English and in Italian which upset some belligerent social democrats close by and a fight ensued. Suddenly the meeting turned into a riot. The police stormed the scene and I was one of those carried off to the police station where, despite showing my press pass, they continued to accuse me of fermenting the disturbance. The inspector in charge of the investigation finally conceded that I had nothing to do with the more violent side of the riot and I was allowed to go. To my horror the next day, the leading Rome daily, *Il Messaggero*, gave a slanderous version of the incident implying that I had been jailed for twenty-four hours. I insisted on them printing a correction, but everyone who knew me was convinced I had been in the Regina Coeli prison. It made quite a hero of me in Trastevere. I wondered what would be put on my file in the foreigners office which, until then, had only been given copy by some of my more salacious mishaps. I hoped this new escapade wouldn't compromise me when I finally had to register as a Roman resident.

In November, I did two nights on an Alberto Sordi film called *Una vita difficile* (It's A Hard Life) where I was little more than an extra but the film seemed very promising. The director was Dino Risi who, until then, had mostly made comedies, like the one I'd seen being made in Sorrento where I first interviewed Sophia Loren. Risi had made the two box office hits of recent seasons, those starring the Trastevere muscle boys, Maurizio Arena and Renato Salvatori. This new film was a very dramatic story of a Roman who was trying to swing with the new economic miracle but who was too honest at heart to cope with the kind of political corruption that that was essential to success. I was one of the guests at a party given in the villa of the corrupt business tycoon for whom the Sordi character has been working. For once, Sordi's acting seemed less over the top. My scenes were shot in a splendid villa in Grottaferrata but it was a harrowing nocturnal experience for which fortunately I was well enough paid to resign myself to the humiliation of not having any lines.

Finally, Antonioni let me see the first rough cut of *The Eclipse*. Despite some uneven moments which would be polished up when the film was mixed and very well dubbed (Delon was speaking in French), I was deeply moved. As with *L'avventura* and *La Notte*, it was amazing that an unsentimental film, on the theme of the failure to communicate, could manage to make you feel deeply for the characters. The details that the camera lingers on in every shot are not there for visual effect but help you to understand what the characters are feeling. There are stupendous filmic sequences, such as those I had seen being filmed at the Borsa and around the lake at EUR, and a quite startling scene that surprised and puzzled me when Monica and a girl friend indulge in dressing up as Africans and do an erotic tribal dance together. That same week, I saw Resnais's *Marienbad* film, which was also dazzling to look at, but which in comparison was abstract and cold.

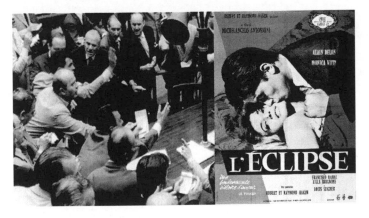

When Christmas came I still had no news of *Cleopatra* which seemed to be running into delays but I had other film roles coming up for the New Year. I wondered if there was any hope for me getting something on *The Leopard*, the start-date of which continued to be postponed? I ran into Visconti at a film event and asked him "When can I see you?". To which he replied curtly: "Well, you're seeing me now aren't you!". Very disagreeable. Fellini was much more accessible and seemed to be getting closer to the start of his new film of which we still knew absolutely nothing. He asked me where my "vampirish Scottish friend" was and I told him Ian was still in Paris looking after Edith Piaf. Federico told me he wanted Ian for a part in the film and said he would let me know when to summon him to Rome. I didn't tell Ian this for now, for fear he would take the next plane to Rome. I certainly couldn't put him up.

Early in 1962, I did a brief cameo in a film by Valerio Zurlini called *Cronaca familiare*, based on an impressive semi-autobiographical novel by the much-admired Florentine writer, Vasco Pratolini, which I had read after seeing Carlo Lizzani's film of another of Pratolini's novels, *Chronicle of Poor Lovers*. I played an American officer in a brief scene at the start of the film in which Marcello Mastroianni is sitting in the background. Marcello was very surprised to see me doing something so insignificant and this confirmed my impression that it was becoming rather degrading for me to do these stints. But I needed the money. I was always behind with the rent especially since my tenant, John K,. was out of work.

But my cameos sometimes provided exhilarating experiences. Such was the case with a small role I played in a muscleman film called *Maciste in Hell* directed by Riccardo Freda, who was very popular with producers because he could shoot costume spectaculars very economically in a few weeks. Maciste, the first muscle man hero of the Italian cinema, had first been seen in the great silent epic, *Cabiria* (1914), which many film scholars think inspired Griffith's *Intolerance* (1916). The first actor to play the role was a

John Francis Lane and Kirk Morris in 'Maciste in Hell'.

burly docker from Genoa, Bartolomeo Pagano. Among the many silent Maciste roles Pagano played was a *Maciste in Hell* made in 1926. For the 1962 version, Maciste was played by one Kirk Morris, who was not a real American but a Venetian called Adriano Bellini. The success of Steve Reeves meant Italians now expected the stars of the genre to be American. The film told the story of Maciste's descent into Hell in order to bring back to earth a wretched Scots lass who had been accused of being a witch and burnt at the stake. I was the village coachman who bursts into a tavern one night to warn the crowd that Martha Gunt, the name of the supposed witch, was 'coming'. The crowd of mostly Brits and Americans playing the Scottish revelers in the tavern broke up with laughter when I deliberately pronounced the witch's surname with a 'c' instead of a 'g'. Freda, a sophisticated playboy type always surrounded by women and dogs, spoke a little English but didn't understand why everyone was laughing. He was angry until I apologised and explained why. He saw the joke but still accused me of not being professional. Fortunately it was one of the few occasions when he was not trying to shoot the whole sequence in one take. Many years later, when Freda had become a cult with the French critics, someone would write that the English critic who had played cameos in films by Fellini, Antonioni and Marco Ferreri, among others, in order to watch them at work, had also wanted to appear in a Riccardo Freda film. I replied in an article that I had done the film for the money. Freda read this and was deeply hurt. But when he died I did try to do justice to his cult reputation by writing a flattering obituary that was published in *The Guardian*.

I managed to find time to write my introduction for the book on *The Eclipse*. Michelangelo said it wasn't quite what he'd expected but nevertheless he enjoyed the article. He got Tommaso Chiaretti, an intelligent communist critic, to write a more analytical study of how the finished film differed from the script. My piece was perhaps too anecdotal but written in a style that would be easier to read than the usual aesthetic studies that Italian intellectuals write. Perhaps I had made a mistake writing it directly in Italian but when Chiaretti corrected the piece he only changed the occasional grammatical lapses and cut a few of my gossipy comments. A few people were irked by my suggestion that Antonioni, by showing the superficiality of the bourgeois society and the inferno of the stock exchange, was perhaps more Marxist than many who preached communism in their films.

The producers of the Antonioni film, the Hakim brothers, were now making a film by another director who was becoming a cult with French critics, Joseph Losey. Though the Hakims were clearly not intellectuals themselves, they wanted to keep up with the fashionable trends of the moment. I went rather tepidly to the press conference for the launch of Losey's film *Eve*, knowing that Losey had written a letter to *Films and Filming* complaining about my sarcastic remarks in reference to his adored Stanley Baker. Both were present at the press conference and, to my relief, Losey greeted me politely while Baker didn't seem to recognise me. Also present was Jeanne Moreau whom I'd met in Milan on the Antonioni film. I'd recently seen her in Truffaut's *Jules et Jim* in which she was again adorable. I promised myself to be kinder to Losey (and maybe even to Baker) in future, though I'd appreciate Losey's subsequent film, *The Servant*, more than this *Eve*, which was Antonioni-ish without the same thematic and emotional depth. I wouldn't join the growing Losey cult until I saw *Accident* (1967). The scripts by Harold Pinter for that, and for subsequent Losey films, certainly helped to give more credibility to his work.

I did my best to make it known in Rome and London that the 'special correspondent' who wrote the Pasolini and Antonioni articles in *The Times* was JFL because I had many rival journalists eager to write about the new wave in Italian cinema. *The Sunday Times* published a rather misinformed article on Italian films by Derek Prouse, while *The Observer* ran an article on Antonioni by my friend, Ian Dallas, the result of a dinner we had had with Michelangelo, which was a bit of a betrayal because that meeting had not been intended as an interview. Fortunately the article was respectful. Ian, meanwhile, had arrived in town, having found out himself that Federico definitely wanted him for the part in the new film and he was eager to sign a contract. He flew in from Greece carrying tantalising stories of his conquests there.

Federico invited me and Ian to see his episode for the *Boccaccio '70* film which was quite delightful. It seemed too that the censors didn't dare to cut a film that was obviously Federico's revenge on the Italian prudishness brigade. Eduardo De Filippo's brother Peppino, a great comic actor, played a middle–class prude who has sexual fantasies over a billboard image of Anita Ekberg. She's at her most erotically luscious in the film when the poster image of her on a billboard comes to life.

After the film, Federico said to me: "Now I hope you won't accuse me of being employed to make propaganda for the Vatican". I didn't know I had ever said that he did! Over dinner I tried to find out more about the new film he was planning but he continued to be evasive and mysterious. I suspected that he himself didn't really know what it was going to be, and he admitted as much, saying he would be inventing the film as it went along. He seemed to have been given carte blanche by Rizzoli. He promised he'd find something for me to do in the film, probably to play a journalist again. The part he had in mind for Ian promised to be more substantial, of course, though Fellini couldn't say how long Ian would have to stay in Rome. Many actors, even quite famous ones, were agreeing to appear in the film without really knowing much about their role or how long they'd be working. I told Ian he couldn't complain. Thus the JFL entourage acquired another impoverished intellectual for the coming year.

When I celebrated my eleventh anniversary in Rome in March, Ian was still waiting to shoot his first scene in the film. We had heated arguments about how materialistic life was in Rome. Materialism was something I had learned to accept, even to cherish. It was the History of Rome. Ian, a Hellenist at heart, was an unrepentant romantic. My own materialistic self-indulgence got a boost when the *Cleopatra* people finally summoned me and I signed a contract to play the part of Bacchus, which I felt it was one step towards playing the role in which I most dreamed of being cast as, Nero. At Cinecittà I was given personal attention by Edith Head, one of the legendary Hollywood costume designers. The costume of course was scanty, a few fig leaves and lots of gold dust. The publicity guys were alarmed by me being hired. They knew I was a journalist and the world press gossip surrounding the Taylor and Burton affair was getting hotter every day. I reassured them that on set I would be an actor not a journalist.

I had a more interesting film story to write about that month. I was invited to Sicily for the Sicilian premiere of Francesco Rosi's stunning new film about the bandit, Salvatore Giuliano, which I had already seen at a private preview. I flew to Palermo with other journalists for a press conference and public debate at which I met the Rome-resident American actor, Frank Wolff,

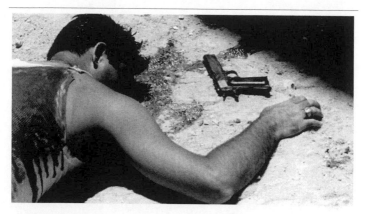

who plays Giuliano's cousin and supposed killer, Gaspare Pisciotta. There was an animated debate with Sicilian journalists and leftist politicians. They were impressed by the film and it's hints that the official version of how Giuliano was killed was not the real story. The premiere was to take place in Montelepre, Giuliano's home town, in the hills above Palermo. When we arrived at the local cinema, only a fleapit, it was already crammed full of locals who had occupied the place and refused to budge. I never found out whether this occupation of the local fleapit had been engineered by Enzo de Bernart, the very smart publicity man for the distribution company, but Rosi and his producer, Franco Cristaldi, insisted that the screening had to go ahead and that it would have to take place in the main square of the town. Someone was dispatched to Palermo to fetch a projector. An improvised screen was set up on one side of the piazza as the townsfolk brought out chairs and now occupied the piazza. We visitors were offered wine and snacks of local cheese and salami while we waited. It was nearly 10pm before the screening began. Naturally there were almost no women in the audience and we were told that the bandit's family were barricaded inside their home. A cold March wind had blown in after sunset and it got steadily colder during the two hours screening, with several interruptions to change reels. The film was received in almost total silence. The only reaction came during the scene when the police arrest all the men of the town and their women protest. The real women of Montelepre had refused to appear in the scene so Rosi's assistant, Franco Indovina, who was sitting near me, explained that they had been obliged to round up women extras in Palermo, mostly among the whores of the port area, whom the men of Montelepre recognised. Some of them protested among themselves that it was an insult to their women. But there was no other reaction and at the end there was no applause. They all gathered up their chairs and slunk back home. The Giuliano of Rosi's film was not the Giuliano that had been a hero for their village. I was almost dead from the cold and had wrapped round my head a scarf that I had fortunately brought with me. The next day, a photograph of me appeared in a Palermo paper with the caption "an old woman of Montelepre during the screening of the film". The publicity man was so amused by this that later he'd have a silver medallion struck of the 'old woman' and it was given to all the visitors who'd come from Rome for the event. I was sad that my treasured copy was among the 'valuables' stolen from my flat in Trastevere not long afterwards.

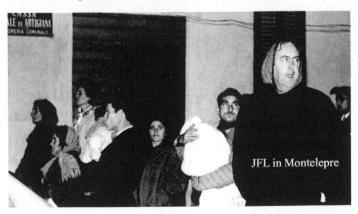

JFL in Montelepre

I'd been waiting eagerly for a call to do my cameo in *Cleopatra* and finally I was summoned to Cinecittà. The casting director took me immediately to the office of no less a personage than the producer, Walter Wanger. He told me gently that he was obliged to cancel my contract, for which I would be paid the full sum promised me, because Mr. Burton didn't want any journalists on the set. "Either in costume or not", he added with an apologetic smile. On my way to pick up my money, I passed by Edith Head's office. She embraced me warmly saying she was quite dismayed at the news. "You would have been a perfect Bacchus!" she exclaimed. It almost consoled me and I felt very flattered.

I was having a bad week. My flat had been burgled. Gone was not only the gramophone but all my precious records, including the one that Dietrich had given me and signed a dedication on the cover. Also gone were some clothes and other souvenirs. The door had not been broken open so it was someone who had the keys. I summoned Enzo but didn't feel I could blame him. Indeed I realised that a spare pair of keys was missing and only later would I discover who had taken them. As I had wisely taken out a theft insurance, Enzo was clever enough to help break the door lock open so I could report the robbery to the police and make a claim. This and the disappointment over *Cleopatra* gave me private doubts about staying on in Rome. I would have liked to take off for Greece but I used the *Cleopatra* money instead to pay my immediate debts including the back rent. I felt that I had to give Rome a new try.

Early in April, when Spring was supposed to have arrived, a 100km an hour gale swept through Trastevere. John K. and I had a hard time hanging on to our badly made upstairs windows, especially the one in his kitchen which threatened to be blown in. On a calmer evening, watching television, I saw an interview with Franco Citti filmed at his home in the fishing village of Fiumicino.

When the woman interviewing him asked Franco if she could play one of the LPs in his impressive-looking record collection (obviously to show how intellectual this sub-proletarian was becoming!) what should the record be but the one with Lotte Lenya singing songs from the Brecht-Weill opera *Mahagonny* in German, not the sort of record you would expect a Franco Citti to possess. It was indeed one of the records which I had been most distressed to lose among my stolen collection. It was likely that I was the only person in Rome who had a copy. Suddenly, I remembered that my keys were probably stolen by someone of the Citti clan whom I'd entertained and he had found a buyer in Franco. I complained about it to Pasolini. He had a good laugh but promised he'd mention the matter to Sergio. I was relieved that at least I had solved the mystery and couldn't any longer suspect Enzo of being involved. I could admire the literary works of Genet (and Pasolini) but I had no ambition to emulate their private fascination with the criminal classes.

In Hollywood, in April 1962, the only Academy Award won by *La Dolce Vita* went to Piero Gherardi for costume design in black and white. Meanwhile in Hollywood-on-the-Tiber, *Cleopatra* was continuing to dominate the attention of the world's press, more than anything for the 'scandalous' Taylor-Burton affair. The very day they were shooting the scene at Cinecittà in which I was to have appeared as Bacchus, Taylor's husband, Eddie Fisher, announced in New York that he was divorcing her. I would have been the only journalist in the world on the set that day and I could have recorded the couple's reaction. I wonder if I would have been tempted to offer a story to a London paper with the by-line: 'Bacchus date-line Cinecittà, Rome?'.

Towards the end of April, I had another story in *The Times* about Pasolini, or rather about the film made from his novel, *A Violent Life*. He didn't direct it himself, but the director's assistant was Sergio Citti, PPP's invaluable authority and contact with the

Roman sub-proletariat world. In the lead role, Sergio's brother, Franco confirmed the promise shown by his debut as Accattone and, I think, this time he dubbed himself. Obviously, he was one actor "taken from the streets" who could hope for a professional future. A still of Franco looking very tragic was published with my article. I was tempted to take a copy of it out to the Citti home at Fiumicino to show him, and challenge him about my stolen records. But he was currently acting in *Mamma Roma*, Pasolini's new film with Anna Magnani and had just been arrested and jailed for drunken driving so it wasn't exactly the right moment to disturb him.

Fortunately, I had plenty of work to do before going to Cannes in May. I had done the English commentary for *The New Angels*, one of the most delightful new Italian films of the moment. Directed by Ugo Gregoretti, *The New Angels* was that rare thing in Italian cinema, a satire about Italian eccentricities made by a humourist who didn't depend on sub-Commedia Dell'Arte horse play to make you laugh. Gregoretti had proved himself to be a witty observer of Italian mores. Francesco Rosi asked me to do the subtitles and an English commentary for *Salvatore Giuliano*, a translation of his own commentary which described the historical background and showed how the Mafia and the pro-American separatists took control of Sicily after the liberation.

Ian was back in town still waiting to be called for his first day of shooting on the Fellini film which was gradually getting underway, or so it seemed. With Federico nobody ever seemed to know if he was really shooting or just doing tests. Ian had come back from London with the friend in whose Chelsea apartment I had stayed, Hugh Donaldson Hudson. Hugh was setting up a production company to find backers for a fascinating film story Ian had written about a British footballer playing with an Italian team. Ian's story was obviously inspired by John Charles, known in Italy as *Il Gigante Buono* (The Gentle Giant), Juventus's legendary

Welsh player. Being a Scot, Ian had made his hero born North not West of the border. Hugh wanted me to be his partner in the new company and I accepted his proposal willingly as his project seemed very promising, though Italian producers would tell me that subjects like soccer were surprisingly not box-office in a sports-crazy country like Italy.

The Eclipse, due to be in competition at Cannes, opened in Italian cinemas and was hailed by most Italian critics as Michelangelo's best film to date. Even Ian liked it. In interviews, Antonioni said that Vittoria's problem was that she needed spiritual as well as physical love. The young man, played beguilingly by Delon, who did give her 'a good lay', doesn't know how to communicate with her. When Ian and I discussed the crazy scene in which Monica-Vittoria does the tribal dance with her girl friend, we agreed that there was a suggestion of Lesbianism as an escape route for a young woman who doesn't feel satisfied by her male companions. This film completed Michelangelo's trilogy on what everyone was now calling 'alienation'.

My *Eclipse* book, which was being distributed at Cannes, was ready in time for the festival. I was hoping it would benefit me. I was hoping too that my production partner (!) Hugh Hudson, and I would find a producer at Cannes who was interested in our football film project. I had hospitality for the second week because I was covering the festival for *The Observer* but, during the first days, Hugh and I had to make do with a cheap off-Croisette hotel and, when we couldn't get invited to official bean feasts, we ate in the smaller restaurants in the back streets. Fortunately my friend, David Robinson, who was covering the festival for the *Financial Times*, took us to a 'small' restaurant off-Croisette where indeed we ate fabulously without spending much.

In Rome, I had committed myself to giving a helping hand to Dino De Laurentiis who wasn't too happy with the American publicity guys from the company which was about to release

Barabbas. The film was being released first in London where Dino wanted me to join him. It would open the new Odeon Haymarket. Dino was quite happy that I should keep my 'helping hand' anonymous as he hoped I could give him a boost with the intellectuals who, I'm sorry to say, he was over-optimistic enough to think the film would appeal. He was pitching *Barabbas* at an up-grade market though, from the private screening of the film in Rome which I attended with Ian (and had to restrain him from making outrageous remarks at scenes which we both felt were frankly preposterous), I had my doubts about the film's prospects for success as a serious subject for discussion, even if it had been based on a novel by a Nobel prize-winning Swede. Anyway, when I went to see Dino at his suite in the Carlton he sent the others away and told me frankly that he was counting on me to help boost the film. He promptly put a wad of 100 franc notes into my hands and said he'd pay my fare to London after the festival. After my last adventure in publicity I had sworn I wouldn't get involved again in this not-always-honest activity but this time my contribution would not be discernible (I hoped!). The 'dirty money' was certainly welcome in Cannes. Although I was now hosted by the Festival in a decent hotel I still had to pay my own way on the Croisette. Hugh had left having had difficulty finding anyone interested in our project. "A script about a Scottish soccer player in Italy? Not bloody likely!" was the general reaction. I'd introduced Hugh to Dino who was a football fan. Dino told us that if Hugh could get Albert Finney to play the footballer he'd sign a contract immediately. Hugh knew that Albie was now too busy on one side of the Atlantic or the other and was unlikely to be available for some time. Hugh himself would soon give up being a producer and dedicate himself to direction. Eventually he'd make a film on a sports subject, the Oscar-winning British film, *Chariots of Fire* (1981).

The Eclipse didn't go down too well at the festival though it got the intellectual critics raving. It would only win the Jury's special prize which it had to share with Bresson's impressive *Jeanne d'Arc* film. I was told by French friends that the reason why *The Eclipse* didn't get the top prize, even though some members of the jury supported it, was that the most influential voice on the jury was that of *Nouvelle Vague* leader, Francois Truffaut, who hated Antonioni's films. The Golden Palm went to a soon-to-be-forgotten Brazilian film which had gone down very well with the public, *O pagador de promessas* (The Given Word) by one Anselmo Duarte. In my report for *The Observer* I described it as "one of those typical Latin American parables heavily loaded with sex and religion". I added that there were at least six other films more worthy of the coveted Palm. Among these, in addition to *The Eclipse*, was Sydney Lumet's adaptation of the (long!) O'Neill play *Long Day's Journey into Night* which we all admired. The cast, Katherine Hepburn, Ralph Richardson, Jason Robards Jr and Dean Stockwell won the best acting award, shared with Rita Tushingham and Murray Melvin, the two young stars of Tony Richardson's film of Shelagh Delaney's play *A Taste of Honey*. I thought the Delaney was better on the stage than it was on the screen.

Another theatrically inspired film competing in the festival was my friend Michael Cacoyannis's film of *Electra*. At least he added a few cinematic effects to the theatrical original, some of them borrowed from Eisenstein. It was a pity, however, that he was too faithful to Euripides in leaving it to the Messenger to describe the death of Aegisthus rather than show it taking place. Irene Papas was magnificent in the title role and would have deserved the best actress award if there hadn't been such competition from the English-speaking thespians.

Early in June I went to London. Hugh kindly met me at the airport and was putting me up in his Chelsea home overlooking the cricket field. The first evening after an excellent dinner (London restaurants seemed to get better every time I visit) he took me to the fashionable club of the moment, The Establishment, where I ran into Ken Tynan and his wife. Tynan said how much he liked my piece on Cannes in *The Observer*. In the revue at The Establishment, the comedians sent up the Queen and were scathing about the new Coventry Cathedral and everyone roared with laughter. Four letter words got the biggest laughs. Was this the hallmark of the 'new' permissive London?

I tried to console myself by seeing films, first *Sweet Bird of Youth* from Tennessee's play which came close to condemning American fascism. It had a superb performance by Geraldine Page and an alluring one from Paul Newman. Then I had to prepare myself for the arrival of Dino and lower myself by trying to help 'save' *Barabbas*. I had begged him to change the placing of the opening credits which were shown over the scourging of Jesus, a scene I remembered Fleischer had been so proud of, but Dino refused to move them. But bad taste seemed to be chic in London in those days so maybe I would be proved wrong?

Dino arrived in town and I arranged for him to be interviewed by David Robinson. Realising that I'd have little chance of influencing the British critics to be kind to *Barabbas*, at least I could interest the more prestigious papers in the personality of the new mogul of Hollywood-on-the-Tiber. Dino gave a small dinner party in honour of his British representative and I found myself sitting opposite Christopher Fry and another playwright, John Whiting, whose play *The Devils* would be expanded into a famous film by Ken Russell. Fleischer's wife, Mary Dickson, was sandwiched between the two dramatists and I tried to help her keep up a conversation with them on theatre. Fortunately she didn't remember that she had caught Ian and I giggling during that private screening of *Barabbas* in Rome. I felt sorry for Dino who was eager to keep up with the intellectuals but had to keep flying in a different orbit. But he had great intuition and was learning fast how to do the right thing. I remembered telling him one day in his office opposite the Quirinal Palace in Rome when I caught him reading

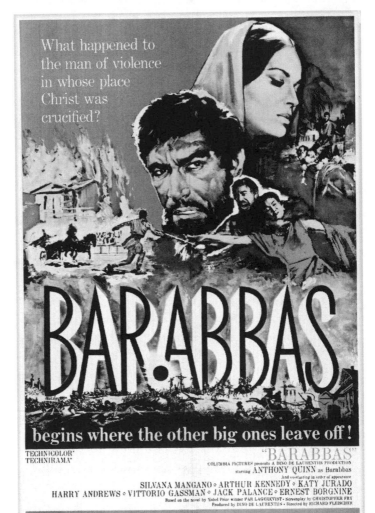

the Naples daily newspaper that he ought to be reading or anyway pretending to read the *New York Times* or at least *Variety*. I noticed he followed my advice because both papers were in evidence on the lounge table of his hotel suite at London.

At a press luncheon for Dino, which I had persuaded James Quinn of the BFI to organise in his honour, he made quite a 'bella figura' even if I soon gave up trying to convince the *Express* man that *Barabbas* wasn't as dreadful as he seemed to think it was. At the press showing I had been embarrassed when there were snoots during the opening credit titles but I was tactful enough not to let Dino see I was thinking "I told you so". Fortunately, David's glowing profile of Dino had appeared in the *Financial Times* that morning so I felt I had earned my money without humiliating myself. At the luncheon I sat next to Penelope Houston, now the editor of *Sight and Sound*, and we talked about Antonioni whose films she adored, obviously more so than the films of Richard Fleischer.

Among the many films and shows I saw in London that week, the one I gave most attention to in my diary was a British film, *I'm All Right Jack*, made by The Boulting Brothers. It was a very negative 'comedy' which sent up both the bosses and the trade unions. It was part of the 'new' London I suppose? Better was the outrageous musical revue called *Beyond the Fringe*, though many people in London were saying it was "merely undergraduate" humour. Perhaps. But it provided good laughs and the artists were very talented. Peter Cook, Dudley Moore, Jonathan Miller and Alan Bennett became household names in Great Britain. I also enjoyed an original entertainment called *Stop the World I Want to Get Off* by a vivacious young performer named Anthony Newley, a former child actor who had been the Artful Dodger in David Lean's *Oliver Twist*. And I was excited by Arnold Wesker's new play, *Chips with Everything*, which confirmed his early promise and seemed to me to be the most pungent play of the 'angry' school. It truly got to the depth of the class war from which poor ex-Great

Britain was still struggling to disentangle itself none too successfully. The audience didn't know how to take it, embarrassed by its
desecration of all that is 'holy' in British traditions. The audience
were Establishment-friendly unlike the members of the club of
that name which Hugh had taken me to. In Wesker's play, when
the Union Jack is raised in the final scene, in the air force camp,
and the national anthem was played, I had an awful feeling that
many in the audience were wondering whether they ought to stand
up. Fortunately they applauded a few moments later after the
black-out. English audiences applaud good theatre when they see
it and, unlike the Italians, don't get too worried about political
content. Ibsen may have upset bigots but Bernard Shaw gave his
audiences too much pleasure for them to worry about his criticism
of their society. Anyway Wesker's play, along with Pinter's *The
Caretaker*, was the most compelling theatrical experience I'd had
in London for a long time.

During my last days in London, Hugh drove me up to Coventry
to see the new cathedral which had been built on the site of the
old one destroyed when the city was razed to the ground by German
bombs. I was impressed by the way the architects had merged what
was left of the bombed building with a new modern church and
couldn't understand why the revue at The Establishment Club had
been so cynical. On the way back to London, Hugh drove rather
recklessly in his left-hand drive Alfa Romeo sports car which had
Italy on its number plates. When he overtook English cars waiting
patiently in line we got racialistic abuse shouted at us which
amused us both enormously. I behaved like Alberto Sordi and gave
them the finger.

Before leaving London, I went to an exhibition at the Tate
Gallery of paintings by Francis Bacon whose work I had not seen
before. There were several paintings which caricatured Velasquez's
portrait of Pope Innocent X, the original of which is in a gallery
in Rome. There was also a hint of sado-masochism in Bacon's

obsession with the Crucifixion. I saw that Bacon was influenced by films, too. Clearly the terrifying face of a woman screaming had been inspired by the Odessa steps sequence of *Battleship Potemkin*. Here was a painter of the post-Great 'New' Britain who had something important and original to contribute. On one of my last afternoons in London, Hugh took me to a club in Soho where members and their guests can drink in the afternoons when the pubs close. Among those who had obviously been drinking for hours was Francis Bacon who was introduced to me. A good-looking burly young man at his side was obviously his boyfriend. However, I was beginning to feel I had seen more than enough of the 'new' London of which Bacon was not enough to make me feel I wanted to become part.

I broke my journey back to Rome by spending four days in Venice where I had been invited by the Biennale for their art films festival, and though I had hoped they'd put me up in a hotel on the Grand Canal I found myself back on the Lido. Still, in the non-film festival season it was pleasant to be over there and travel backwards and forwards across the lagoon. More appealing than the art films was the splendid costumed regatta of the four ancient republics. I'd already attended the event in two of the other maritime republics, Pisa and Amalfi, but here in Venice in June it was much more exciting for its colours and backgrounds (I'd never attend the regatta in the fourth of the republics, Genoa). I also managed to get to La Fenice where I saw a production of *Carmen* with my favourite tenor, Franco Corelli. The production was a bit too folkloristic but at least the dancers were authentic Spaniards.

Whereas in Venice the sunshine had been welcome, back in Rome the heat was already beginning to be suffocating, at least until after sunset when eating out of doors was such a delight, especially with all the young men, and particularly those in uniform, dressed more enticingly than they are in winter when overcoats cover them up too much. They were quite happy to be admired.

Now that it was the season for summer wear, I decided I must try to lose weight, especially as being portly didn't seem to be helping me to get film roles for which there was always a Laughton or a Welles available, or else one of their Italian look-alikes.

I called on Monica Vitti to do an interview that had been commissioned in London by the magazine *Town*. She and Michelangelo still lived on the top floors of a modern apartment house in the street named after Alexander Fleming, which climbs up the hill at the beginning of Via Flaminia. They have a splendid view over the Tiber and the area where the Olympic Games were centered two years ago. But Monica now lived in the lower apartment and Michelangelo was on the upper floor with a spiral staircase separating the two. I didn't see him on this visit because, as Monica said with a smile pointing to the spiral staircase, "He's up there working on the script of his next film!". Will you be in it? I ask. "Of course" she replied. Monica was not the apparently neurotic example of alienation that she plays so well in Antonioni's films. I had long suspected that Monica herself was eager to find more cheerful roles but I doubted if it would be the one Michelangelo was writing for her that day, which would be *The Red Desert*. She'd have to wait for "cheerful roles" from other directors.

There wasn't much of cultural interest going on in Rome that summer of 1962. The 'dolce vita' was still carrying on around the Via Veneto but it was becoming a parody of itself and a tourist attraction. The interesting people were escaping to other parts of town or to Spoleto for the Festival of Two Worlds now in its fifth year. In spite of my ever-present financial problems I managed to visit Spoleto several times during its three weeks. The theatre and musical events were a mixed bag. An Italian ballet company had been put together especially for the festival by the eclectic Florentine theatrical jack-of-all-trades, Beppe Menegatti, the husband of the great new Italian ballerina, Carla Fracci, but her appearances provided the only good moments in that company's programme.

More rewarding was Menegatti's delightful festival production of Rossini's *Il Conte Ory* performed in the exquisitely restored 18th Century Caio Melissa mini opera house, so much more suitable to camera-sized operas. The Festival's drama events included an Italian play by Joppolo called *I Carabinieri*, an out-dated pastoral anti-war parable, not given much pep by Roberto Rossellini's conventional direction. Oddly enough, Jean-Luc Godard would make an excellent film of the play.

The most interesting theatrical event of the festival was *The American Dream*, a one-act play by the young American dramatist, Edward Albee, presented on a bill with several other one-act plays, including a rather dull one, *The Alligators*, by Elia Kazan's wife, Molly. Menotti told me that the festival had commissioned a play from Albee two years before, but the resulting short piece entitled *The Sandbox* had not been staged. *The American Dream* was fascinating for its first hint of the drastically cynical assault against the American family which this brilliant writer would carry to greater depth in his subsequent full-length plays. The collapse of the American dream was portrayed here by the Mum and Dad trying to identify the son they would have liked in the handsome young stud who suddenly appears in their home. The lad tells his story of a lost twin brother to Grandma, superbly played by Mildred Dunnock, to whom he confesses that his only talent is his body which he is happy to let people "draw pleasure from". Some time later, I bought a book with several Albee one-acters, including *The Zoo Story* which I was about to help a young Italian actor, Francesco Gerbasio, to stage. I would discover that the characters in this earlier play, which Spoleto never saw, were the same as those in *American Dream*, except that the young stud in *The Sandbox*, wearing only a bathing costume because the setting is a beach, is explicitly described as the "Angel of Death".

I attended some sessions of a seminar Lee Strasberg was holding for young actors and was rather startled to hear his wife, Paula, say that Marilyn Monroe was one of the greatest actresses that had ever studied with them. And I saw the 'world premiere' of a new play by Tennessee Williams, a loyal friend of Menotti's. It was the first version of *The Milk Train Doesn't Stop Here Anymore*, which was never to become one of Tennessee's most memorable works despite several re-writes. There were some flashes of the dramatist's magic in this grotesque tale of a fading beauty, a latter day Blanche du Bois, writing her memoirs and trying to recapture youthful fires with a handsome young man in leather breeches who turns out to be after her soul rather than her body, and who beats a hasty retreat without obtaining either. Hermione Baddeley's cabaret-style performance was enchanting. She made the character a cross between Elsa Maxwell and Winston Churchill.

At one of the parties given by Giancarlo Menotti, in the palazzo out of the centre of the city to which he had now moved, I finally had a chance to meet Tennessee Williams. He was Menotti's guest there. As I didn't feel like talking about the play I camped it up a bit and said we had mutual friends, one of whom was Leslie E., an American beachcomber who always behaved as if he and Tennessee were good friends. I knew Leslie from my Piazza di Spagna days when he'd often behave disgracefully in public and would usually annoy celebrities he barged in on. But Leslie could be a fun person. I told Tennessee that I owed it to Leslie that I had discovered Baron Corvo, for on one of the occasions when the errant wanderer was fleeing his hotel because he couldn't pay the bill, he had left me his copy of *The Quest for Corvo* by A. J. A. Symons. Tennessee laughed and agreed that Leslie could be a nuisance but could also be good company for a short while. "I often amused myself", he said, "by being nice to Leslie to annoy other people who treated him as a balls-breaker".

Menotti had kindly let me sleep in his palazzo in the cathedral square, the one where John Gielgud had received me so graciously the year before. I didn't sleep very much because it was too tempting to look out on the moonlit city at night when the piazza, so busy during the day, was deserted. I found time to explore what would go down in the history of Italian cultural summertime attractions, a quite unique exhibition of modern sculptures which included, among others, works by Moore, Marini, Manzù, Calder and Pomodoro which the curator, Giovanni Carandente, had imaginatively placed in the piazze and back streets of the medieval city, creating, especially at night, magical contrasts between the ancient and the modern, rather like what had impressed me so much about the new Coventry Cathedral. At least one of the sculptures, by Henry Moore, would be given to Spoleto and remain a fixture of the city for decades to come.

Spoleto Cathedral

Chapter 17

I went out to Cinecittà to visit the set of Federico's new film which had at last taken off and I saw that, for the moment, on the clapper board it was being called *8 1/2*, which was the sum of his films to date. I watched him shoot a scene between Marcello and a Cardinal which was a fascinating lesson in film direction as he told them from behind the camera, at times gentle, at times a bit aggressive, how to play the scene, rather like directors did in silent film days. I warned Federico that my friend Peter Daubeny, who had been asked to interview leading European cultural personalities for an English Sunday newspaper, was coming to Rome the following week and hoping to interview him. I explained that Peter was not a journalist but a theatrical impresario who brought the Moscow Arts Theatre and the Berliner Ensemble on their first visits to Britain. Fellini told the American woman hired to do the publicity on the film to arrange the meeting. I was writing a Rome cultural column for *The Observer* but I realised that all I could say about Fellini's new film was that it was a mystery to almost everyone in Rome, even those who were acting in it.

When Peter arrived in Rome to do the interview with Fellini, I took him out to Cinecittà to meet Federico who invited us to lunch. Present also was Ian and another of the film's dilettante 'actors', a charming man, one of Italy's most distinguished industrialists, Guido Alberti of the Strega liqueur firm. Alberti was also a patron of the arts (sponsor of the prestigious 'Strega' annual literary award). He had never acted before but, thanks to this debut in Federico's film, he would become an important character actor in Italian cinema (I'd be responsible one day for getting him the part of Rossini in a BBC film, a part that had been offered to me but which I felt Guido would be much more suitable for). By now we knew that the new Fellini film was autobiographical, about a film director who after the success of his previous film didn't know how to follow it up. I'd already seen him shoot a dream sequence in which the director, called 'Guido' and played, of course, by Marcello dressed rather like Federico, was walking amidst floor-level steam down the corridor of cabins in the thermal spa where much of the action seemed to be taking place. Guido Alberti played the producer of the film within the film. The scene I watched him play that day was obviously part of another dream.

Guido Alberti in Fellini's *8 1/2*.

At lunch, Federico enjoyed talking to Peter who was a showman himself and who obviously had done his homework as he knew much about Federico (he told me he had read a long article in an American magazine). Indeed, Federico said to me teasingly: "Your friend seems to know a lot about me. Ask him to tell me the meaning of my life. It may help me to finish the film". Talking about FF to Peter and Ian at dinner that evening, Peter said he had been struck by the fact that when he mentioned Peter Ustinov, whom he knew well, Federico had commented: "He is a good person". We agreed that this seemed an inadequate description of a person as versatile as Ustinov but, in the final analysis, it was probably the greatest compliment one creative artist could pay another.

Oddly enough, talking about Federico to the adorable Anouk Aimée, on another day on the set, she too used the same expression, referring to Federico as "très bon". When the conversation with Ian and Peter turned to the Wesker play, which I had admired so much in London but neither of them had liked, Peter complained that the author of *Chips With Everything* might have at least conceded that there could be a 'good person' among the upper class officers in the air force camp. Peter Daubeny was a 'good person' himself but he was a bit of a snob.

On another evening, Guido Alberti drove us up to a picturesque 18th century village called Feliciano, sixty kilometers north of Rome along the Via Flaminia. The cluster of houses must have been the 'borgo' (adjacent dwellings) of a family castle. It was against this bewitching background that Federico was shooting another dream sequence, involving the film director played by Marcello and the girl of his dreams played by the ravishingly beautiful Claudia Cardinale. Everyone enjoyed chatting with us over wine and savoury tit-bits in a local tavern. Claudia was still a bit shy because of her poor English (one day I'd be her dialogue coach on Jerzy Skolimowsky's *The Adventures of Gerard*, by which time her English was much better). But like Marcello, whose English was also pretty bad, both of them loved to try it out. Marcello told Peter he was hoping to convince Sophia Loren to do *The Taming of the Shrew* in the theatre with him, a project that unfortunately would never be realised.

While Peter was in town, I also took him to meet Vittorio Gassman. We talked about Danilo Dolci whom Vittorio had been to visit in Sicily. He wanted to include in his upcoming TV programme about theatrical heroes (and eventually a theatrical tour of the same) a dramatised excerpt from one of the books by Dolci describing his social activity. I could see that Peter wasn't part-icularly interested in Dolci but seemed excited by the idea of Vittorio's anthology of 'Heroes', who included Edmund Kean.

He promised to return to Italy to see Gassman's show as he was looking for an Italian company to invite to the festival he was organising the following year, at the Aldwych, for the Shakespearian quatercentenary.

A week after Peter left Rome, I was on a plane to Palermo where I had been invited to visit the location of Visconti's film *The Leopard*, an adaptation of Lampedusa's novel. On that very hot day, in the last week of July, I was met on arrival at the airport in Palermo by the driver of a production car, unfortunately not by a handsome young Sicilian, but by a grim-looking mafioso type who seemed offended when I made the gesture of sitting up front with him. This made him think I was an American but when I said I was English he further insisted that I sit behind. Suddenly he became embarrassingly obsequious and, to my astonishment, said: "We Sicilians and you English have a lot in common". I asked him where he found this 'similarity'. He replied: "We are both island peoples who like to keep aloof from the continent. Our gentry and the working people keep their distance but respect one another".

I had read Lampedusa's novel when it was first published in Italian and thought then that Visconti, a 'gent' himself but one with sympathies for the communists, was obviously the right person to film a book about the Risorgimento seen from the point of view of a nostalgic Sicilian aristocrat and his more enlightened nephew. Visconti was back in the era he had depicted so magnificently in *Senso*, where the young Austrian officer wastrel, played by Farley Granger, scathingly prophesies to the Venetian countess who has been his lover: "We Austrians won a battle today against your Italian patriots but our class will soon count no more".

The driver didn't take me into the Sicilian capital but to the beautiful Villa Igiea, a five-star hotel overlooking the sea just outside Mondello, the fashionable beach of Palermitan society. I was welcomed by someone from the publicity office and told that my meetings with Visconti and the cast of *The Leopard* would be arranged as soon as possible. After a rest and something to eat, they told me I could visit the palazzo in Palermo where they were preparing the set for the ballroom sequence which was due to start shooting within the next weeks. In the afternoon I visited the palazzo, then owned by the Gangi family, and one of only three palazzi still in decent shape in Palermo. The others had either been bombed during the war or restructured as hotels or regional offices. The interior decoration of the whole film was to be accredited to Giorgio Pes, and a young woman from the noble Hercolani family, but, the afternoon I was there, I was introduced to a charming young man whom they told me was the Count of Mazzarino. He was supervising the works and he very courteously showed me round. He spoke perfect English. I'd discover later, when he was being called what I thought was Joe but which was Giò, short for Gioacchino, that he was in fact the adopted son of the *Leopard* author and had been hired as an historical consultant.

Gioacchino Lanza di Lampedusa (his full name) was destined to become a very distinguished Italian literary and musical authority. Many years later I'd attend a seminar in Palermo where Giò, and others of his generation, would describe so vividly the literary salon of the real Prince, which they had been privileged to frequent as young bloods of the city, before the aged Lampedusa wrote his memoirs as a novel to be published after his death. Giò told me that the rooms of the palazzo didn't need a great deal of touching up because much of the 'faded gold' described in the novel was conveniently still present. However, the candelabras would have to be restored to their original form with real candles which would have to be kept alight all night during shooting. "Obviously they'll make for hot nights even by the standards of the Sicilian summer!" I commented. Giò smiled, with a somewhat apprehensive sigh, adding, "I guess so!" At that point I was rather relieved that there'd been no follow-up to a vague suggestion by Luchino, some months before, when I'd asked if there were a part for me in the film, and he'd replied almost menacingly, "Well I suppose you could be one of the guests at the ball". After this Palermo visit, I had already decided to go on to Taormina for the film festival, a more inviting prospect than staying on for the hot nights at Palazzo Gangi.

But first, of course, I had to do what I had come to Palermo to do, a journalist report for *The Times*. That evening I had dinner at the hotel with Alain Delon's dialogue coach, John Alarimo, whom I knew from Rome. John had to prepare Alain for the scenes shot in English with Burt Lancaster. He told me Alain was not shooting that week; he was driving around Sicily in his Ferrari with Romy Schneider, who was staying with him in a villa by the sea that had been rented for him. During the day they were racing round the bay on his motorboat. I knew Claudia Cardinale was not there either, for I had seen her the week before in Rome where she was shooting the Fellini film. But at least I was going to meet Burt Lancaster.

The next day it was arranged for me to be driven up to the hills, thirty miles inland from Palermo, where I could watch Visconti shoot an important scene with Serge Reggiani playing Don Ciccio Tumeo, the local landowner, who feels nostalgic for the Bourbons. I prepared by looking up the scene in the English translation by Archibald Colquhoun which I had brought with me. Colquhoun was in the same car that took me to the location and I was pleased to be able to talk with him about his experience (of which he would write a brilliant short article for *Films and Filming*). He was working as a 'super dialogue consultant' on the film and told me that it was being shot in English only where Lancaster and other English-speaking actors were involved. The rest of the film was being shot in Italian or French. "The people at 20th Century Fox will have to cope with turning it all into English, or probably American" he said somewhat sarcastically. I told him of the problems I had had with dubbing *La Dolce Vita* into English. But it was fascinating to hear Mr. C., whom I respected also for his translation of Manzoni's classic, *The Betroved* (I Promessi Sposi), talk about the unexpected intelligence and dedication that Lancaster was putting into his performance, especially as everyone, starting with Visconti himself, had been sceptical when the American co-producers had proposed him for the role.

After an hour or so along the country roads we transferred to a jeep which took us over dusty footpaths to the location. We watched Lancaster and Reggiani playing the last part of the scene in which the Prince and Don Ciccio, resting from the morning's hunt, sit under a cork tree and discuss the outcome of the referendum in which the Sicilians have voted in favour of the new kingdom emerging from Garibaldi's conquest of their island. Don Ciccio admits he voted 'No' and refuses to share the Prince's resignation that things will have to change if they are to remain the same. The 'change' in Donnafugata will mean accepting the access to local power by the new bourgeoisie personified by the somewhat pompous Calogero Sedàra (played by Paolo Stoppa). Don Calogero is the father of the beautiful Angelica (Cardinale) who will marry Prince Fabrizio's nephew Tancredi (Delon) who, having fought with Garibaldi's redshirts, had been the one to convert his uncle to the idea of the necessity for 'change'.

Burt Lancaster in Visconti's *The Leopard*.

Lancaster seemed to be having some difficulty in getting the scene right, but Visconti patiently discussed it with him (out of our hearing), and they did fifteen takes before both were satisfied. That evening, I had dinner in the hotel with Archibald and we talked more about Manzoni than about Lampedusa. I confessed that I didn't think much of Manzoni's play, *Adelchi*, which I'd seen recently with Gassman but that I had appreciated *The Betrothed* in his translation. "Did you feel it seemed too like Walter Scott?" he asked modestly, adding "As you seem to know Italian well, I suggest you read it in Italian. You'll appreciate more how wonderfully Manzoni described the mood of Northern Italy and how the people suffered under its 17th century occupiers".

On Sunday afternoon, I was finally received in audience by Count Visconti. The production office told me I was very privileged as I had been invited to tea at his villa, which had been Nelson's headquarters in Bourbon times, and where the Count rarely received journalists. Luchino was very cordial and this time I was not a subject for his ironical jibes. He didn't tell me much about the filming that I hadn't already heard from others but he did admit that he hadn't been enthusiastic about the casting of Lancaster, "How could one who played cowboys and pirates play a Sicilian Prince?", he had wrongly thought. He had been pleasurably surprised at the intensity of Burt's dedication to reading up on everything about 19th century Sicily; what Luchino described as "Burt's determination to feel the part". He told me that Lancaster would be dubbed in the Italian version by an Italian actor, preferably a Sicilian. (In fact the part would be dubbed superbly by the great Turi Ferro. Luchino would show no interest in the eventual Anglo-American version). At the Visconti villa that evening I could see there was some preparation for a dinner party where probably Alain and Romy would be present. I was not invited to stay on but I could hardly expect to be. I had long ago gambled my likelihood of becoming a member of the Visconti clan and I could feel honoured that at least he'd received me on his day off.

The next day, I took a local flight to Catania where I arrived too late in the day for transport to Taormina so I had to stay the night. I was glad of an excuse to take a look at this principal city of Eastern Sicily which I'd never visited. I was fascinated by its Baroque sombreness, less romantically Mediterranean in feeling than Palermo. It seemed a bit frightening at night so I didn't prowl around but I made a promise to myself to come back. I could see that the young men looked much more interesting (and interested) than in Palermo. The bus ride to Taormina proved rewarding, above all because we passed through places which I'd have liked to take a closer look at, such as Aci Trezza where Visconti had shot *La Terra Trema.*

In Taormina, when I reached the hotel booked for me by the Festival, near the gate at the other end of town from where the bus had left me, I was given a single room without a view and protested so indignantly that they reluctantly gave me a double room overlooking the sea. The first evening at the Greek Theatre I saw a disturbing Japanese film called *The Naked Island* which impressed me very much. It was a beautiful film, in the Flaherty tradition, in which nobody spoke until the ending when the mother opened her mouth to make a poignant wail at the death of her child. By then most of the several thousand people in the audience had left noisily. They'd enjoyed the earlier part of the evening's entertainment, with the presentation of some popular stars and a comic act, but this film, the tragic saga of the daily life on a bare rock of an island, was too much for them. And it certainly wasn't easy viewing for those of us eager to watch, who were distracted by a Sicilian crowd climbing noisily down in the dark towards the exits. The film was certainly an unfortunate choice for an audience of this kind. This strange 'festival' wasn't a festival at all. They called it a Rassegna, a "review", but it was really a collection of previews of the new films for the next season, the better ones obviously being kept for Venice a month later. It seemed a pity that they showed films which would only be shown, if at all, in arthouse cinemas. But the people who organised it had to try to produce an alibi for calling it a 'cultural event'. Taormina did have a normal cinema where, some evenings, we could see previews in its vast spaces with a roof that opened up after dark to let in some air but also the stupid comments of locals leaning out of their windows to look down. Many years would pass, indeed decades, before Taormina would get an air-conditioned cinema palace where one could see arthouse-style competition films in comfort. And the real international festival wouldn't take off in Taormina until Italy's wizard festival organiser, Gian Luigi Rondi, took it over in 1970. It gathered even more prestige when another distinguished Rome critic (and dramatist) Guglielmo Biraghi, took charge for a few years. Both Rondi and Biraghi were destined to become directors of the Venice Festival.

The first events of the 1962 festival had been held in Messina and those of us who had arrived for the second week had to go to Messina too, for a couple of evenings, a harrowing journey there by coach, driven through the villages while the crowds promenade in the streets. But the night I had the honour of escorting the star of the evening, the French sexpot, Martine Carol, they had found a new means of transport to Messina. It still meant getting into evening dress at 6 pm when it was still hot. They had hired an aliscafo, the newly invented hydrofoil motorboat, to take us by sea. But they had forgotten that, at that hour, the fishermen were already pulling out for the night's catch, so our magical new means of transport had to run at a snail's pace. Since there was no air-conditioning in the hydrofoil and, of course, no space for poking our heads out for some air, by the time we reached Messina we were all in a bad shape, particularly the ladies. I had to insist on taking poor Martine to a hotel to freshen up and she was surprisingly patient about it, much more than I was. When we finally were taken to the dismal open-air theatre on the sea front, the lovely view across the Straits to the flickering lights of Calabria was more comforting than that of the noisy impatient crowd waiting to hear me ask Martine the imbecile questions that had been prepared for me. When it was all over we were supposed to watch an awful film directed by Roberto Rossellini, *Anima nera*, adapted from one of Giuseppe Patroni Griffi's dullest plays. We managed to creep out at the interval and got the Messina people to take us to a local restaurant to eat a good fish meal, then drive us back to Taormina by car, easier going at that hour, when the locals had gone to bed.

The last night of the festival was held, of course, in the Greek theatre where we had to sit through the ceremony for the awarding of the Davids of Donatello, one of which went to Marlene Dietrich. The poor darling had to cope with descending a precarious staircase by herself, starting from the top of the ancient ruins, with a spotlight blinding her sight, while we heard her recorded voice singing *"Ich bin von Kopf bis Fuß"* from *The Blue Angel*. She had told us rather naughtily during a press conference earlier in the day that it had been a role that she frankly hadn't enjoyed playing. "I hate playing vulgar women". That night in Taormina she was lucky that the compère of the show had the quick wits to realise that the divine Marlene risked not seeing the last steps and he climbed them to give her a hand.

The most disappointing film of the week was Jules Dassin's *Phaedra*, a modern version of Euripides' *Hippolytus* in which Raf Vallone's Theseus becomes a shipping magnate, Onassis-Niarchos style. His wife Phaedra (Melina Mercouri) is repulsed in disgust by Theseus's bastard son, Hippolytus (Anthony Perkins) and, in revenge, she accuses him of trying to rape her. The poor lad is so upset he drives to his death in his Aston Martin. This crowd loved the film but the critics fled. Yes, the film was a mess but I stayed on because I felt sorry for Perkins who I knew in real life probably wouldn't have wanted to be seduced even by such a bewitching lady as Mercouri.

My stay was given a boost when the organisers took us (in one of those suffocating hydrofoils which are even worse in daytime) on a tour of the Aeolian Islands. The first we visited was Stromboli, where Rossellini had made his film, so titled, with Ingrid Bergman. Next up we visited Volcano, where Anna Magnani had made her revenge film to spite Rossellini's abandonment. The islands were both more appealing than the films which bore their names. I spent the day in the company of a German colleague and, after a brief look at the two 'film star' islands, we decided not to get off at Volcano where our fellow festival day trippers wanted to swim and be richly fed. We stayed on the hydrofoil till the next island, Salina, where we ate modestly but deliciously and enjoyed ourselves with some of the eager to be entertained young locals, before returning on our own to Messina by a ferryboat at sunset. I vowed I'd go back to Salina but I'd never succeed in doing so.

On another day, my German friend hired a car and we drove up to Etna which was puffing rather modestly that summer. It was exciting to peer into the crater close to. On the way down we took a footbath in the icy waters of the Alcantara Gorge and then went to Aci Trezza for lunch. The fishing village was a bit less primitive than in the late 1940s of Visconti's film, but most of the inhabitants, whether elderly or young, still looked like players in the film.

My stay in Taormina that year was given a heart-warming epilogue by my acquaintance with an elderly American lady staying at the same hotel as me. She had lived in the town since the end of the war and wouldn't hear a word against the Sicilians, especially when I told her I was reading Danilo Dolci's latest book, *Conversazioni.* She snorted something about these 'social workers' who think they can change things here. She showed me a clipping from an American newspaper which reported a vain attempt to stop the showing on television of a documentary about Sicily called *The Inferno,* claiming to describe the "Living Hell" of life in a Sicilian village. "That's not the image of Sicily that Americans should see," she ranted. This dear Taormina resident was a relic of Victorian times, a latter day American equivalent to those English ladies who still lived in Florence and Rome and were impenitent Romantics. Even so, some of these ladies did contribute much to local development. One such was Florence Trevelyan, who won an honoured place in Taormina's history in the late 19th century. She had married the Mayor of Taormina and helped to expand the modest Hotel Timeo which, by our times, had become very chic. In what had been an abandoned area underneath the cliff on which the Greek theatre had been built, she had created a magical public garden complete with a pagoda and exotic flora. In that garden, one summer, I would persuade the Taormina theatre festival people to put a stage up among the trees. I organised a festival of Shakespeare in English, staged mostly by American and British experimental companies including Cheek by Jowl.

The Greek Theatre at Taormina

Chapter 18

I flew back to Rome in time for the last night of the Trastevere festa in honour of the Madonna of the Carmelites which, though no longer such a novelty for me, was still a reminder that Rome could still offer the best illustrations of the Lampedusa theory of how 'change' could leave things much as they were. In this case pagan rituals into Christian ceremonies. I found that while I was away, Ian had done a couple more days work on the Fellini film but, since there was no certainty about when they would shoot the final sequence (in which I too was due to appear), he was taking off for a few days in Greece.

Early in August we were all shocked to hear that Marilyn Monroe had died, apparently through an overdose but what really drove her to it remained unclear. Certainly after her marriage with Miller ended there had been stories that she had become more and more unhappy and not even the Kennedy brothers had been able to console her. In July, I had been able to see in Rome (in English) the film which Miller had written for her, *The Misfits*, directed by John Huston. I had written in my diary: "A moving attempt at acting by Marilyn". John Huston's film gave me an idea of what Paula Strasberg had seen in Marilyn as a young actress, but I added: "It is probably a good thing for the American arts that Marilyn and Miller have broken up. He is too great a writer to waste himself writing this kind of film and Marilyn needs to straighten up her life". It was sad that she never succeeded in doing that, even if Miller would try to do it for her in a play after she was gone. In 1964, when that play, *After the Fall*, was performed in an Italian production by Franco Zeffirelli, with Monica Vitti playing the Marilyn role, I'd go to Naples to see it and have dinner with Miller and his new wife afterwards. It was a pleasant evening even if Miller got food poisoning from the excellent (for us others) fish meal.

In August, I visited the set of the Fellini film again. He was shooting another dream sequence in which Marcello as Guido (the character representing Fellini) remembers his childhood and then, gradually, all the women in his early years reappear, those who had cockled him as a boy. But the dream turns into an erotic nightmare, a harem. In the scene I saw being shot that day he was chasing round the house all the real and fantasy lovers including his wife, the latter role played by the enchanting Anouk Aimée, who was certainly more attractive than Fellini's own wife. Marcello took the whip to them while the music of Wagner's *The Ride of the Valkyries* played, the same as would be heard in the finished film. Both Marcello and Federico seemed to be enjoying themselves enormously, the actresses perhaps less so, with the exception of Barbara Steele who kept shouting: "Delicious!". I didn't know whether the line was in the script or whether she invented it herself. Marcello had once told me: "Federico lets you do the things you have always dreamed of doing". I didn't ask if that included the whipping of his girlfriends!

Marcello Mastroianni and Barbara Steele in *8 1/2*.

Also, that August, I went to Viterbo, a beautiful city just north of Rome, where the Popes once resided. John Karlsen was in a scene being filmed there at what was supposed to be Guido's school. John played one of the priestly teachers we also see in a later scene on a beach where he chases after little Guido, an errant schoolboy with his mates ogling at the fat whore, Saraghina. The August heat in Rome became unbearable, worse than in Sicily where at least the sea was close at hand. For the mid-August bank holiday weekend, I went to spend a few days beside the cool lakeside of Bracciano where my actress friend, Tamara Lees, now a star in Italian films, had lent me her villa while she was in Greece. When I got back to Rome, I found that Ian had returned from Greece. He too had suffered from the heat and he had not been able to find the rapturous lover of his previous visit to one of the islands of the Aegean. As I too was still sorry I had to abandon an island (but in the sea of Magna Graecia) where there were rapturous young men waiting to be seduced, we tried to console ourselves by reading Ian's copy of an excellent English translation of Cavafy's poems in which homosexual love was idealised metaphorically.

We had dinner one night with the Greek actor, Spiros Focás, and his wife. Spyros was the sort of rapturous Greek we could all dream about, but I got a bit irritated to hear him so eager to defend his country. We all love Hellas but I find it difficult to understand why the Greeks of today seem to have an inferiority complex and are always on the defensive. Spyros's wife worked with the Greek National Theatre and she told us they'd rehearsed the chorus of their latest production for five months. Afterwards Ian told me he'd seen that production and frankly didn't feel its standards were high. During the summer at Ostia Antica we had seen a production of *Electra*, by the Piraikon Theatre, which was quite extraordinary and the chorus was impeccable probably without needing five months rehearsal because it wasn't a state-subsidised company.

Fortunately that summer, to quote Michelangelo's sonnet again, 'lustful arrows' did fly in my direction again and in an unexpected way. It happened at the Volturno, a cruisy cinema near the railway station where the star of the variety show was a drag queen called O'Brien, a more talented performer than the one I had seen at the Altieri with Zavattini, who had been intrigued by the sexual ambiguity on display. This time, thanks to O'Brien's performance, I made the acquaintance of a carabinere sitting next to me. I had to work hard to convince him that the artist we were watching was a man. As a result he became very friendly. When we were outside I gave the carabinere my phone number and he promised to call the next day which he did. Though he was a bit complicated at first, and got aggressive at times, feeling guilty over this first homosexual experience, we were to develop an affectionate relationship that would carry on for several years. I'd get to know O'Brien when I saw him playing a dramatic role in a Strehler production at the Piccolo Teatro in Milan and, in later years, I'd meet him, or rather her as he became after a sex change in Casablanca. I became very friendly with Giorgia, as she had become, and also with her husband, the head waiter at a Rome restaurant. Giorgia would tell me the story of how, as a boy born in Palermo, he'd suffered a lot, teased and sexually abused by his mates. I would tell her what happened to me in that Roman cinema that August afternoon. She told me she often had men pursuing her when she came out of the theatres where she performed, even when she wasn't in drag.

I never got to the Venice Festival that August. I was particularly sorry because Pasolini's second film, *Mamma Roma*, was showing, as was *La commare secca* (The Grim Reaper), based on a story by Pasolini, the first film by the young man who had been Pier Paolo's assistant on *Accattone*, Bernardo Bertolucci, son of the poet, Attilio, an adorable person whom I had first met in Parma when attending a film seminar there. But I was able to watch the television transmission from Viareggio, of the annual prize-giving ceremony of the prestigious literary awards, where Bernardo, with Pier Paolo as his sponsor, won the young poet award.

Just before the start of the Venice festival I received a visit at my home from Franco Citti, who I had asked to interview. Of course he brought a friend along, probably to protect him. The interview went very well and I was impressed by his surprisingly professional attitude, which no longer seemed that of the sub-proletarian type of the PPP film, so much so that I failed to muster the courage to affront him over the robbery which I knew his younger brother might have been involved in. He told me he was learning French as he had been signed to play a leading role in Marcel Carné's new film. He was off to Venice for the screening of *Mamma Roma* in which he played Anna Magnani's pimp. As he left, I wished him luck and he replied: "If we win the Golden Lion I'll bring you back a paw".

The film didn't win the Golden Lion or any prize. The top award was shared between Zurlini's *Cronaca Familiare*, in which I had played one of my mini-cameos, and *Ivan's Childhood*, the first film by a twenty-three year old Russian director, Andrei Tarkovsky, which sounded promising. I wondered how long I'd have to wait to see it now that I didn't have any friends at the Soviet Embassy? But I soon got the chance to see *Mamma Roma*. It wasn't as striking as *Accattone*, but one could certainly see that PPP was developing a distinctive film-making style. The film had lots of cultural citations, the music this time taken from Vivaldi rather than Bach, while, in the tragic last scene, when Magnani's son (Ettore Garofolo) dies strapped to a grim prison bed he is clearly in the position of Mantegna's Christ. The acting was less naif than in *Accattone*, and Magnani was her usual magnificent self, and surprisingly subdued for her in the big emotional scenes, obviously thanks to her director. Still, it was difficult to believe that such a strong-willed woman, even if necessity had driven her to the streets, would let herself be exploited by such a mediocre pimp (a superb cameo by Franco Citti, this time dubbed with his own voice).

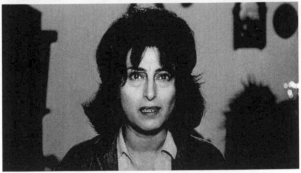

Ettore Garofolo and Anna Magnani
in Pasolini's *Mamma Roma*.

In September, my morale was helped by the appearance of my article on *The Leopard* in *The Times* and by my interview with Monica Vitti getting a nice spread in the monthly magazine, *Town*. My spirits were helped by the cooling autumn air, and by the regular appearances of my new carabiniere friend. And my work prospects were good, with work coming up on the Fellini film and with an offer of a role in the next Pasolini film. I did the English subtitles for the first feature directed by the playwright Giuseppe Patroni Griffi, *Il Mare*, in which a charming new actor,

Dino Mele, plays the third man in a trianglular love story in the offbeat setting of a winter-time Capri. I also did a day's work playing a priest leading spiritual exercises in a Jesuit college for a film called *L'Ape Regina* (The Queen Bee), starring the brilliant comic actor, Ugo Tognazzi. It was directed by a bizarre guy named Marco Ferreri, who had made an amusing little Spanish film, *El cochecito* (1960), which I had seen. He insisted on my speaking in Italian and my voice stayed in the finished film. The film itself would become a *cause celebre*. I was proud to be associated with the first Italian film of what proved to be an illustrious career for a very offbeat and controversial 'auteur'. So when my mother and her husband arrived for another short Roman visit I felt happy to celebrate my new successes with them at our favourite restaurant in Trastevere, the Meo Patacca. There I was surprised to see that the boy who played Magnani's son in *Mamma Roma*, Ettore Garofalo, who had had that Mantegna-like ending, had returned to being a humble but good-humoured waiter, a further attraction for the restaurant which was now occupying the whole piazza.

JFL at the Meo Patacca with his mother and stepfather.

Early one morning, in October 1962, an ominous-looking little man knocked at my door and politely asked to see my passport and residence permit (in those times renewable every three months) which showed that my most recent entry into Italy had been in May when I came back from the Cannes Festival. My heart stopped beating for a moment, fearing that my sinful life in Roma was catching up on me. It turned out that my caller was not from the police but from the city registry office. He asked me if I intended to stay on in Rome and I said, "Yes." "In that case", he said, "maybe it would be a good idea to sign up at the anagrafe (the city registry office)". I told him that to become a Roman citizen was "an honour I dreamed not of" which left him rather bewildered. The next day I went to the Anagrafe and did what he had suggested. There were no problems. So, from October 1962 I became an official resident of the Eternal City. It meant I eventually had to pay rates but they would never prove too onerous.

My first month as a registered Roman citizen seemed to be proceeding well. Under the October sun, on the beach between Fiumicino and Ostia, I did my seven-day-stint on Fellini's *8 1/2* which had become its definitive title. They had built a weird space ship construction which was to be the setting of the film-within-the-film. The sequence of the press conference was supposed to mark the wrap of that film but Fellini shows that the director played by Mastroianni is at a loss to know what to say to the press and imagines himself committing suicide. Ian told me that it seemed unlikely they were going to finish on what, those of us appearing in the press conference scene were told, was our last day. He told me caustically: "He still doesn't know how he wants to finish the film". They had already shot what was supposed to have been the epilogue, with all the characters, including Ian, on a train which was taking them nobody knew where, "probably to Hell" said Ian at lunch at Ostia. Ian was eager to get out of town. He had been in Rome on and off for eight months and had only worked for a few days in the filming of the spa episode, where he performed his tricks as a telepath at a nightclub, and he had filmed a scene of him in conversation with Guido (Mastroianni), in which it becomes clear that they have known each other since they were young. The production company had kept Ian on call for several more months without working but now they were begging him to stay around without offering any guarantees as to how many more days he would work now that his contract had expired. He owed money all over town. The people in the production office had no idea what Federico intended to do with him or the ending of the film. I told Ian frankly that he couldn't abandon Federico at this point. He had to trust him.

I hadn't earned much myself on the film but, after all, I'd only been working a week and I was just a glorified extra, a member of the press shouting questions at the director, Guido, and without even a close-up. An American woman was chosen to be the one who scathingly shouts into camera the film's most incriminating line: "He has nothing to say!". I was always called for six a.m. but after the first day I realised it wasn't necessary to be that early. No one checked whether I'd arrived so obviously my presence wasn't that important. My tenant John Karlsen, who was playing a priest, was called every day without having much to do either but at least he succeeded in joining other bit players in a car being driven out to the location. On days when it wasn't already full on reaching Trastevere I managed to squeeze in. It was an adventure. And as I was in a film which we were all expecting could be become as much a landmark in cinema history as *La Dolce Vita*, I was pleased to stay around and watch what was going on. I felt anyway that my contribution to the film had been in introducing Federico to Ian, who had a key role. A few days after I had finished working, and Fellini was still shooting out at the Ostia location, Ian came back to my place one evening, with John K, and his mood had changed. He declared excitedly: "Federico is a genius. He didn't know how to finish his film, so he is making a film about a director who doesn't know how to finish his film!".

The next afternoon I got Salvatore to drive me in his borrowed 600 Fiat to the location. In my diary I wrote: "October 10 1962. As we drove down the Via del Mare in pouring rain, we were passed by black limousines full of clerical gentlemen speeding into Rome. They were not actors from Federico's film but real clerics converging on Rome for the Ecumenical Council due to open the next day. Arriving at the location I spotted Federico in his blue raincoat and felt hat, what he called his "English outfit". The unit was having what we would call a 'tea break'. The crowds of actors and crew were indeed running to get something warm to drink and eat but also to escape from the rain. Federico only made a pretence at worrying about the weather. In the dressing room tent I met the American writer, Eugene Walter, whom I knew well from the days when I frequented Princess Caetani and her *Botteghe Oscure* literary crowd. Eugene was a permanent fixture there." Eugene and I would appear together one day in an Italianised TV mini-series based on *The Pickwick Papers*, written and directed by Ugo Gregoretti, who asked me to play a cameo as a genuinely English-accented Dickensian traveller meeting the 'Italian' Mr. Pickwick in Bath. In Fellini's film, Eugene played the part of a journalist at the spa who was trying to interview Guido. He told me that Federico had now invented an alternative epilogue for the film, what Eugene called a "happy ending", in which all the characters of this film will be rejoicing around Guido who has abandoned the film he didn't really want to make. I also ran into Mastroianni sipping an espresso and asked him what he thought of the new ending. He seemed a bit confused and said he thought the ending on the train was fine. Marcello told me smilingly: "But it seems your Scottish friend has become the *Deus ex machina* for an alternative circus fade-out".

Images from John Francis Lane's cameo in Fellini's *8 1/2*,
with Ian Dallas (below) leading the parade

Federico was quite happy to shoot in the rain even if nothing shot that day would be in the finished film. The scene I saw seemed to be a mixture of *La Strada* and the last scene on the beach of *La Dolce Vita*. The fat whore, Saraghina, was pathetically dripping from the rain among the crowds of priests, clowns and the ladies of the spa splendidly costumed by Gherardi for the nightmare which turns into the 'happy ending'. The clouds burst and what was only a Tyrrhenian seaside drizzle turned into a Nordic tempest. I took refuge in our car and got the driver to move off in case we get stuck in the muddy sand. As we drove to safety, I looked back and saw that the man in the English outfit, who had invented this richly decorated chaos, was still gesticulating wildly, even if his technicians were wisely turning off the flood-lights. I began to wonder whether the whole film would turn out to be something of a leg-pull aimed not only at his producer, Rizzoli, but also at those critics that expected Fellini to be more 'socially committed'. He had already fired at his critics in the press conference scene in *La Dolce Vita*. Was it true that he had nothing more to say? No, he had a lot to say ... about Federico Fellini! But it remained to be seen if his dilemmas as man and as artist would interest the rest of mankind.

Finished for the moment with the Fellini world, I was ready to move into that of Pasolini in which I expected to feel more at home, though a little more cynical after my recent experiences with some of his street boys. First, however, was a call for a small part in Dino Risi's new film, *Il Sorpasso*. In English it would be called *The Easy Life* which took the bite out of the Italian title, *The Overtaking*, which referred to the tragic ending and had an allegoric significance for the bittersweet lifestyle of its leading character played with great panache by Vittorio Gassman. I played the cousin of a young man, played by Jean-Louis Trintignant, whom Gassman had swept off in his sports car (after picking him up quite innocently!) on a hot summer day in a deserted Roman piazza. Those of us shooting our sequence didn't know much about what they had been doing 'on the road' but now they had turned up at the country home of the young man's uncle. It was supposed to be in Tuscany but it was shot in a villa off the Via Aurelia, not far into the countryside north of Rome. The cousin I was playing was a rather pedantic middle-class provincial solicitor.

Luciana Angiolillo and John Francis Lane in *Il Sorpasso*.

Jean-Louis Trintignant and Vittorio Gassman in *Il Sorpasso*.

During their visit, Gassman guesses I was not sired by the uncle but by their sturdy farmhand who, with us in the drawing room, is treated as one of the family. As I ranted on, I had to twitch my finger in the same way the ageing yokel did. I never knew who was cast first, the farmhand because he looked like me or me because I looked like him!

On the second of my two scheduled day's work, the late afternoon sun was setting before they had done my close-up. I, and the actress who played my wife, were sitting on a sofa in front of a window through which there had been daylight outside. With the daylight now gone, Risi wanted to wrap the day's shoot, which would mean another day's work (and 40,000 lire!) for me so I was quite happy. But no, the wily producer, Mario Cecchi Gori, gave orders to move the sofa so that the camera couldn't see the window which, instead of 40,000 lire, meant for me another two hours work and I was already getting tired. Several takes were necessary before Risi was satisfied that I had spoken the lines exactly in Italian so he'd be able to post-synch me perfectly.

The whole sequence in the farmhouse would become one of the most praised scenes in the film, especially for its conclusion when the two men, the extrovert Gassman and the introvert Trintignant, drive off, and the aunt's sister, with whom Trintignant had been infatuated as a boy, is seen at the window looking like a sad wallflower after having been flattered by the ever-seductive Gassman into believing that, if she let her hair down and wore some make-up, she could really still be attractive. The screenplay of *Il Sorpasso*, which Risi wrote with Ruggero Maccari, and future director Ettore Scola, was a masterpiece of the genre and worthy of the best road movies in cinema history. In a book published in 1992, commemorating the 30th anniversary of the making of the film, our episode was the only one published in full.

My cameo promised to me by Pasolini would be, as in *8 1/2*, a scanty appearance in another story of a film within a film. Even so, it would provide me with two of the most memorable weeks of my whole Roman life. The script of *La Ricotta* had been written by Pier Paolo when a producer commissioned an episode for a film in four episodes to be called *Life Is Beautiful*, but the producer was horrified by what Pier Paolo had written, fearing (rightly as it would turn out) that such a daring approach to a religious subject would cause too much of a scandal. Alfredo Bini, who had produced *Accattone* and *Mamma Roma*, read the script and, as he was having trouble setting up another screenplay that Pier Paolo had written which required filming in Africa, he found a French co-producer interested in joining forces in what became a compendium film project. To Pasolini's story would be added others directed by Godard, Rossellini and Ugo Gregoretti. The film would be called *RoGoPaG* after the initials of the four directors' surnames. But only the PPP episode would make cinema history.

Pier Paolo succeeded in persuading Orson Welles to appear as an American director making a biblical film in Rome. Welles had agreed to appear for only $5000 for two weeks work, a fee which was probably much less than what he was usually paid for a day, but the premise appealed to him and he was eager to work with Pier Paolo. I was supposed to play the part of Welles's assistant, which seemed an exciting prospect for Orson was one of my cinema icons. In the end, however, the assistant became a pivotal character in the story, a scatterbrained Italian running around on the set, shouting orders and looking rather idiotic, as he waved his umbrella. Pier Paolo excused himself saying: "I don't think you'd like to horse around so much would you?". He was right. I remained the more 'serious' foreign assistant hovering around the maestro in some scenes, and I am also present at the cocktail party on the set of the film within the film for VIPs from the Roman literati crowd, mostly Pier Paolo's friends. The party takes place at the end of the episode when we were all witnesses to the surrealistic crucifixion scene. The poor devil playing The Good Robber (Mario Cipriani, the elder of the two thieves who led Accattone to his doom) had given his lunch box to his starving family waiting in a nearby field. And, subsequently, as hungry as a dog, he had gobbled up the contents of another lunch box. Having stuffed himself with too much ricotta cheese, he dies on the cross.

As with *8 1/2*, I was grateful to be paid to be present at the ego trip of another director-genius and this time share the limelight with so many celebrities. And I had the extra satisfaction of getting to know Orson himself. He seemed quite happy to hang around even on the days when he had been told he wouldn't be appearing before the cameras. Pier Paolo would apologise to him and Orson would reply, "Don't worry, it's a pleasure for me to sit around and watch you all at work". It was a pleasure to be able to chat with Orson without trying to do an interview. I knew from past experiences, first with Laughton and then with Burton, that famous actors stop being polite to you and stop talking off the cuff when they learn you're a journalist. On the first day, Pier Paolo had warned Orson that I was a journalist but he seemed quite happy to talk to me. I asked him if I could quote him. He smiled and said "Okay". Only once or twice did he beg me not to quote what he'd said. I published the interview in *Films and Filming*, including some of his not very generous remarks about Visconti and Antonioni which he hadn't told me not to quote. He admitted he'd been one of those in Venice in 1948 who had hated *La Terra Trema*: "Visconti looks at the poor as if they were illustrations for *Vogue*." Of Antonioni he said: "A film about boredom is so boring!".

Orson refused to receive any press people who came to the set. I think I won his sympathy because I was able to tell him that I had seen his double-bill of plays in Paris in the early 1950s, his bizarre re-hash of *Dr. Faustus*, with the then unknown Eartha Kitt, and the other short play, *The Unthinking Lobster*, about Hollywood

John Francis Lane, Pier Paolo Pasolini and Orson Welles on location for *La Ricotta*.

being turned into a second Lourdes after a real miracle happens during the filming of a saint's life. A looking glass reflection, of sorts, of Pasolini's film. Orson said it had been years since he had met anyone who had seen those one-off performances. I'd notice that while sitting around on the set he'd be reading something by Melville. In the finished film, however, we'd see Orson, the director of the film-within-the-film, reading aloud the last lines of a poem by PPP published in his diary of the making of *Mamma Roma*,

Alan Midgette reads, whilst John Francis Lane sits in the director's chair on location for *La Ricotta*.

some of which was shot on the same location. In the film, Orson's voice would be dubbed by the Italian writer, Giorgio Bassani. The lines begin: "I am a power from the past...", and include, "I am running around the Tuscan Way like a mad man/ And the Appian Way, like a stray dog."

During those two weeks in the sun, in the fields between the two modern roads between and named after the ancient Roman highways, the Appia and the Tuscolana (the latter where the Cinecittà studios are situated), I tried my best not to get too friendly with the crowd of PPP types on the set, some of them quite attractive and most of them enjoyable company. I didn't want to take any further risks. The most interesting casual acquaintance I made on the set was a young American called Alan Midgette, who would become famous in America as a look-alike of Andy Warhol, whom the pop artist would employ as a stand-in when he didn't want to bother attending social events. We shared a fascination in watching a real poet like Pasolini engaged in inventing cinema according to how he saw it, not in accordance to studio formula. Alan would play a leading role in *Before The Revolution*, directed by a visitor to the *RoGoPaG* set, Pier Paolo's friend and former assistant, Bernardo Bertolucci.

Two weeks after we finished shooting we were called back. A field in Cinecittà was being used as the setting for a linking shot close-up of Orson Welles. He had flown back from Paris two days earlier than was needed, and nobody had thought of telling him that we were shooting at Cinecittà, so he had climbed to the top of the Appian hill and found nothing but the mushroom growers. The close-up took about ten minutes to shoot. Then Orson went back to Paris to tackle Kafka. He was making a film of *The Trial*.

That October ended with bad news from the real world, which I had been ignoring during the blissful PPP festive fortnight. First was the death of Enrico Mattei, killed in an air crash flying back to Milan from Sicily. The crash was rather mysterious. Many felt immediately that it was not an accident but an assassination organised by the petroleum cartels who objected to the way he had been doing private deals with the oil-producing countries in Middle East on a 60-40 percent basis in the Arabs' favour. Mattei, (who Time Magazine described as 'the most powerful Italian since Caesar Augustus') had been the only public figure in Italy whose chief interest seemed not to be pocketing profits for himself or his friends, but in getting the satisfaction in assuring that his actions were helping the nation to protect the interests of the majority, and without political rhetoric.

Pasolini wrote a canvas for a novel called *Petroleum*, published posthumously by his heirs, in which in addition to homoerotic fantasies that he might have cut if he had lived to publish the book himself, is his hypothesis about those who might have been responsible for Mattei's death. That part still causes controversy today. In 1972, ten years after Mattei's death, Francesco Rosi, many of whose extraordinary films have recounted the ambiguous Italian realities of the second half of the 20th Century, made a film about Mattei, and the mystery of his death, called *Il Caso Mattei* (The Mattei Affair) co-scripted with Tonino Guerra, in which Gian Maria Volonté, as Mattei, gave one of his greatest performances. Another unsolved 'Italian mystery' emerged from Rosi's film. A Sicilian journalist called De Mauro, who had been commissioned by Rosi to research the Mattei affair, disappeared and was never heard of again after a phone call with Rosi in 1970.

The other worrying news came from Cuba where Kennedy was imposing a blockade to stop the Soviets from setting up missile bases. Khrushchev had replied that the Americans had missile bases in Turkey, which was as much within range of the Soviet

Union as Cuba was to the U.S. The world was in a panic again but the crisis would be settled by compromise. The Third World War of the century was once again postponed.

Another acting cameo came my way in early November, offered to me by Gianni Buffardi, the producer for whose *Il Mare* I had written the subtitles. Buffardi was making a film with his father-in-law, the self-proclaimed Prince of Byzantium, Totò. The film was *The Two Colonels*. Totò was the Italian colonel. His English counterpart, in an exchange of military and philandering frolics, was Walter Pidgeon. I was a British sergeant and I had some amusing scenes in which I went over the top, as usual. The director, Steno, a respected maker of popular comedies, didn't seem to mind.

With Walter Pidgeon in *The Two Colonels*.

Of course, Pidgeon was bewildered by the whole experience, but I told him what Dietrich had said to me when she was acting with De Sica: "Darling, I've been through the war so I am fortified for the Italian way of making films". Our 'war' was pretty chaotic and the dialogue in English was silly but we managed to cope. As I had found when I did my cameo with Totò and Magnani in the Monicelli film, the comedian was rather sour off screen but very funny when he started making his usual facial comic grimaces in the great Commedia dell'Arte tradition which always provoked ribald giggles from his Italian audiences. Nino Taranto, who played my counterpart, the Italian sergeant, seemed to me a more versatile comic actor.

I had difficulty getting my money out of Buffardi and Titanus who were backing the film but, in the end, I earned enough in those weeks to cover my current domestic and amorous expenses. I had managed to find time to see what, for me, was the best Italian film of the new season, Nanni Loy's *Four Days of Naples*, a sort of *Open City* Neapolitan-style but, of course, more melodramatic. My German friend, Johannes, who had joined me on my excursions in Sicily the summer before, saw the film with me and was probably right when he said the Germans had already decided to retreat to Cassino by the time the Neapolitans started the uprising against them. But this didn't lessen the emotional impact of the battles in the streets and the sacrifices being made by people of Naples. They were like characters from Eduardo De Filippo plays, acted superbly even by those who were not professionals. I wrote an enthusiastic piece about it for *The Times* which got a nice spread.

That autumn I went to the British Council, which then was situated in the magnificent Palazzo Drago, just round the corner from the Quirinal palace. I went to hear a talk about William Blake given by the poetess, Kathleen Raine. The lecture was very boring but useful to me because it gave me a few hints on how NOT to deliver a lecture. It helped me to prepare mine, on the British documentary movement, which I was due to deliver there shortly afterwards. My lecture would go down well perhaps because I spoke on a subject about which I felt passionately and I was able to keep my listeners interested by telling personal anecdotes. I told them about my meetings with John Grierson at the Venice Festival. I endeavoured to be informative without seeming too scholastic. I'd repeat the lecture the following week, in Naples, where I was even more relaxed probably because I am always happy to be in Naples. After the Nanni Loy film I had seen a new play by De Filippo called *Il figlio di Pulcinella* (Pulcinella's Son). Though the reviews were less enthusiastic than was customary for Eduardo's plays, it had impressed me enormously. It ended symbolically with the actor playing Pulcinella (Eduardo himself, of course) tearing off his mask and saying he was going out into the streets to face real life. Perhaps it was a bit rhetorical but there was an essential truth there. I had learned from my own experience that the Neapolitans are too inclined to wear masks to hide their real selves.

Naples remained much in my mind that month because I was asked by Francesco Rosi to translate the synopsis into English of what would be his next film to be shot in Naples. For the moment it was called *I padroni* (The Bosses). It was a powerful story of political bosses conniving with speculators to build monstrosities that ruined the city's skyline and town planning. Rosi sent it to Rod Steiger whom he wanted to play the boss of bosses. Having already seen Rosi's *Giuliano* film, the project appealed to Steiger, who agreed to do the film without waiting to see the script.

On December 1st, I had hoped to return to Naples to spend my birthday there basking in the sun and seeing an opera at the San Carlo. Instead I was called for another film, again produced by Buffardi, this time a parody of Dumas's *The Three Musketeers*, now retitled *The Four Musketeers* (I quattro moschettieri); a vehicle for the great comic actor, Aldo Fabrizi, who had played the priest in *Open City*, and Nino Taranto (with whom I had played in *The Two Colonels*), and also for Peppino De Filippo with whom I'd play my scene. The film wasn't due to start shooting officially until the New Year but Peppino wasn't free then, so it was necessary to film his scenes now. He played Cardinal Richelieu. Our scene was shot in the freezing cold castle at Bassano di Sutri where Fellini had filmed the nobility party scene for *La Dolce Vita*. For my cameo, as the rather stupid fiancé of the pretty Milady, I was being paid the same miserable fee as in *The Two Colonels*, even though Buffardi was gloating about the fact that that film had been bought by an English distributor and he said my dialogue would be left in the film in English. I suppose he intended to make me feel flattered.

JFL in *The Four Musketeers*; Peppino De Filippo as Richelieu (right)

Once I had finished that job, and picked up what was still owed to me by Buffardi from the previous film, I took off in the opposite direction from Naples. I had to go to Milan to repeat my lecture for the British Council there. In spite of its aura of bourgeois prosperity, but maybe because of it, this metropolis was still progressive Italy's most stimulating centre of creative activity. It was the home city of another of Italy's great actor-dramatists, Dario Fo, destined to become world famous (and even win the Nobel Prize for Literature). Fo was much in the news for he and his talented and glamorous ex-showgirl wife, Franca Rame, had been guest starring in the popular TV show, *Canzonissima*, which, at the end of every year, becomes the showcase for the Epiphany national lottery. Some of Dario's sketches were daringly anti-conformist for Italian television and I wasn't surprised to hear that the censors had objected to his very left-wing satire. Television at the time was totally under the whipping hand of the Christian Democrats. Anything risky got cut. Naturally, Dario and Franca refused to accept being censored and withdrew from the programme. They wouldn't appear again on TV for another two decades. These were difficult times for artists fighting political battles. I would one day be privileged to get to know and work with Dario when Alan Yentob engaged me as the interviewer and Associate Producer for a BBC programme, directed by Dennis Marks, which we began shooting during carnival in Venice, where Dario performed his *Mistero Buffo*, and which took us across Umbria to Dario and Franca's home, near the Adriatic coast, where we completed the interview.

In Milan, my lecture went down even better than it had done in Rome and Naples. At the dinner party in my honour afterwards, I had an unexpected gracious female companion in my niece from Broadstairs (my step-brother's daughter, Josephine). She was studying ceramics in nearby Cremona. Also attending my lecture, even though he didn't understand much English, was my friend Guido Aristarco, to whose home I was invited to lunch. As usual we had heated arguments over the new films. He didn't consider the Resistance in *The Four Days of Naples* to be "historically accurate". And he didn't approve either of Zurlini's *Cronaca familiare* which, to him, seemed a too novelettish treatment of Fascism. I had a great admiration for Guido, and the theories he was expounding in his *Cinema Nuovo* magazine, but I was beginning to feel he was expecting too much from the cinema. It's rare that a film could touch the heights of the 19th Century novel which he and György Lukács, the Hungarian-born Marxist aesthetics professor, expected of it. He gave me an new edition of his *History of the Theories of Cinema*. I don't much care for cinema theories and was sure I would never be able to translate it for him even if we found an interested publisher.

Thanks to the director of the British Council, I had the good fortune to be invited to the glamorous ceremonial inauguration of the new Scala season on December 7th, the feast day of the city's patron saint, Ambrose, in whose honour the city gives itself a public holiday. The opera chosen to open the season was *Il Trovatore*, starring my two favourite singers of the moment, Franco Corelli and Antonietta Stella. Both were in good form even if it was sad to see that the handsome tenor was beginning to put on weight. He and Stella were upstaged, on this occasion, by a new contralto, Fiorenza Cossotto, and the baritone, Ettore Bastianini. The production was not exactly up to Visconti standards even if it was staged by one of his protégés, Giorgio De Lullo. I was frankly unimpressed by the glitterati first night audience, the ladies there to flaunt their jewels and their new fashions. Fortunately I was not the only one wearing a blue lounge suit. I had mine with me for the British Council lecture and dinner.

In Milan, I also attended a recital by the famous Greek actress, Katina Paxinou. I was disappointed to find that instead of the heartfelt peasant acting style, which we had appreciated in *For Whom The Bell Tolls*, here she seemed to be trying to emulate the

Duse school of acting and was dressed up like a grand society dame. Indeed, the sophisticated Milanese audience seemed to appreciate her. They got very angry with an academic-looking gentleman who heckled her because she was performing in modern Greek. To most of us it was all Greek anyway. I got more enjoyment in Milan from a concert by Juliette Gréco which made me feel very nostalgic for my student days in Paris.

Returning to Rome, I stopped off in Florence where I'd been invited to the 'Festival of Peoples', which specialised in showing films of social significance. When I arrived, I found an urgent message from the Buffardi office. They wanted me to return to Rome immediately to redub some of my lines in *The Two Colonels*, which Titanus wanted to bring out as a Christmas attraction. So I left the nice warm hotel in Florence, where the festival was putting me up, and I took the train down to Rome early the next morning. I did the chore quickly, shouting my silly lines to the soldiers in the piazza which had been lost when they filmed the scene, and I hurried back to Florence that same evening, after a quick visit from my carabiniere, who was glad to find me in town because he was going on leave for Christmas and, as always, had a problem. He had to pay a debt before leaving town, he said, or he'd be arrested. Of course we were able to give each other what both wanted. I hadn't been to Florence since 1956 when I covered the farcical wedding of Anita Ekberg to Tony Steel. On this visit it was very cold, so I wasn't tempted to cruise around that lovely city. I concentrated my attention on the films and the food, both of which were excellent. I was asked to speak at a debate on the sociological significance of the cinema and, fortunately, I still had my British documentary talk in my head so I translated it ad-lib into Italian and they seemed impressed. I'd always enjoy attending this festival. On a future occasion, I'd write a review for *The Guardian* of *Which Side Are You On?*, the Ken Loach film about the 1984 miners' strike which was banned in the UK and hadn't been shown to the press. And one day I'd be on the festival jury. I knew by now that I would never find a justification for settling permanently in Florence, as I had dreamed of doing when I first visited the city of Michelangelo in 1949, but I was always glad of excuses to come back. Before leaving I managed to see an operatic rarity, a performance of Verdi's early *Attila*, the title role magnificently sung by Boris Christoff.

In Rome, Christmas was already in the air. Among the new film releases, the only one I was particularly intrigued to see was the Russian film which had shared the Golden Lion in Venice, *Ivan's Childhood*. It proved to be a stunning debut by Andrei Tarkovsky, who looked a great charmer when I saw him on TV picking up his Golden Lion. His was a rare cinematic talent blessed with a truly poetic streak. His film told a story about what the Soviets called the "Great Patriotic War" and ended with the Soviet army entering Berlin. But there was none of the rhetorical propaganda usually present in Soviet war films. The main part of the film was about the delicate relationship between two officers of different generations and their tender affection for a 12 year-old blond boy they use as a reconnaissance scout. The boy doesn't return from the last mission they send him out on, among the birch trees through which the Germans are firing. Tarkovsky clearly had an innocent love for children and, like De Sica, knew how to direct them sensitively. Perhaps it wasn't difficult to read a homoerotic feeling behind the relationship between the two men but Tarkovsky brought a girl soldier into the story to make sure we didn't get the wrong idea.

Later in the 1960s, on my first visit to Moscow, I was working at Mosfilm Studios and I found that Tarkovsky was much respected there even if feared by the Soviet authorities. Thanks to Sean Connery, with whom I was working in Moscow (on the film *The Red Tent*), I'd have a chance to meet Tarkovsky and to see a very private screening of *Andrei Rublev*, still at that time a forbidden film, but destined to be seen round the world and win acclaim as a cinema masterpiece. Like Maxim Gorky, earlier in the century, Tarkovsky would end his days in Italy.

That Christmas, I was one of the journalists who received generous gifts from film producers showing their gratitude for the attention we had given them during the year. My friend, Guglielmo Biraghi, critic for Rome's leading newspaper, *Il Messaggero*, told me it was a regular custom and none of them considered it a bribe. Dino De Laurentiis sent me a case of six bottles of whisky. Alfredo Bini, the producer of *Accattone*, sent me two bottles of champagne. Gustavo Lombardo, who should have been grateful for my articles on *The Leopard* and *The Four Days of Naples* in *The Times*, didn't even send me a Christmas card. However, the big event of 1962's end-of-year festive period for me was an invitation to Rome's biggest theatre, the Teatro Sistina, for the first night of a new show by the authors and impresarios of Italy's most famous musical comedies, Pietro Garinei and Sandro Giovannini. The show was *Rugantino*. The score by Armando Trovajoli included several hit songs including one dedicated in dialect to Rome, *Roma nun fa' la stupida stasera* (Rome Don't Play Stupid Tonight). The show starred Aldo Fabrizi as Mastro Tito, the last executioner in papal Rome. One of his last victims was a goodhearted lack-adaisical Trastevere lad, Rugantino, an historical figure who fell foul of the nasty young 'dolce vita' Roman aristocrats of those years. Rugantino was played and sung by one of the most talented and sympathetic young Roman actor-singers of those times, Nino Manfredi. Rugantino's girlfriend was played by Lea Massari, the actress who played the girl who disappears in *L'avventura*. I wrote an enthusiastic review of the delightful show and immediately sent it off, with a photograph, to *The Times*.

So the year in which I had finally become an official Roman resident was ending well for me. I felt I had honoured my adopted city. The latest issue of *Films and Filming* (dated December 1962) contained a long piece I had written on the 'Italian Decade'. In spite of the stupid title given to it by the editor, Peter Baker ('Oh! Oh! Antonioni!') I felt I had made a good summing up of the impress-ions which had matured since I started writing about and living with the Italian cinema of those years. I was sorry that I had never followed up the encouragement given me by Tom Maschler in London to write a book on my first-hand experience of the neo-realist cinema and the new generation that was emerging afterwards. Like most of the literary projects I had in those years, I was too absorbed in living the experience to write more than a diary record of what I was doing and the people I was meeting. Over the years, many others would write the story of the period which they had not lived in, those 'dolce vita' years about which I'm now writing here. But for the moment, I was too distracted by the 'dolce' and 'amaro' of my life as a Roman.

To see the New Year in, I had bought a ticket in advance for the Foreign Press Club party where our annual film award would be announced. I knew it was going to *Salvatore Giuliano*, a film that had been part of my 1962, and I had promised Francesco Rosi I'd be present. So I put on my tuxedo and took the bus over to the club where I found the party warming up. Rosi was with his wife, Giancarla, and they insisted I join them at their table, where Cristaldi had already ordered the champagne, but, because I had to take part in the ceremony, I moved to another table for the supper, which included turkey and lobster, because I didn't want my colleagues to see me being too friendly with the winner of our top award. After the end of the ceremony, and the explosion of New Year wishes to everyone (we were indoors of course so could only imagine the hoodlum going on outside), I left the party and managed to find my way on foot back to Trastevere, picking my way carefully through the rubbish that people had thrown out of the window when the New Year came in. Rather than join the merrymakers in the Trastevere streets, I climbed the stairs wearily and went to bed alone. I was woken up early the next morning by a phone call from the station from my carabiniere lover who said he would come straight over even if there were no buses running on New Year's Day. He stayed until the late afternoon when he had to report to the barracks. It was the best way I could have started 1963. I wasn't sorry to see him go because conversation was starting to run short and we'd made love twice. Left alone for the evening, I was able to listen on the radio to a performance from La Scala of Rossini's *Semiramide* with the magnificent Joan Sutherland. I don't think my friend would have appreciated it.

My enthusiastic review of *Rugantino* appeared in *The Times* on January 1st but I didn't find out until the day after when the paper arrived in Rome. My review induced two American impresarios to fly to Rome to see the show, one of whom wanted to translate it into English for an American cast, while the other, who would win his way, wanted to sign up the whole Italian company and take *Rugantino* to Broadway after it finished its run in Rome.

There was further consolation when the 100th issue of *Films and Filming* arrived in January 1963. It had Peter O'Toole in *Lawrence of Arabia* on the cover. Among the contents of this bumper 100-page edition was a fascinating by-line piece by David Lean himself writing about the making of *Lawrence*. At the time of *Brief Encounter* (1945), when I was a young man in England, Lean was the contemporary director who meant the most to me. Subsequently, I found others to admire more but I continued to have great respect for Lean's professional and imaginative flair, of which *Lawrence of Arabia* would remain a prime example. The January 1963 issue also included articles about the four international sex symbols known in the media by their initials, France's BB (Bardot), the US's MM (Monroe), the UK's DD (Dors) and Italy's CC (Cardinale). The piece dedicated to CC was written by me. I predicted for her new heights of stardom in 1963 thanks to Fellini and Visconti. I didn't know then that Fellini would be the first to let her dub

herself with her own disarmingly raucous voice. In the article I
mentioned that the novelist, Alberto Moravia, who liked to consider
himself Italy's leading authority on the female body, had published
an interview with CC which had begun with him addressing her
with these words: "I don't want to know what your opinions are
on politics, love, art, women, men, Italy, the United States, the
movies, religion, cooking and so forth. Nor does it interest me to
know how you live or with whom you live, what pictures you have
made to date and what your plans are for the coming months or
the coming year". He admitted that he wanted only to write about
her body. I, a humbler interviewer than Moravia, when received in
Claudia's delightful presence, would have liked to ask her about
the very matters that had not interested the author of *Woman of
Rome* and *Two Women*. I wrote that I thought of asking her to
describe Moravia's brain as he had described her body. But though
Claudia had a lively sense of humour it would have probably
embarrassed her. She was about to star in Citto Maselli's film of
Moravia's first novel, *The Time of Indifference*, so she must have
read that at least. On the table in the room where I interviewed
her there were newspapers with headlines about the Cuban Missile
Crisis and the threat of World War Three. But Moravia was right.
How could one talk about serious matters to a young woman
whose beauty and smiling charm were so overwhelming even to
one like myself, who was more inclined to go into raptures over
her recent co-star, Alain Delon, than over her (I didn't write that
in my F&F portrait). However, I did write that I was sure that CC
would still be a great star when the papers had all forgotten about
the Cuban crisis and Fidel Castro. I described how the CC myth
had been created in the years following her trip to Venice in 1957
as a Tunisian teenager who had been given a free trip to the film
festival because she had been chosen as the most beautiful Italian
girl in Tunisia. At the time I interviewed her she was playing
opposite David Niven and Peter Sellers in *The Pink Panther*, the

setting of some sequences of which had been transferred from the South of France to Italy, because Blake Edwards wanted her for the exotic role of an Indian Princess. Indeed I was to quote her as saying that, after only four years in films, she had discovered that it wasn't necessary to go to Hollywood to have a career in American cinema: "They come to Europe to make films these days".

Early in the New Year I called on Fellini at the dubbing studios and found Marcello doing post-synch on the two endings of *8 1/2*. A month before the film was due to open Federico still hadn't decided which one he was going to use. I sent stills taken on the set by the photographer, Paul Ronald, to Peter Baker to include with my article on Italian cinema for his upcoming series on 'The Face of 1963'. The article began with me saying that the future of the Italian film industry in 1963 would depend much on the outcome of the three 'colossals' made in Rome: the Italian, *8 1/2* and *The Leopard*, which cost three million pounds between them, and the American *Cleopatra*.

The Sunday Times called and asked for some extra paragraphs and pictures for an article about the Fellini film I'd written for them. Their request coincided with a telephone call from Ian Dallas asking when there'd be a screening. He sounded sorry for himself for his sudden departure from Rome. He had left without paying back some of the money he'd borrowed from friends. I was fond enough of him to forgive him. As I had not mentioned him in my original *Sunday Times* copy, I was now able to add in a bit about how he came to be cast. Better that I should tell the real story of how he met FF rather than let Ian invent his.

Soon after the Epiphany of 1963 I was to interview, for the first time in many years, another Italian star who was making her name in the American cinema without settling permanently in California, Sophia Loren. I was received by her in the palazzo opposite the Capitoline Hill where Carlo Ponti had his headquarters. Sophia gave me a warm reception and reproached me for having put on so much weight since she last saw me. "You like our pasta too much, eh?" she said in English. Indeed we hadn't seen each other since early 1958. We had a laugh about that unconvincing melo, *Legend of the Lost*, on which I'd worked at Cinecittà. It had been beautifully filmed in the desert and the magical ruins of the Roman city of Leptis Magna in what was then the Kingdom of Libya. I complimented Sophia on her English and on her acting which was better than that of her co-stars John Wayne and Rossano Brazzi. I also complimented her on *El Cid*, adding rather naughtily that maybe her Neapolitan accent in the Italian dubbed version was not appropriate. We'd been speaking in Italian till then but she suddenly burst into broad American again, exclaiming to the publicity people in the room with us: "Look who's talking! This guy has been around in Italy for I don't know how long and he still speaks Italian like an English governess!". I deserved that!

Carlo Ponti, Sophia Loren, and Oscar.

The interview proceeded in English and the meeting ended amicably. Sophia would always greet me warmly in future years and I'd always admire her but, with hindsight, it is interesting to note that though she made scores of American films, often with great directors, and she won acclaim as one of the great stars of the century, as had Gina Lollobrigida, and would probably be the case with Claudia Cardinale, it would be for their Italian films that they would be most remembered.

The following evening I went to the premiere of *The Two Colonels*. The producer, Buffardi, who was there with the star of the film, his father-in-law Totò, made me pay for my own ticket though my name was on the up-front credits. My lines, and those of Walter Pidgeon and the other English soldiers, were left in English with subtitles, but Pidgeon spoke in Italian with Totò and the other Italians. It sounded like his own voice. Indeed he had in fact dubbed himself into Italian. The audience seemed to enjoy the film but I felt a bit embarrassed and didn't think it stood much chance of being shown abroad even if Buffardi boasted that it had been bought by a British distributor. In that week's *Variety*, a review of the film appeared, written by the Rome correspondent, Hank Werba. He kindly gave me a flattering mention: "Francis Lane neatly shapes a tongue-in-cheek version of the duty-bound British sergeant." (January 16, 1963). My 'career' as an actor was indeed blossoming. *Il Sorpasso* was the hit of the season at the box-office (and would remain a cult classic of Italian film comedy). Some time after the film opened, during a visit to Tuscany, while dining with Anglo-American friends in a restaurant outside Siena, a fellow diner, hearing me speak English, came over and asked: "Excuse me, sir, aren't you the actor who played in *Il Sorpasso*?". When I nodded an affirmative, he enquired caustically: "Please tell me. Are you a Tuscan pretending to be English or were you an Englishman pretending to be Tuscan in that film?". Obviously I had been well-dubbed. The Tuscan accent was not mine.

I saw a preview of Marco Ferreri's *L'Ape Regina*, its Italian title modified into the meaningless *Una storia moderna* (A Modern Story) to placate the censors. The film had run into trouble with the censors even before it had opened. I could see why. It was a very black comedy with a cruelly ironic attitude to religion. Ugo Tognazzi's acting was superb. My cameo as a Jesuit priest giving a lesson on ethics came over very well. I had re-seen Marco's *El cochecito* which I appreciated even more now that I was familiar with him and his iconoclastic style of film-making. Its satire was more bizarre than in his new film, but the transfer into his own world of tongue-in-cheek anti-clerical irony was a success.

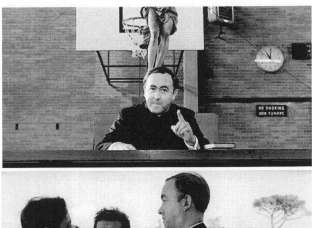

John Francis Lane with Ugo Tognazzi in *L'Ape Regina*.

It heralded the arrival of another major director for the Italian cinema and a hat trick for me as a bit player. I had no qualms in displaying enthusiasm for the film, even though I was in it and my name was on the titles, in a piece that was published by *The Times*. Likewise, *The Times* had printed my article on Bini's film, *RoGoPaG* of which the 'Pa' episode was the only one about which I wrote positively. Pasolini's film deserved particular defence because of the violent reactions against it from clerical circles, who accused it of blasphemy, and because it was a small masterpiece. I was less pleased with a piece, subsequently published in *The Times*, about the new Fellini film which I had still not seen. It was perhaps not surprising that arts page editor, the dear old Mr. Laurence, had cut all references I made to the film being autobiographical. He was probably afraid that I'd got it wrong and that Federico might sue the paper. Little did he know how right I had been.

In the first month of 1963 I was reading a book which had just been published in Britain by Michael Davidson, a freelancer friend who often stopped over in Rome on his way to foreign trips. I had spent much time with him during my first period at the Foreign Press Club and he had helped me to get my first assignment as a stringer for a London paper. On the flyleaf of his book, Arthur Koestler was quoted: "Michael Davidson's autobiography, *The World, the Flesh, and Myself* starts with the sentence: 'This is the life story of a lover of boys.' It is in fact the twofold story of a courageous and lovable person's struggle to come to terms with his Grecian heresy and of a brilliant journalist's fight against Colonial jingoism from Zululand to Cyprus". An impressive tribute from such a distinguished writer. Michael and I often lunched together, exchanging anecdotes about our journalistic experiences and our communal 'Grecian heresy'. His boys were much younger than the ones I enjoyed the company of and, in the afternoons when we parted, we'd go to different cinemas in search of the company that suited our tastes.

Images from Fellini's *8 1/2*,

Chapter 20

When I was finally invited to a screening of *8 1/2* my first reaction was one of disappointment. Maybe I was too aware of how Fellini was playing tricks in order to disguise the truth that he hadn't anything to say other than: "You see, you all took me too seriously with *La Dolce Vita*. Maybe I took myself too seriously. Now you know that I just want to enjoy myself making a film, putting into it all the things that I have liked most in my life, some of them real some of them just dreams". As Angelo Rizzoli had made so much money out of the previous film which, as producer, he never really believed in, and had not been generous in terms of salary with Federico, it was considered poetic justice that the money should be found to produce a film which mass audiences would probably never understand even if, inevitably, it would please directors who could envy a colleague who had found a producer to let him take such a costly self-indulgent ego-trip.

After that first screening, while stunned by the beauty of it all, I felt let down. The ending, with Ian as a sort of ringmaster bringing on all the people we have met in the director's story, the most fascinating of whom come from Federico's own adolescent memories, all surrounded by clowns to the strains of Nino Rota's wondrous melody, was visually stunning but it was a cheat. The pessimistic alternative ending, in which we would have seen them all on the train disappearing into the tunnel and not knowing where they were going, would probably have been more honest. Only when I saw the film a second time, at the end of the same week, did it come to me that perhaps Federico was indeed being more honest in this ending, admitting that he was unable (or unwilling?) to offer a way out. But it seemed to me too easy to escape this way.

I had an invitation to the gala premiere so I put on my smart clothes and went to see the film for the third time in a week. Whereas I appreciated even more the purely aesthetic qualities, the visuals, the sound, and most of the performances, including Ian's, I got rather bored and I felt this was the reaction of the majority of the audience who only applauded politely. On the way out, I ran into Michelangelo and Monica and they too seemed to be unenthusiastic. What lets the film down most, in my view, was that it's difficult to believe in the director, played too impassively by Marcello, who is dressed like Federico but who does not have Federico's fascinating personality as a director and as a man. This is Federico's greatest leg-pull. Nobody could say that 'Guido' could have made films as great as *I Vitelloni* or *La Dolce Vita*. Was he just a Henry Hathaway or a Delmer Daves, to name two Hollywood professionals I had seen at work close to? But perhaps I knew too much about the problems of the film's creative progress and I would have to wait a while to try and be more objective about it.

In mid-January 1963, I visited one of the most magnificent art exhibitions I'd seen in Rome in the past decade. Dedicated to Mexican art, it brought back memories of that stop-over in Mexico City in 1936 when my father took me and my mother on a transatlantic cruise to the West Indies and Central America. The whole Mexican experience, including the visit to the Aztec pyramids, had remained etched in my memory. The exhibit also reminded me of a more recent experience in Italy. In 1955, I had co-translated into Italian the biography of Eisenstein by Marie Seton who had known the great Russian director well. In 1932, in Moscow, she had seen how depressed he was after his return to the Soviet Union after three years on the American continent. He was deeply embittered that he had not been able to finish his film about Mexico. He had shot only the prologue, the epilogue, and some other sequences, before the American left-wing novelist, Upton Sinclair, who had found backing for the project, withdrew his

Images from *Time in the Sun*, Marie Seton's film assembled from footage shot by Eisenstein.

support and refused access to the footage Eisenstein had filmed with his great cinematographer, Eduard Tisse. Marie Seton wrote in her biography that, in 1929, Eisenstein had been given permission to travel abroad to lecture and study the consequences of the newly invented sound film. In the U.S. he was obliged to abandon a first project to film Theodore Dreiser's *An American Tragedy*, to which he wanted to give what was considered a too anti-American slant. His interest in Mexico had been aroused apparently by a young Mexican film student he met when he was lecturing in New York. Marie Seton wrote: "as a mature man in his middle thirties, (Eisenstein) poured all of himself into this Mexican project... (the film) was to express his most intimate thoughts and emotions, his personal philosophy, his idiosyncrasies and his concept of a civilization". She added: "as Eisenstein planned it the film would have been the most gigantic anyone ever attempted in the film medium." (I'd add 'since Griffith made *Intolerance*'). In 1939, Seton went to New York and did everything in her power to try to obtain the material, still intact, and get it back to Eisenstein, but she was not successful. A bowdlerized version of Eisenstein's footage was released in the USA and the UK with the title *Thunder Over Mexico*, which film intellectuals, including John Grierson, protested had little to do with Eisenstein's original project. Seton would eventually succeed in purchasing 16,000 feet of the original 170,000 feet of material shot and, with Paul Burnford, in the 1940s would put together a medium-length film called *Time in the Sun* which didn't pretend to be Eisenstein's original film. When Marie Seton came to Rome in March 1955, for the launch of our Italian translation of her Eisenstein biography, she showed her film. On the flyleaf of my copy of her book, she wrote: "To John-Saint Francis, who nearly sacrificed himself to save the day". I don't remember why I deserved such thanks but probably, as usual, I was taking sides in some Italian controversy that conflicted in this case with her interests.

After seeing that marvellous Mexican art exhibition which, like Eisenstein's project, illustrated the whole of that country's history from ancient times to the dictatorship of modern times, I returned to my Eisenstein studies. I looked up my copy of the original script outline of *Que Viva Mexico*, which I had bought when it was published in 1951. It had a well-informed introduction by Ernst Lindgren explaining the whole saga of how Upton Sinclair panicked when his backers refused to provide any more finance for the Russian director's Mexican follies. In a review of Seton's book, when it was published in England in 1952, Thorold Dickinson had written that: "Eisenstein made the mistake of assuming that the average audience has a brain and can react en masse to an intellectual argument". I still had Eisenstein in my mind when I attended the gala premicre of Fellini's film. I felt that I was beginning to understand it.

The weather, which had been Spring-like in January, turned very cold in February and Rome suffered a cold spell even worse than the 1956-57 winter I had spent in my rented room in the streets behind the Piazza Navona. In Trastevere we were freezing indoors without adequate heating, but John K. and I, and our funny little dog we called 'Horse', had fun in the snow on our communal terrace and we appreciated the view of the snow-covered rooftops. Less entertaining was the fact that the fragile water pipes, exposed on the roof to the freeze-up, were inclined to burst and the landlord's rather jaded old handyman, named Machiavelli, had to climb precariously to the roof above to fix them.

In March, I went to Naples to visit the set of Francesco Rosi's new film, now called *Hands Over the City*. As a guest of the production company, I was given a room in the glamorous Excelsior Hotel which overlooked the Castel dell'Ovo below and which gave a view of the whole bay beyond. I was told that Rosi was not yet back from Paris where he had gone for the premiere of *Salvatore Giuliano*. The PR man, Enzo de Bernart, a good friend who had organised that dramatic public screening in Giuliano's home village in the hills above Palermo, took me, and other reporters who had arrived, to dinner at the hotel. We argued a lot about *8 1/2* and, to my surprise, I was the only one defending it. Later, in the TV lounge, we watched communist leader Palmiro Togliatti at a press conference for the upcoming elections. The employees of the hotel kept nipping in to watch but the American guests in the hotel were dismayed when they realised we were all watching a communist leader and that he was getting such exposure. Togliatti had all the replies for the questions about the failure of the government to resolve Italy's problems and he reproached them for agreeing to join NATO's multilateral nuclear force. He didn't find it so easy to reply to questions about the growing dissent in the Iron Curtain countries.

Rosi arrived at midnight and we had a brief chat. He told me that *Giuliano* had been rapturously received in Paris and he hoped I'd be in London for the opening there of my subtitled version. I asked how he was getting on with Steiger and he hinted there had been problems but that all was working out for the best. "You'll see when you come on the set," he told me.

The next morning, Steiger wasn't working when I arrived at a picturesque backstreet near the harbour, where Rosi was preparing a take with the inhabitants themselves playing extras. This was the street behind the building that we see collapsing in the film. The sequence was being filmed from a height at one end of the street. It was an introduction to the daily life of the inhabitants who were to protest because they were to be evicted so that the building speculators could construct a new housing estate. There wasn't much space from where I could watch the shooting so I didn't stay long. When I came back in the afternoon I found them preparing a tracking shot along the street. The director of photography, Gianni Di Venanzo, and his cameraman, Pasqualino De Santis (whom I had watched working with their customary skill on *The Eclipse* the year before) were shooting almost without lights because they wanted a documentary effect. They had placed some lighting inside a few doorways. In one of them it served to show a typical good luck horn hanging at the entrance which the set decorator hadn't needed to add. There were problems with the crowds who were being paid a modest sum as extras but who were inclined to be temperamental. For example, in the scene showing the police throwing them out of their homes, the male extras, in particular, were expressionless. For them it was just a job and they were beginning to look bored by the natural slowness of shooting. Franco lost his temper. The assistant called for silence which he got. Franco then took a megaphone and delivered a homily in a Neapolitan dialect, reminding them that he was making the film to help them and their children have a better future and not become victims of those who were speculating at their expense. "Can't you get it into your thick skulls that I'm making this film for you?" There were some shouts from the women, more than the men, saying they understood and would do their best to help. Franco turned to me and winked. The shooting went ahead and he got the reactions he wanted without any more trouble.

During the break, I talked to some of the real actors who were not locals, including a Sicilian actor who had played a police chief in *Giuliano*, and a handsome young man who was playing a policeman. When the handsome young man saw me, he came over to speak to me. We recognised each other. He had played a carabiniere in the sequence of *La Dolce Vita* shot at Ciampino airport when Anita Ekberg arrives. At the time he was a student actor at the Centro Sperimentale film school near Cinecittà. He remembered with a smile that he and a fellow student, also dressed in carabiniere uniform, had posed as if they were arresting me for a photograph taken with my camera by my friend, the future director, Gianfranco Mingozzi. The boy told me he had given up acting, and returned to being a fisherman at Fregene, and was on a visit to relatives in Naples, where he had found the Rosi crew filming, and had obtained a few days work. From some of the remarks the boy made I got the feeling that he had found working in films too "degrading", which made me suspect that he must have been the victim of attempts at seduction. Not surprising seeing his good looks. So I prudently gave up any attempt to pursue a similar 'degrading' objective. The photograph remains as a testimonial to our 'dolce vita' encounter.

On the Saturday evening, I had arranged to get an invitation to the San Carlo opera house for the first night of a new production of a Verdi opera I didn't know, *Luisa Miller*, the first time it had been seen in this opera house since its first performances there in 1849. It was a rather heavy melodrama, based on a Schiller play, but given almost a Neapolitan feel thanks to Verdi's lusty score. Even if not as overwhelming as *Il Trovatore*, it was still worth listening to when sung as well as here and given such an excellent production as that by Franco Enriquez, a director, I gathered from the opera programme, who had been a Visconti assistant. The San Carlo company was due to take the production to the Edinburgh festival that summer. I had not yet met Enriquez and did not know that, one day, he'd invite me to Glyndebourne to see his production there of *Don Giovanni* and, on that occasion, ask me to find an English actor who could speak Italian. I offered my services and he cast me as the Milord in his production of Goldoni's *La Vedova Scaltra* with his company at La Fenice theatre in Venice in 1967.

On the Sunday morning in Naples I went to the Royal Palace to see an exhibition dedicated to 'Caravaggio and the Caravaggeschi'. I ran into Pasqualino De Santis who commented that those few paintings on view by the Maestro himself were enough to give a lesson in lighting to any cinematographer. I had hoped to have lunch with Rosi but he was busy seeing rushes, and had arranged instead a meeting for the evening, so I bought a seat for the matinee at the San Carlo and saw their production of Offenbach's *Orpheus*

Lane as 'Milord' in Goldoni's *La Vedova Scaltra* at La Fenice (1967).

in Hell, which they were filming for RAI-TV. The cameras caused quite a disturbance. *Orpheus* is more an operetta than an opera, and the choreography seemed rather like that of an Italian TV show, but the audience enjoyed it and, in the end, so did I. It didn't finish till quite late so, to my embarrassment, I found that Franco had been waiting for me, a bit impatiently, at the hotel. We had something to eat and we watched the political election debates on television. He seemed tired and I didn't get much of an interview from him. There were others at the table and they talked about politics. I did at least manage to ask him again how Rod Steiger was fitting into the Italian way of working. "It hasn't been easy" he admitted. "Rod is an intellectual, a Method actor, and isn't used to working with non-professionals and, of course, he's acting in English but he's adapting well".

The other pressmen left the next morning but I was allowed to stay. I got to dine alone with Franco in the Excelsior restaurant. He introduced me to spaghetti 'alla puttanesca' which gets it's name 'whorish-style' because of its piquant Neapolitan sauce with capers, peppers and black olives. Franco had pepperish things to say about his approach to film realism. He admitted it was difficult for him as a Neapolitan to get beyond the sentimentality of this city which he had left, as a young man after the war, like most of the Neapolitan intellectuals of his generation who had ambition. Every time he came back, he admitted, he had to try to behave less like a Neapolitan, maybe "more English", Franco added smilingly. I asked him how different this film would be from *Salvatore Giuliano*. "The material in that film was more obviously dramatic. There was the moving story of the picciotti, the Sicilian peasant lads, who were victims of the abuse of power by the police, and also by the politicians and by the bandits, who offered resistance. And there was the stuff of heroism in their struggle. The material of *Hands Over the City* is much more complex, though no less realistic in inspiration. This time I have to seek out the human factor on which to hang my story. I can no longer be an objective observer. I want the characters to be functional, without any fiction attached to their lives. If it is a business man I must show him at work where he does business. The same whether he be a city councillor, a policeman, a bricklayer, or a journalist. To convince an audience that these problems are real, I must show these characters as they really are". I quote these words from my article which *Films and Filming* published in the August issue just before the film was shown at Venice where it won the Golden Lion. A piece about my visit to the location was also published in *The Times*.

In Rome I started writing articles on my Neapolitan visit and another invitation to visit Naples came a week later, this time to attend the inauguration of the new studios there of RAI-TV. I couldn't resist the temptation to accept. The studios were situated in the area beyond the tunnel that runs under the promontory of Posillipo, the most beautiful part of Naples, where there are many ancient and modern villas, including one in which Oscar Wilde lived for a while, when he had abandoned England, after he came out of prison. It was there that he hosted Bosie when they were not supposed to see each other again, if Wilde was to continue receiving an allowance from his wife.

The new residential and industrial area, which one finds after emerging through the tunnel under Posillipo, is known as Fuori-grotta (Beyond the Grotto). In one of the grottos under that hill, Virgil is supposed to have been buried. Among the modern structures of Fuorigrotta is a trade fair and park which I'd one day visit with a BBC crew to film a communist rally jamboree. This time, however, I was there to see the inauguration of the television studios, impressive in themselves, even if the ceremony was a bore. It turned into a promotional election event with the Prime Minister Fanfani making a tedious speech.

I took advantage of this second Naples visit to seek out the Rosi crowd again and this time found them shooting on the top floor, the 30th, of Naples's only skyscraper, partly a chic hotel. Rosi was filming in the restaurant, part of which had been cordoned off and transformed into the offices of Nottola, the character played by Rod Steiger. As Rosi had explained in his interview with me the week before: "if my character is a business man I want to show him where he works." Nottola, a building speculator and a right-wing councillor, is seen in the film during tumultuous council meetings in the city hall but here we see him in his office where he plots his speculating real estate projects. His offices are not in that unattractive new industrial area 'beyond the grotto'. He has a penthouse flat with a view of the whole Bay of Naples. I was finally introduced to Steiger who was polite but I could feel he didn't want to be interviewed. There was no point in telling him that I knew his wife, Claire Bloom, and had worked with her when she was an unknown actress in London.

Rod Steiger in Francesco Rosi's *Hands Over The City*.

Instead, I was glad to lunch with my friend Guido Alberti, the liqueur entrepreneur who, thanks to Fellini, was now pursuing a successful career as a spirited character actor. In *Hands Over The City* he has an important role as a politician of the Nottola clan.

There were urgent jobs waiting for me when I returned to Rome, among which was a commission from Alfredo Bini to do the English subtitles for *RoGoPaG*, still very much in the news because of Pasolini being denounced for offending religion. I was present at a public debate in defence of PPP and Bini, not as one who had appeared in the film but to voice my support as a foreign journalist. I received the first copies of the issue of *Films and Filming*, dated April, which had my article on the Italian Cinema for Peter Baker's series on 'The Face of '63' in leading film producing nations. I wrote that 1963 would be the year in which the Italian cinema was destined to win new prestige with films like *8 1/2*, *The Leopard*, possibly De Sica's *Condemned of Altona* and (I hoped) *Hands Over the City*. And, of course, I found space for some irony over the fact that there was a dubious future for 'colossals' produced in Rome like *Cleopatra*, the costs of which had raised exorbitantly the prices of filming in Rome for the major American companies. Perhaps Hollywood-on-the-Tiber's days were indeed over? Proof of the crisis was that the first Hollywood historical spectacular of 1963 in production in Europe, *The Fall of the Roman Empire*, was filming in Madrid (!). I persuaded a cameraman friend in Rome to shoot some footage for a film about the crisis, which I hoped to sell the next time I went to London.

In March, there was a press conference in Rome for the MPPA President, Eric Johnston, who admitted that the Americans would be making less films in Europe (viz. Italy). The Italian industry itself was already suffering the effects of the crisis and thousands were out of work. Titanus boss, Goffredo Lombardo had overspent not only on *The Leopard* but also on co-producing Robert Aldrich's *Sodom and Gomorrah*. Dino De Laurentiis was launching his new studios with a production of what he ambitiously announced as "The Bible", and for which he optimistically hoped to persuade Fellini and Visconti and maybe even Bergman (!) to direct episodes. And he had proudly announced he had signed up a new star, none other than the ex-Empress Soraya. At the press conference for her, we frankly found it difficult to believe that she would become a new Ava Gardner. Was this the best way of affronting the crisis?

Shortly after the Ides of March, my 12th in Rome, I finished reading the script of Vittorio Gassman's stage version of *The Heroes* which was having a lot of success as a TV mini-series. The show had been performing all over Italy with his Italian Popular Theatre company. Vittorio had prepared this version with his regular (left-wing) theatrical collaborator, Luciano Lucignani, and co-written the commentary with Ghigo De Chiara, theatre critic of the Socialist party newspaper, *Avanti*. I was asked to give my opinion on the commentary they intended to have translated into English and French if it went to London and Paris as now seemed likely. I was embarrassed because on reading it I realised that it certainly wouldn't go down well with an English theatre audience, even less with the critics, who would resent being given a lecture on theatre history. What should I do? Peter Daubeny had invited the show to represent Italy at the Aldwych, where the Royal Shakespeare Company was sponsoring his festival to celebate the Shakespearian quatercentenary. I knew that Peter would not be happy with it as written, but would Vittorio resent my objections? The day I was invited to lunch with Gassman and Ghigo to tell them what I thought about it I plucked up courage and decided to be honest with them. What had I to lose? Fortunately, they were intelligent enough to admit that I was probably right. I came up with an idea that allowed the production to move forward. Vittorio's Peoples Theatre Company had often given performances for working class audiences all over Italy who didn't normally go to see classic theatre. I suggested they present the performance as if it were being given to a factory audience in the Italy of the 'economic miracle'? They liked the idea and immediately began work on the new version.

During the following weeks, I had a one day stint on an American film in the Gidget series, in which I was paid rather well to say one line: "Did you see *La Dolce Vita*?". The lead actor in the film was the glamorous young star, James Darren, whom I was told had threatened to sock me after the sarcastic thing I had written about him in my report on my visit to *The Guns of Navarone* location in Rhodes. Fortunately he didn't recognise me and, on the day's call sheet, I was only named as "Mr. Dolce Vita".

I was briefly distracted that spring by the return of my cara-biniere. He had discovered that his girlfriend in Rome was having an affair with one of his colleagues so he felt less guilty about dedicating some of his passion to me. When his visit was over, I concentrated my attention on preparing for the Gassman show. Vittorio invited me to his house-warming party at his lovely new home on the Aventine hill where he had built a pocket stage from which he entertained his guests. I didn't feel I was really one of his court, and I could see that he realised I was not girl-crazy like most of his hearty friends, but at least he seemed to be grateful to me for what I was doing to help him. Thanks to Gassman I got a small part in a film in which he was starring that Spring, *Il Successo*, directed by Dino Risi even if the credit was being given to Mauro Morassi, one of his ex-assistants. On the night we shot the scene in which I appeared, we were working late in the garden of a villa up in the hills above Rome. I had very difficult lines which I would have liked to have rehearsed with him. But it was getting very late into the night, and Vittorio, who was probably tired too, didn't bother to help me, even treating me sarcastically as if to say: "If you want to be an actor you have to look after yourself!". Fortunately I managed to cope. At that point I was glad that there was no longer talk of my speaking the commentary at the London performances. But I was invited to London and Paris with them.

The Italian elections at the end of April surprised everyone. The Communists had increased their vote considerably but the Centre-Left, though weakened, still had to try to put together the same coalition as before. It was comforting anyway to know that the new generation of Italians was dissatisfied with the way the Christian Democrats and their cronies were running the country, and it was unlikely that a new edition of the previous government would last for long. I wanted to find a paper for which I could write again about politics as maybe the political climate in Italy was at last changing. Before leaving Rome, to meet up with Gassman in Paris, I ran into Fellini. It was the first time I had seen him since my none too flattering piece had appeared in *The Times*. He had seen it. He greeted me angrily and made me get into his car. He drove me out of town towards Fregene where he had a villa.

I didn't feel ready to argue with him as I hadn't yet got over my first reactions. There was a moment when I wanted to get out of the car and find my own way back to Rome but he softened a bit and drove me back, telling me that he was sure I would change my mind. *8 1/2* would win Fellini the top prize in Moscow that summer, while *The Leopard* would win the Golden Palm at Cannes for Visconti. Unfortunately I thought Visconti's film was something of a let-down too. I was to regret this somewhat negative hasty reaction but, in an article published in the Summer 1963 edition of *Sight and Sound* under the title: 'A Case of Artistic Inflation', I put my feelings on these two films, and also on the De Sica-Zavattini *The Condemned of Altona*, a much more serious creative botch. In *Encore*, Ian Dallas had reviewed the Paris production of Sartre's play, with Serge Reggiani "electrifying" in the role of the son dully played by Maximilian Schell in the film. He had described the play as "the most important written in Europe since the war".

In Paris, the Gassman show went down well with the French audience, a bit less well with the snooty critics. We got a few hints as to last minute changes we might make. For the speaker of the commentary in London they found an actor named Jamil, a charming and intelligent boy who, I think, was from Lebanon. Though I was kept busy rehearsing him, I did manage to see one important new film, *Le joli mai*, the new TV-style documentary by Chris Marker. It seemed to me to justify the whole *cinema verité* movement which, for the French, was their reply to neo-realism, and obviously aimed more at TV than cinema audiences. The 'joli' May of the title was that of 1962, the first after the signing of the treaty which ended the conflict with Algeria. The commentary, spoken engagingly by Yves Montand, was full of wit as well as pungent political significance, like the images. Marker had agreed to cut it for cinema release from three to two hours. This was the version I saw in a cinema on the Champs-Élysées where the audience reacted very favourably. It was amazing that such a powerful political film could be made and shown in De Gaulle's France which, maybe, wasn't quite the dictatorship leftist opinion was accusing it of becoming.

In mid-May I was in London, once more 'looking after' an Italian VIP, this time Vittorio Gassman. I stayed again at the Chelsea apartment of Ian's friend, Hugh Hudson, who was away. There was, inevitably, a great social whirl organised around Vittorio, most of it by Peter D. As in Paris, the show went down very well with the first night audience and, surprisingly, with the critics of the more conservative papers like the *Daily Mail* and the *Telegraph*, who accepted, and seemed amused by, the idea of it being performed before an Italian factory audience. Particularly appreciated was Vittorio's hilarious performance as an English 'hero', Edmund Kean, in a scene from Sartre's adaptation of Dumas's play. Vittorio had performed the play on the stage and in a film adaptation (which was more about Gassman's histrionics than Kean's). The 'technical direction' of the film was credited to Francesco Rosi.

Among the heroes that Vittorio and his collaborators included in their show was a contemporary Italian who was theatrical only in his public 'performances' as an agitator. This moving tribute to Danilo Dolci was a scene taken from the social reformer's book, *Waste*. The idea of including it had not appealed to Peter Daubeny when we discussed the show in Rome, because it was not a scene from classical theatre but, as it went down very well with the London audience, Peter didn't complain. For the opening night Peter had succeeded in convincing John Gielgud, Paul Scofield, Peggy Ashcroft and Edith Evans to be present among the celebrities at the Aldwych who applauded Vittorio and his company. Vittorio's flamboyance seemed to have been particularly enjoyed by Lord Harewood, the only culturally competent member of the royal family, who came backstage and said he wanted Vittorio to come to his Edinburgh Festival to play a speaking role in an opera.

For the last night, Olivier came up specially from Brighton, even though he was suffering from gout, and he was very kind to Vittorio afterwards. During the week, Arnold Wesker had come to see the show and suggested that I bring Vittorio to visit the Centre Fortytwo which he was setting up in the Roundhouse, a Victorian engine shed in Chalk Farm, a project very much on the lines of Vittorio's TNP. Vittorio did in fact go with me one morning and was enthusiastic about what Arnold was doing to try to move the magnet of London's theatrical attraction away from the West End, even if a lot of money had to be raised before it could take off. Arnold depended very much on the trade unions but they didn't have the sort of cash that Arnold needed. A commercial success in the West End would remain a playwright's only hope of raising big money. It was sad that Wesker was looked down upon by the snobbish theatrical Establishment in London, even by Peter D. I'm sorry to say. Arnold's Centre Fortytwo would never take off as he had dreamed despite some support from Harold Wilson's Labour Government. However, The Roundhouse itself would carry on and, one day, I'd succeed in bringing to it one of the most enthralling Italian avant-garde shows, Giuliano Vasilicò's fantastical version of *The 120 Days of Sodom*.

When the Aldwych stint was over, with a dull very formal dinner party at the Embassy, I was relieved to feel free at last. I went straight to Eastbourne to stay with my mother and her husband. It was there that I read the Sunday papers and the inevitably nasty review by Harold Hobson in the *Sunday Times*. He wrote he did not want to be treated as an Italian worker going to see classic theatre for the first time. Even Ken Tynan was lukewarm in *The Observer*. But the Sunday papers were full of news from Rome where dear old Pope John was dying. I was sorry not to be there to share the general grief for a Pope who even non-Catholics like myself had admired. I had so many very personal memories of his short but historically important papacy.

I was staying on in London, during the first week of June, because I was still hoping to find a TV company interested in the footage I had shot to illustrate the end of Hollywood-on-the Tiber. But, since we hadn't recorded any interviews, at screenings I could only read my commentary on the crisis as I showed the footage. The only place I got a positive reaction from was the BFI where my friends, James Quinn and Penelope Houston, wanted it to be shown as part of a campaign sending up the expected fiasco of *Cleopatra*, which was due to open any day now in the States. At least by staying on a few more days I was able to see Joan Littlewood's wonderful show, *Oh, What A Lovely War!* which impressed me not only for the quality of the invention behind Joan's production, but also for the way the audience reacted so positively to this striking musical with its mockery of patriotism over our war-hungry century. I hadn't been able to follow all that had been taking place at Joan's Theatre Workshop, to which I had been only once,

Murray Melvin
in Joan Littlewood's
Oh, What a Lovely War!

© David Sim, The Observer

but I knew how important Joan's contribution had been to the changing face of London's theatre-going habits, something that Wesker was struggling to do in his way. Joan's show would have a success in the West End, on Broadway, round the world, even in Italy. I wouldn't meet Joan until 1966 when I went to Tunisia to see *Who is Pepito?*, a show she staged there with local performers. Joan had fled to those shores after the flop of a Robin Hood show called *Twang!* which she had made the mistake of presenting first in the West End!

During my extra week in London, I also enjoyed an evening dining in Islington with David Robinson, the film critic for the *Financial Times*, who was to publish the best biography ever written about Charlie Chaplin. We ate in an Italian restaurant, the Portofino in Camden Passage, next door to the antiques shop David ran with a friend. The food was good and the atmosphere friendly. Rather than talk about films our conversation turned to the bric-a-brac which I'd seen on sale in David's shop, and to the curious hobby of a friend of David's who was eating with us, a collection of pot and pan lids. I could understand now why David had given Visconti's over-opulent *The Leopard* such an enthusiastic review.

On June 4th, we learned that Pope John had died the night before. The funeral, and the subsequent frenzy over the election of the next Pope, would occupy all media attention out of Rome that month, so I knew there was little hope of rousing further interest in my 'film' on the Italian Cinema crisis. I arrived back in Rome on the day that, as had been expected, Cardinal Montini was elected Pope Paul VI. My cameraman, who had spent money of his own on our projected film, was upset that I hadn't been able to find anyone interested. I had lots of other problems too, mostly over debts, and I realised that I faced a difficult summer. I would have to accept as many festival invitations as I could, hoping that my 'crisis' would pass in the autumn before I celebrated my first year as an official Roman resident.

Chapter 21

The first invitation was to Trieste for the Science Fiction Film Festival which Bill Pepper, a fellow Trastevere resident, had asked me to cover for *Newsweek*. He was their Rome correspondent. Trieste had been very much in the news in the early 1950s when the Italians got quite hysterical in a rhetorical nationalistic campaign to have it 'returned' to Italy after post-war squabbles over which nation it belonged to. The return had finally happened in 1954, with a compromise all round, but I gathered that the return to Italy hadn't benefitted the city's prosperity as much as it would have if it been turned into a free port available to all surrounding nations. I had two friends in Rome from Trieste, the film critics Tullio Kezich and Callisto Cosulich. Italians whose surnames end in 'ich' are usually from Trieste. Before starting this visit I refreshed my memory of Trieste's literary connections. I knew that James Joyce had lived there as an impoverished young man when his brother, who was doing business there, had got him a job teaching English at the Berlitz school. I looked up my copy of Richard Ellmann's monumental biography of Joyce and found I had underlined passages in the chapter about 1907 when Trieste was still under Austrian rule. Ellman tells us that one of Joyce's pupils was Ettore Schmitz: "the middle-aged manager of a company that made an anti-corrosive paint for ships' hulls". Joyce became friendly with Schmitz and his wife. One day, Schmitz admitted to Joyce he had started writing books himself, in Italian. He gave two to Joyce to read. One was called *Senilità* (As a Man Grows Older). Joyce read it and was so impressed that he encouraged Schmitz to go on writing. Schmitz would adopt the pen name 'Italo Svevo' and would become one of the most respected Italian novelists of the early 20th century, always recognising that he owed it to Joyce that he had continued writing.

In 1961, I had discovered the writings of Italo Svevo thanks to an exquisite film adapted from *Senilità* directed by Mauro Bolognini. The film benefitted much from the photogenic presence of Claudia Cardinale, made up to look like Louise Brooks. Very appropriately seeing that, though the novel was set at the end of the 19th century, Bolognini had moved the period to the 1920s. However, the dazzling images of Armando Nannuzzi's black and white cinematography were unrecognisable as the taxi took me along Trieste's rather drab modern main street to the Jolly Cavour Hotel where the Festival was putting me up. I'd later discover the city's more alluring areas. Before exploring them I first had to take an interest in Science Fiction, of which I was not an addict, either as a reader or a filmgoer. The screenings were held at night in the courtyard of the castle on the hilltop built in the 15th century and often rebuilt. I was bored by the first films I saw, but the festival (and Science Fiction in general!) were saved for me soon afterwards by a Czech film called *Icarus XB 1* which would share the top prize (named the 'Golden Spaceship') with a new film by *Joli Mai* director Chris Marker, *La jetée*, a chilling, sad, time-travel photo-story. The Czech film told of a spaceship voyage two centuries from now. Its most significant scene came when the voyagers land on a distant planet and discover the relics of a spaceship from 1987. Inside, alongside the remains of the crew, they find a group of what were presumably rich 'dolce vita' travellers. One of the crew of tomorrow's spaceship tells a younger fellow crew member: "In the 20th century they committed such historic crimes as Auschwitz and Hiroshima. They had no values". In my diary I wrote: "reading the newspapers of 1963 it seems we live in suspended time. How absurd it is to still give such importance to Monarchies and Religions. We are making no plans for the future. The myths of Science will be our new religion. No wonder Science Fiction was becoming so popular". I was obviously being converted, even if it was clear that we would have to depend more on the realities of

Science itself than the fantasies of Science Fiction. We'd have to wait another five years before Stanley Kubrick reconciled science and fiction with a cinematic masterpiece.

That I did finally manage to see quite a lot of Trieste was thanks to the enthusiasm of another festivalgoer, an American friend from my Parisian student days, Elliott Stein. Of course we visited the famous Miramare castle on a promontory just outside the city, built in the mid-19th century by the tragically destined Archduke Maximilian, brother of the Habsberg emperor, Franz Joseph. The castle itself had a lovely view over the bay but it was dull inside, very 19th century mittel-European bourgeois in taste. However, in its museum, Elliott and I were able to unravel the fascinating story of Maximilian who had it built as his love nest for the Belgian princess, Charlotte. But, perhaps wishing to prove to the Habsburg family, who had discarded him, that he too had imperial potential, he accepted an offer to become Emperor of Mexico. Though he'd always been a liberal at heart, he was to be assassinated as a reactionary by the republican rebels. Elliott and I would explore other parts of the city but I soon got the impression that his main concern was to make erotic masculine conquests. His conversation made me feel that my own exploits into that kind of promiscuous obsession were much more innocent or anyway at least less dangerous and more humanly rewarding. For me I was just sorry that, during that first Trieste sojourn, my carabiniere friend who was stationed there had been transferred elsewhere to train for a boxing tournament.

From Trieste I went to Verona where I had accreditation for the annual summer Shakespeare Festival. I went there, in particular, to see the much respected Italian stage actor, Giorgio Albertazzi, play Hamlet for the first time. Albertazzi had recently been seen on the screen as the handsome but rather gelid lover in Alain Resnais's *Last Year at Marienbad*. To do the production for *Hamlet* he had brought over a rather academic English director, Frank

Hauser. Though Albertazzi gave an intense performance it was only a try-out for the more impressive one he would give later this same year in a more imaginative production of *Hamlet* by Franco Zeffirelli which, in 1964, would be invited by Laurence Olivier to the National Theatre at the Old Vic in London.

Verona was certainly well worth visiting, another Rome in many ways, with a similar very materialistic feel, but less chaotic. Its Colosseum is the Arena. In the summer they present spectacular opera productions inside it to vast crowds who come from all over the world. In the piazza, in front of the Arena, known as the 'Bra', the locals can sit at the cafes or stroll about without the kind of traffic disturbance you get in Rome itself. Verona's river, the Adige, is much cleaner than the Tiber. And of course, in this city which has inscribed over its entrance gate Romeo's line: "There is no world without Verona walls", Shakespeare is a major tourist attraction, starting with 'Juliet's balcony', a must for visitors especially romancing couples with cameras in hand. Verona is full of enchanting balconies. The *Hamlet* I had come to see was performed in the open-air Roman Theatre, where I also saw a rather lacklustre production of *A Midsummer Night's Dream* starring the ballerina, Carla Fracci as Titania, a great dancer but not much of an actress. Another dancer with a Slavonic name and accent played Oberon. Gian Maria Volonté, destined to become one of the greatest Italian actors of his generation, was rather unfunny as Bottom, while the dull Puck was another future star of Italian theatre and cinema, Giancarlo Giannini. On my next visit to Verona I'd see him as Romeo in Zeffirelli's Italian production of Shakespeare's tragedy.

Back in Trastevere, the end of July's pagan-cum-Christian festive week was in full swing. I enjoyed it with my carabiniere who was passing through on leave and stayed for a few nights, sleeping in my bed with me for the first time. For once, he was more a lover than military trade. Sexual obsession, for which I had reproached Elliott Stein in Trieste, was okay when it was on these terms even if, on those hot summer nights, I didn't get much sleep. I was not sorry when he had to proceed to his home in the South. It meant I could sleep alone for a few nights before enjoying a new festival invitation, this time from one of my favourite places in all Italy, Taormina.

The weather which was not as Sicily should be, summer storms coming a bit too early. The hotel and general hospitality were not as luxurious as when I was there before, and the films were not much better. On the beach, however, to my surprise, I ran into one of my best ex-lovers of recent years whom I'd first met when he was a sailor. When demobbed and back home in Apulia he had offered to come back to Rome and live with me. I had declined his offer. Instead he had found an attractive companion, an obviously well-off local girl whom he had married. She was with him in Taormina. He gave me a warm welcome and he and his wife invited me to what would be the best meal I'd have that whole week in Taormina.

The awarding of what were now the most coveted film awards of the Italian year, the Davids of Donatello, was tedious this year without a Dietrich to add some true glamour. The award for Best Producer went to Goffredo Lombardo, who was probably watching the ceremony on TV from the hospital bed where he was suffering from a nervous breakdown brought on no doubt by the crisis into which his Titanus company had been driven by his mismanagement and overspending. But Lombardo had good credit and the banks would save him. Not all his 'investments' had flopped. *The Leopard* had done well at the box office and that's what counted in an industry which celebrates results rather than methods. The winners of the Davids were still very much chosen according to that criterion. Among the celebrities picking up a David was Vittorio Gassman, once again Best Actor for *Il Sorpasso*. Vittorio seemed unwilling to talk to me about future projects. I realised that if he took *The Heroes* on tour abroad, maybe even to New

York, my presence would no longer be needed. Fellini was also there to receive a David and, though he embraced me as always, he soon started the reproaches even if he hadn't yet seen my article about *8 1/2* in *Sight and Sound* (but neither had I). The best thing for me of the whole week, apart from the meeting with the ex-sailor, was that I was invited by the producer of the Marco Ferreri film to sail back to Rome (or rather to the port of Anzio) on his yacht, as he had to fly back. He told me to protect his girlfriend, presumably from the crew, none of whom seemed to me attractive enough to be likely to stir up the interest of the fiancée and a girl friend who was travelling with her (or yours truly for that matter!). The girls were good company and we enjoyed the cruise passing Stromboli and Capri in the moonlight.

In Rome I learned that Alfredo Bini had been looking for me again. This time he wanted me to translate, maybe even collaborate on, a script which Ugo Gregoretti was to film for him in London. I thought on reading the synopsis that the leading role of a young English lord would be excellent for Tom Courtenay, who I had befriended at one of Peter Daubeny's dinner parties. Though Tom was a Lancashire working-class type he was a good enough actor to play Gregoretti's non-conventional English aristocrat. I also translated an adaptation of *Le cocu magnifique* (The Magnificent Cuckold) for Bini. I wrote in my diary that the script, set in an Adriatic seaside resort, seemed like a "description of the wet-dreams of a seminarist". Not surprising seeing that it had been adapted by the Catholic dramatist, Diego Fabbri, from a 1920s surrealistic erotic farce by the Franco-Belgian Fernand Crommelynck.

In August, I saw the rough cut of *Hands Over the City* which seemed to me an unquestioned masterpiece for its style and content. Rosi asked me to do the English subtitles for the screening at Venice. I set to work immediately. I would have to wait till I came back from Venice to be paid for my summertime translations but, fortunately, before leaving I received a generous payment from the

BFI for my 'Artistic Inflation' article in the summer issue of *Sight and Sound* of which I had finally received a copy. On reading the article in print, I realised that it would not please many people in Italy. I had nothing but praise for the visual qualities of the new films by Fellini and Visconti but I knew that what I had written might upset their producers. I was critical that they had over-indulged the ego-trips of the great director-artists and had let them overspend. Rizzoli could afford to spend what he had earned from *La Dolce Vita*, but in the case of Goffredo Lombardo the overspending, not only on *The Leopard* but above all on the disastrous co-production of *Sodom and Gomorrah*, had been catastrophic. Would I once again be considered a ballsbreaker? The curse or, as I hoped, the distinction, that had plagued me all my life, and which would continue for the rest of my days, was that I always wrote what I sincerely felt without caring what the consequences might be. When I arrived on the Venice Lido for the festival, at the end of August, I found Peter Baker already there. Not surprisingly he greeted me coolly, complaining about my having written that article for the rival magazine. I couldn't resist reminding him that the most serious article I'd written recently on Italian cinema for *Films and Filming* had been given the absurd title, 'Oh! Oh! Antonioni!'. I was glad anyway that my article had appeared in what could then still be considered Britain's most serious film magazine. That Summer 1963 issue had, on its cover, Orson Welles in Pasolini's *La Ricotta*. It carried an intelligent interview with Peter Brook, who was making interesting films at the time (*Lord of the Flies* was in post-production), and there was a fascinating report by Louis Marcorelles, from a conference-festival in Lyon, called 'The cinema of Immediacy' where, in addition to the extraordinary *Le Joli Mai*, there were new works by directors such as Jean Rouch, Richard Leacock and Albert Mayles. Present in Lyon was Rossellini whom Marcorelles reported as having accused Mayles, and his brother who co-authored his film, of "sacrificing too much to a dangerous modern passion for the formless and the shapeless". This seemed like a dig at Jean-Luc Godard who considered himself a disciple of Rossellini. Marcorelles added that Rossellini's latest film, shown at Lyon, was the: "too beautiful *Vanina Vanini* which showed how dangerous such pointless aestheticism can be". I felt indeed I was in good company in that issue. Anyway, I was glad that Peter Baker was fortunately enthusiastic about Rosi's *Hands Over the City* and, in his report from Venice, would write that it deserved the Golden Lion. He even quoted what JFL had written in F&F about Rosi's film when shooting in Naples.

Peter was also full of praise for Louis Malle's deeply moving film *Le feu follet*, which we had all admired. It only won the Jury's second prize and there was an uproar at the final ceremony when the awards were announced. The protest was created only in a small part by Malle's supporters who thought he deserved the top prize. It came mostly from the pro-Catholic crowd who had objected to Rosi's attack on the corruption by the Christian Democrat politicians in Naples. On the steps outside the Palazzo del Cinema, after the press screening of Rosi's film, I had a violent argument with Gian Luigi Rondi, who would never normally let his hair down in public, but this time his own political feelings as a conservative Christian Democrat make him forget he was an excellent film critic. His very negative review of the film, in the Rome right wing paper, *Il Tempo*, the next day would begin "No, no, no…". In 1961, Pier Paolo Pasolini had included in an appendix of epigrams to his collection of poetry entitled *The Religion of My Time*, one dedicated to Rondi: "You are such a hypocrite that when hypocrisy will have killed you, you'll be in Hell but you will believe you're in Paradise". I was in Venice that year more than anything to offer my solidarity to Rosi and his film, but I was also hoping I'd be able to help set up the Gregoretti film in London. Both Ugo and his producer, Bini, were due on the Lido for the presentation of Ugo's new film *Omicron* and I knew that Tom

Courtenay would be there for Schlesinger's *Billy Liar* (John and I had an amusing time cruising around the Lido). I wanted Tom and Ugo to meet and see each other's films. I gave Tom a copy of my translation of the synopsis for the proposed film to be shot in 'Gregoretti's England', and he was immediately enthusiastic. Unfortunately he told his agent about it and she grabbed Bini as soon as he arrived. I had been planning to bring them all together much more diplomatically. Obviously Ugo was, for the moment, more concerned about the festival screening of *Omicron*. It was understandable that Bini also thought it inopportune that I should be already interfering with the casting. I did succeed in bringing Ugo and Tom together eventually and they seemed to get along well but his agent was still around. I had probably botched my chance of working on the film. *Omicron* did not get the reception that Bini had hoped for, either with the press or with the public. Indeed it lacked the charms of Ugo's previous films. It was clear that the English film project was now unlikely to take off. I would have to wait to get my 'English' experience with Gregoretti, when he made a witty six-part mini-series, *The Pickwick Papers*, in 1968.

For September, I had another festival lined up as an alternative stand-by to my possible work as an actor or a writer. The British Embassy had asked me if I would like to represent the UK on the jury of a festival of films about mountaineering and exploration in Trento. I had told them I didn't think I'd be free but, seeing that the Gregoretti project was now no longer likely to keep me busy, when I met the Trento organizers in Venice I told them I would go. I travelled up by wagon-lit and, on arrival, took an immediate liking to the city. I knew Trento had always been a very clerical city, loyal to Rome from the time of the first ecumenical council held there in the 16th century, the council at which were established the dogmas of the Catholic church, and which confirmed the break from Protestantism, but Trento maintained all the charms of an Italian provincial city. Coming out of the station, the porter told me to walk through the gardens to the hotel and he would bring up my luggage on his bicycle. I passed by a statue that, for once, was not of Garibaldi or Cavour (which one finds in most Italian public gardens), but of Dante stretching out his arms towards the surrounding mountains. Of course Dante was a Catholic icon but he was also Italy's greatest poet and such a statue seemed a fitting introduction, or welcome, to this city. The festival I was attending turned out to be hard going. The films we had to view were mostly tedious. I soon got tired watching people climb mountains or come down them on skis. But in the category of exploration, strangely enough, they screened the Japanese film, Shindo's *The Naked Island*, and I appreciated it even more here in the quiet of a cinema in the company of four other lovers of good cinema than I had done in Taormina with 15,000 impatient Sicilians. We felt we might give it the top prize because it looked like being the only 'work of art' in the programme. But in the jury discussions we had to admit it didn't really qualify as an exploration film. So though we praised it warmly in our verdict we gave the top prize to a French film about Cousteau's men who live under the sea. We also gave a prize to *Il Signor Rossi va a Sciare* (Mr Rossi goes skiing) by Bruno Bozzetto, the most talented and entertaining of the Italian animation filmmakers. Bozzetto's international breakthrough would come with the feature-length cartoon, *West and Soda* (1965).

In Trento, we jury members were taken on a trip on the funivia (mountain railway) up to the summit of Mount Sardagna, from which the view was stunning. I got childish pleasure from throwing peanuts to the bears who were friendly. We were also taken on a trip to a wine festival in a village near Lake Garda where we were greeted by a local band playing *The Merry Widow* whilst the charming local youths showered us with grapes. During a last walk round the gardens of Trento before leaving, for the first time since I had arrived, I got an inviting smile from a sweet young man and we had a quickie in the bushes with Dante's blessing.

In October, the deceiving Roman autumn sunshine (I recalled those glorious two weeks in the sun when PPP was shooting *La Ricotta*) had induced me rashly to take my carabiniere lover, who was on a brief Roman visit, to Grottaferrata, my favourite of the nearby wine-producing hilltop towns. We lunched out of doors in the shade, as a result of which I was soon struck down by a terrible bout of 'flu. I was still feeling very groggy when I left for London later in October with Franco Rosi, his wife Giancarla, and Guido Albert, for the premiere of *Hands Over the City*. The film company had paid me for the subtitles, and were paying my round trip to London, while Guido Alberti had kindly offered to pay for my stay with them at the Savoy. The film went down very well at the festival screening and I was kept busy with Rosi and Co. for five days. In London, the winter was already making its presence felt. I was still feeling the worse for that flu' so I went to a doctor in Covent Garden. My health service card was still valid so I didn't have to pay for the visit or the prescribed penicillin which had an immediate positive effect. I didn't feel particularly pleased to be back at the Savoy after the stay with my tailor friend, Litrico. However, lunching at the Grill, after discouraging the young Italian waiter whom I'd met on the previous visit, who was too visibly displaying his joy at seeing me return, during the meal with Rosi and co. I had the satisfaction of suggesting to the Italian maitre d' that he add a drop of Strega liqueur to the vanilla ice cream we had ordered. It went down so well that he said he'd put it on the menu as one of the deserts. Naturally Guido Alberti, Signor Strega, was delighted and I felt I had earned his hospitality.

I would have liked to return to Rome with the Rosi crowd but, as I had been trying to organize a screening of *Hands Over the City* at the House of Commons, and the Labour Party MP with whom I was in contact had told me that she wouldn't be able to arrange it while Rosi was still in London, Franco begged me to stay on and I agreed. Of course I moved out of the Savoy and found myself a more modest lodging. The Commons screening kept being put off. In the end I had to leave the organization to the BFI. I did go to an event at the House of Commons, however, for an Old Boys dinner for my Worcester school, a very English (and rather stuffy formal) evening where I had hoped, but in vain, to meet up with the prefect I had been enamoured of. At one of the Rosi events, I had met an intelligent communist journalist from Bologna, Giorgio Fanti. He was pleasing company and he'd introduced me to Richard Clements, the editor of the leftist Labour political weekly, *Tribune*, who said he'd be willing to commission an article from me the next time the Italian government fell.

Among the new films I saw in London was *Tom Jones*. I was happy that my adored Finney finally had the popular success he deserved. I also saw *Cleopatra* and thought it as ghastly as we had all expected it to be, even if Rex Harrison was an impressive Caesar. And I saw Sean Connery's second James Bond film, *From Russia With Love*, which was fun even though I willingly admit I have read nothing by Ian Fleming. It contains a shamefully over the top performance by the great Lotte Lenya who was probably in need of cash. I would one day work with the director, Terence Young, on his adaptation of Conrad's *The Rover*, filmed on the Island of Elba, with Anthony Quinn and Rita Hayworth among its stars. I'd play a cameo in a scene with Quinn.

On another occasion I'd play a cameo with Sean Connery. It happened at the end of the 1960s when I was in Moscow writing a press book for Franco Cristaldi's Italian-Russian-American production *The Red Tent*, in which Connery starred with Peter Finch and Claudia Cardinale. Connery was playing the Norwegian explorer, Roald Amundsen, looking for General Nobile (Finch) whose airship had crashed in the Arctic. I had an amusing experience with Connery and Cardinale in Moscow. I had to accompany Claudia and a photographer to the Kremlin after it closed for the night. She was being filmed with Sean visiting the Tsar's treasures

The Red Tent with John Francis Lane (above)
Claudia Cardinale and Sean Connery (below).

in the museum. But we arrived at the main entrance from Red Square and I had some trouble explaining to the guards on duty why we were there. They finally understood and one of them was instructed to show us the way through the grim deserted alleyways of the Kremlin to the museum to which we should have arrived by a back entrance. Sean was there waiting a bit impatiently for our arrival beside some of the big-wigs of the capital of World Communism who, of course, had come to see the beautiful Italian star not to meet James Bond!

I was becoming aware that if the autumn of 1963 was to be the beginning of a new course for my life, the end perhaps of my 'dolce vita years' to which this memoir has been dedicated, it might be because I was eager to get more closely involved in theatre again. While in London I had run into Tom Courtenay who was sorry the Gregoretti project never took off. He very kindly took me to the National Theatre's production of *Hamlet* at the Old Vic starring Peter O'Toole for which it was impossible to get seats. Olivier's production was adequate but it didn't seem to have anything new to say about the play, except that Hamlet only seems to become interesting after he meets the players, but that may have been due to O'Toole's otherwise dull performance till that moment. Tom was about to start rehearsing at the National for a play called *Andorra*, by Max Frisch, under Lindsay Anderson's direction. Frisch was one of most progressive German language dramatists of the moment. At the National, during this autumn visit, I'd seen a play by another of the new German dramatists, Rolf Hochhuth. His controversial but compelling play, *The Representative*, accuses Pope Pius XII of not having done enough to help the Jews in German-occupied Rome. Naturally the play would be banned in Rome. When the actor, Gian Maria Volonté courageously presented it at his members only theatre club near the Piazza di Spagna in Rome, I'd be in the audience which the police forcibly obliged to leave the premises before the performance had begun.

At the National Theatre's *Hamlet* I had been amused to see that the young girls in the audience, who'd obviously come to see O'Toole, recognized Tom and came squealingly to ask for his autograph. On another day in London, I'd stop in Leicester Square to see why there was a crowd of girls squealing outside the cinema, where a Royal Performance was taking place. I'd find out that they were squealing at the presence of a musical quartet with long hair from Liverpool who were the rage at the moment. I just caught a glimpse of these 'Beatles' when they came outside to wave to the girls. I thought these lads would be unlikely to provoke squeals from me. Indeed, when I did manage to get to see them again in person, when they gave a concert in Rome, I would, however, appreciate hearing and seeing them perform to an audience that listened to their music enthusiastically with a minimum of squealing going on.

Chapter 22

In November, while I was attending a rehearsal of Albertazzi's new *Hamlet*, at Rome University's Theatre, Giorgio suddenly burst onto the stage, in the middle of a scene in which he himself was not rehearsing, to tell us that Kennedy had been assassinated that morning in Dallas. The rehearsal was suspended. I was supposed to be catching a train to Trieste that night, and had left my bag at the station nearby, but I cancelled my departure fearing what might happen in the world. However, the day after I did take the night train to Trieste where my carabiniere friend, in uniform because he was on duty, was at the station to embrace me. We would have some pleasant meetings together during this brief stay but I felt our story was perhaps beginning to wear out because, in spite of his occasional outbursts of passion, he kept finding excuses (probably invented) to ask for money. I still didn't know if this was to appease his conscience but, anyway, it was convenient for me too as I had no intention of letting our relationship become anything else.

Fortunately, in Trieste, I found a more intellectually stimulating distraction when I visited the local civic theatre for the first time, and saw an enchanting production of a bawdy comedy called *Gl'ingannati* (The Deceived Ones) by an unknown author of the 16th century. Whether the author was English or Italian I don't remember but it was easy to believe that the author of *Twelfth Night* knew it. I went backstage and introduced myself to the director, Fulvio Tolusso, a charming young Triestino who had trained with Giorgio Strehler at the Piccolo in Milan. He invited me to dinner afterwards, with him and others of the company, and they were delighted that an English critic had come to see their show. I said I hoped to write a review of it for *The Times*.

Before returning to Rome I stopped over in Milan and saw Peppino De Filippo bring the house down with laughter as he played a Neapolitan-style Harpagon in Molière's *The Miser*. Peppino told me that if he was invited by Peter Daubeny to London in the Spring, which seemed likely, he wanted to invite me to come with the company.

While attending the *Hamlet* rehearsals, I had become very friendly with his new director, Franco Zeffirelli, whose *Romeo and Juliet* I had so admired at the Old Vic in London. His production of *Hamlet* would open at Rome's Teatro Eliseo in early December and would be an immediate hit, above all with audiences but also with most of the critics, even if the ones who dedicated more space to literary rather than theatrical reflections felt obliged to be a bit snooty about Gerardo Guerrieri's translation, which seemed more Tennessee Williams than Shakespeare. However this was the way Zeffirelli had wanted his *Romeo and Juliet* to be at the Old Vic, where he had helped ordinary English theatregoers to appreciate Shakespeare's more bawdy lang-uage, especially that spoken by the Nurse and Mercutio but also the vehement words shouted at Juliet by her father, Lord Capulet. The poetry had suffered a bit in that English production. In this Italian 'Amleto' the poetry was also often sacrificed but, because it was a translation, that perhaps mattered less to Italian audiences. Franco had wanted Gerardo Guerrieri to give the translation a contemporary feel and it was appropriate. It sounded like a case history from a Jungian shrink's notebook and was given such visual impact that it could have been designed by Edward Munch. But, like his leading actor, Franco Zeffirelli was a Florentine so a Renaissance spirit was always guaranteed in design and performance in spite of the modernisms. Certainly it was a bit jarring for a Shakespearian scholar to hear Amleto say: "essere o non essere, tutto qui?" (To be or not to be, is that all?). I'd be in the National Theatre audience in 1964, at the Old Vic, when Olivier, eager to show that they too, like the RSC, wanted to invite foreign companies to join in the celebrations of the Shakespearian quatercentenary, even if it was two years later, presented the Zeffirelli-Albertazzi *Hamlet*. To my surprise, and even relief, Franco and Giorgio, probably panicking at the last moment, put the 'problema' back into the famous soliloquy.

Zeffirelli's production had many stunning inventions, including a ghost who doesn't come clanking on stage in armour but is only seen as a flickering light, first on the ramparts at the beginning, when the night sentries think they see and hear him in the foggy Elsinore night, and when Hamlet has his own hallucinations either alone or in the closet scene with his mother. Albertazzi gave his Hamlet that extra psychological depth, which had been lacking in the more traditional performance in Verona, but he was aided rather than abetted by the technical and visual creation (not special effects) that his imaginative new director provided. The other performances were all excellent, especially Giorgio's customary stage partner, Anna Proclemer, as a sensual Gertrude; Mario Scaccia as a humorously meddling petit-bourgeois Polonius; and Carlo Hintermann as a Machiavellian Claudius.

The recorded voice of the ectoplasmic Ghost of Hamlet's father was that of one of Italy's best actors of the time, Enrico Maria Salerno. During the same season, Salerno would give one of his greatest performances, opposite an actress of equal stature, Sarah Ferrati, as Edward Albee's terrible couple in Zeffirelli's superb Italian production of *Who's Afraid of Virginia Wolf?*, of which Gerardo Guerrieri's translation won unanimous praise. These two productions were the biggest theatrical hits of the 1963-64 season and they entitled Franco Zeffirelli to feel that he had graduated to the level of, even if not yet overtaken, his ex-maestro, Luchino. Instead of being proud, Visconti would seize every possible occasion to be sarcastic about his protégé's successes.

Before Christmas, the Italians finally got a new government. Ever since the elections in April, when the Christian Democrats had lost votes and the communists had made gains, there had only been a caretaker government without a proper majority, presided over formally by the Chamber of Deputies President (the Speaker). The Christian Democrat secretary, Aldo Moro, had failed to form his proposed government in May, though the Socialist Party leader, Pietro Nenni, was ready himself to join a more decisively progressive Centre-Left coalition. Nenni couldn't convince the rest of his party to abandon the party's alliance with the communists. After the summer it became clear that the standby government, which the Italians had dubbed somewhat euphemistically 'balneare', i.e. 'just for the sunbathing season', had to go. It was November and the sunbathing season was well and truly over. The assassination of JFK had caused increased international tension. There was a risk that the Italian President would call new elections which nobody (except the communists perhaps) wanted. So Moro tried again. This time, a majority of Nenni's socialists agreed to join an Italian government for the first time since they'd abandoned the first post-war coalition of parties who had taken part in the anti-fascist resistance. They had preferred to remain in opposition alongside the communists. The more leftist minority of Nenni's party abstained in the voting for Moro and would soon form Italy's third socialist party. Nenni became Moro's Deputy Premier. Saragat, secretary of the more moderate pro-American Social Democrats, became Foreign Minister.

Richard Clements, of the *Tribune*, kept his word and commissioned me to write an article which appeared in the 13th December issue with the title: "Italy: Can the Centre-Left Coalition Work?". Of course the answer to that would be 'No!'. Six months later, Moro resigned without succeeding in getting through much-needed legislation, including one which the film industry was clamouring for to regulate its state funding. As Christian Democrat chief for many years to come, Aldo Moro would go on trying to form or promote other Centre-Left governments until, at the end of the 1970s, he was on the point of forming one which even had the communist party's support. This prospect upset a lot of people from all political sides. As a result, this remarkably progressive and humanely sensitive politician would be kidnapped and assassinated. To this day one still doesn't who exactly was behind the Red Brigades who were put on trial and found guilty of Moro's murder. My article in *Tribune* on Moro's first Centre-Left government was the last one I'd ever write about Italian politics, except when it involved questions of the entertainment world's regular crises.

At the beginning of 1964, *The Times* published my enthusiastic review of the Trieste Theatre Company's *Gl'ingannati*, and my new friends gave me a big welcome when I revisited Trieste early in the new year. My carabiniere was, of course, glad to see me arrive and, in spite of my having decided to treat him less warmly, I had to admit I was pleased to find him waiting for me at the station. He was still the most satisfying lover I'd had since Salvatore and even if now he had a local fiancée it didn't diminish his passion or his requests for money. I could now afford to be generous anyway as I had received a further instalment from my inheritance funds. Naturally I had to be careful not to squander it too recklessly.

On this Trieste visit, I discussed Shakespeare with Fulvio Tolusso. He had told me on my previous visit that he wanted to inaugurate their next season with a Shakespeare play, maybe one of the Bard's twilight plays. I suggested *The Winter's Tale* which I had studied closely over the end of year holidays. I suggested to Fulvio that we could maybe justify Shakespeare's supposed geographical error about Bohemia having a sea coast by setting it in Trieste. Instead of a character's improbable exit "chased by a bear" I suggested that maybe he was chased by the notorious wind "la bora" that often swept in from the sea to 'chase' Trieste citizens 'off-stage'. But it would require translating the play into local dialect which Fulvio felt wouldn't do justice to the Bard's verses or to the company's local policy. They were the "Italian" theatre of the city. Another local civic theatre performed in the Slovene language. We decided to seek a compromise solution.

From Trieste I went to Ravenna, via Ferrara, to visit the set of Antonioni's new film, his first in colour, *The Red Desert*, starring Monica Vitti and Richard Harris. When I arrived in Ravenna I found Michelangelo in a desperate state. He wanted a grey sky whereas in spite of the cold it was blue. He told me immediately that he couldn't understand how he'd ever been able to shoot films in black and white. Seeing how much everyone had admired the blacks and whites of *Il Grido*, and his 'alienation' trilogy, it seemed unbelievable. But Michelangelo was always eager to re-invent the cinema. Watching him film interiors I was amazed to see that he was not satisfied with 'natural' colours. His director of photography, Carlo Di Palma, was excited by the challenge and told me that he didn't know why, or even ask Michelangelo, the reasons for the choice of colours he had to light. Michelangelo's excessive nervousness was felt by everyone and this would reach a highpoint in his relations with Harris whose contract would expire before all his scenes in the script had been filmed. Harris's agent persuaded him to forgo the unfilmed scenes and leave for Mexico where he was due to start a new film, a Sam Peckinpah western, *Major Dundee*.

What I saw them filming was certainly not the ancient Ravenna I already knew and loved, that of Dante and the Byzantine mosaics which Byron had adored. It was the new Ravenna of which I had had a glimpse when I came for the inauguration of the natural gas refinery which Enrico Mattei's ENI had opened there. Indeed the transformation that had taken place in the past decade was symbolised by the factories which had sprung up in the pinewoods between Ravenna and its beach on the Adriatic coast. The canals which flow into the sea, from the tributaries of the Po, had once provided havens for weekend fishers. The huts which these fishermen built along the banks of the canals (which I was told they used as much for amorous escapades as for fishing expeditions) were now derelict shacks or bungalows like the one in which Giuliana, the character played by Monica Vitti, spends time with her friends and her husband, the manager of one of the local factories. The husband was to have been played by Enrico Maria Salerno who, when the start of the film had been delayed, chose instead to tour the Albee play with Zeffirelli. In his place, Antonioni had found a local non-professional, Carlo Chionetti, who proved to be such a natural actor that he'd even be asked to dub his own voice. Harris played the part of a visiting engineer who becomes Giuliana's lover. Antonioni would tell me, in June when I visited him in Rome in the cutting rooms, that after "the flight of Richard Harris" (as the Italian press described it) he had been obliged to cut a second love scene between the couple, "but in the finished film," he said, "we'd see all we need to see of them to explain what their passionate encounter meant to Giuliana and her neurosis".

The only clue that Antonioni gave me to his use of colour is that his intention was "to make a violent attack on reality". He hadn't been able to paint the sky grey but I saw them shoot a scene in which a whole street was painted grey, including the man behind a fruit stall and even the fruit he was selling. This will be seen through Giuliana's eyes when she comes out of a shop she is about to open where we will have seen her choosing colours for its decoration. She has just been shaken by Harris's lively and imme-diately seductive appearance in the shop. When she comes outside everything in her life seems grey. Her neurosis is also expressed through grey spots she sees on the red walls of the hut where she and her husband are giving a party. The others don't see the spots. Nature is also transformed in colours to show the deadness of the new Ravenna landscape. But it was impossible to understand the significance of all the colours being invented until one saw the finished film. I suspected that the formal aspect of the film might overwhelm the content. When I had interviewed Monica, when Michelangelo was writing *The Red Desert*, I had got hints that she might be eager to change genre and maybe even director. Only later did I find out that Monica and Carlo di Palma had begun an affair during the Ravenna shoot. As I was a great Antonioni fan, I was glad I had not yet seen the finished film and could restrict myself to describing it's making for an article published in August in *The Sunday Times* magazine just before the film was to be shown at the Venice Festival. The jury awarded it the Golden Lion, in preference to Pasolini's *The Gospel According to Matthew*.

Richard Harris and Monica Vitti in Antonioni's *The Red Desert*.

Early in February I had rashly accepted to be on the jury of the Comic Films Festival in Bordighera on the Ligurian Riviera. The year before I had declined to attend because they expected me to write about and speak at a seminar on British comic actors about whom I remembered little. I had to go to London afterwards and I could fly to London from Nice after stopping off for the carnival. Bordighera was an unattractive winter resort full of aged people, a sort of Eastbourne. Though the sun was shining it was freezing cold. The hospitality was okay but the comic films were not funny and I had no adventures in the town, even if the waiters in the hotel made a great fuss of me. They were not worth trying to seduce. The only consolation of being on the jury was that a fellow member was the Spanish director, Luis Berlanga, whose *Bienvenido Mr Marshall* in 1953 had delighted everyone. We became good friends and did our best to enjoy ourselves. When the festival was over they supplied a chauffeured car to drive us over the Grande Corniche to Nice where Luis was taking a plane to Rome (where I think he had to direct the dubbing of his new film, *The Executioner*, in which Nino Manfredi played the lead). I took a hotel in Nice where I had thought, mistakenly, I would enjoy the Battle of the Flowers and the carnival celebrations, and maybe find other attractions. But I was unlucky and I wasted money which I could now afford to spend, unlike my previous visit to Nice at the age of seventeen.

On the plane to London, the presence of the Scotland soccer team didn't offer much consolation. Those sitting near me didn't attract me and, anyway, I couldn't understand a word they were saying. In London in mid-February it was naturally even more depressingly grey and cold, and I didn't feel comfortable in my Gloucester Road boarding house where I stayed again even though I could have afforded better lodgings. To cheer myself up on the first night I went to see a truly comic film, an improvement on those I'd been seeing in Bordighera, *The Pink Panther*. Peter Sellers was fabulously funny but I was sorry to see that Claudia Cardinale, while looking lovely, showed very little personality. Capucine was more striking. The next day I went to see a film called *The Leather Boys* which had made an enticing cover for the *Films and Filming*. Peter Baker's review of the film was favourable even if he found the ending inconclusive (the young married boy leaves his fellow leather boy lover to go back to his wife, played by Rita Tushingham). Frankly I found the whole film inconclusive perhaps because the controversial sex scene between the two boys had been cut by

films and filming

JANUARY 1964 3s

THE LEATHER BOYS

conflict between convention and taboo

the censors in the version I saw in a cinema full of sex–obsessed young men. I supposed that if I had stayed in England I would have ended up enjoying the leather boys circuit. I was better off with my Italian uniform fetish. *Films and Filming* was becoming not only as the masthead proclaimed, "Britain's largest circulation film magazine", but also Britain's "No. 1 magazine for sexy photos" which admittedly were often provided by me. I was glad to see, however, that the February issue dedicated much space to defending the distribution of foreign films with subtitles which didn't always find cinemas outside London.

Before I did anything else, I decided to treat myself to as much good theatre as possible in London. I was eager to catch up with the season's major attractions and, above all, hear Shakespeare in English. My first visit was to see the much–acclaimed Peter Brook-Paul Scofield *Lear* which seemed to me too cerebral and obviously inspired by the theories of the Pole, Jan Kott. I still considered Donald Wolfit's *Lear* the best I'd ever seen even if, but maybe because of, the production and company supporting him hadn't the inspired but not always convincing 'genius' that Peter Brook offered us. Peter Daubeny invited me to go with him to the National at the Old Vic to see Tom Courtenay in the Frisch play, *Andorra*, and I found it very moving. The production by Lindsay Anderson was soberly impressive, respecting the author and getting a good performance from Tom, even if perhaps he was miscast. Peter and I went backstage, he to embrace Diana Wynyard (who I thought had been less convincing, too theatrical) while I went to Tom's dressing where I found Lindsay, who greeted me rather coolly. I didn't know why, probably because he preferred not to discuss Richard Harris's 'flight from Ravenna'. Lindsay had apparently recommended Richard to accept the part. His inclination was obviously to defend his friend while I would defend mine so we talked about Frisch and Tom's acting.

But my greatest theatrical experience in London on this visit, and indeed the most memorable since the times as a teenager when I saw my first Shakespeare in London, was Peter Hall's quite extraordinary serial version of the Bard's historical cycle, three evenings at the Aldwych dedicated to *The Wars of the Roses*. A splendid Royal Shakespeare Company cast and ingenious but respectful editing of the texts. An exciting theatrical event and so much better than the similarly edited production of the same plays by Strehler which I'd one day see at the Milan Piccolo Teatro and write a scathing review. Peter Hall had done honour to Shakespeare with his historical cycle.

Meanwhile, Peter Daubeny, who had begun the Quatercentenary celebrations the year before at the Royal Shakespeare Company's London home, the Aldwych, to which he had brought Gassman's *Heroes*, was now preparing under RSC sponsorship the first of his World Theatre Seasons at the same theatre.

For the moment, I had given in to him over my dream of bringing Eduardo De Filippo, conceding that Eduardo himself would rather wait until he was reviving one of his plays which would be more suitable for a non-Italian audience. I was quite happy that Eduardo's brother, Peppino, was coming to London with a production that Peter had seen at a Paris festival which I had heard was hilarious, an adaptation into musical comedy of an old farce called *Metamorphoses of a Wandering Ministrel*, so I decided to stay on in case Peter needed help. I called in at the office of *The Times* where dear old Mr. Lawrence was quite happy to commission me a piece on Peppino's *Harpagon*, which I had seen in Milan (and one about the films of Richard Leacock).

When Peppino arrived, I arranged to take him to the BBC but I ran into trouble with the woman who edited the *Tonight* programme (who had turned down my film crisis idea on my last visit). She wanted to interview Peppino who, of course, didn't speak English. I thought up a gimmick that both she and Peppino liked. We had him eating an English meal of fish and chips and looking sour, then smiling radiantly when offered a plate of macaroni Neapolitan-style and looking happy. I borrowed the idea from a famous scene in the Alberto Sordi film, *An American in Rome*, which Peppino evidently hadn't seen for he thought it was an original idea. It went down well. We watched it all together during the coffee and liqueurs at one of Peter and Molly Daubeny's wonderful dinner parties.

I stayed on another week as Peter had invited me to go with him to Dublin to see the productions of the Sean O'Casey plays staged by the Abbey Theatre Company which, from his refuge in Devon, the great Irish playwright had given Peter his consent to bring to London, even though O'Casey had broken with the company long ago. In his autobiography, Peter would write: "But when I actually went with John Francis Lane to see the plays in Dublin I experienced a degree of dismay. The Abbey Theatre were performing at the old melodrama theatre, the Queen's, while waiting for the completion of their new building after the old Abbey had been burnt down in 1951... crossing the Liffey to the Queen's (the company) had suffered a deterioration in spirit. It was hardly surprising. The place was like a drill hall and however full it might be, always felt empty. The productions (of *Juno and the Paycock* and *The Plough and the Stars*) seemed crammed with faults: some poor acting and very poor sets... I insisted that changes must be made before the productions came to London".

I never saw the productions in London so I don't know if Peter succeeded in getting the changes made. He usually got his way. Our visit to Dublin was enlivened when he got us invited to supper at the home of Micheál MacLiammóir and Hilton Edwards just outside Dublin. Peter knew them well. He had met them when he was in Dublin working with Peter Ustinov and had brought to London Micheál's brilliant Oscar Wilde recital which I had seen and adored. I was enthralled to meet him at last, even if in the rather Victorian and freezingly cold home where he and Hilton lived. Micheál lit a log fire and opened a bottle of good French wine. He apologised for Hilton, who was not feeling well and was in bed upstairs. Peter introduced me flatteringly and I told Micheál how much I'd appreciated his Wilde recital and his diary of the making of Orson Welles's *Othello* film, *Put Money in Thy Purse*, many of the adventures of which took place in the Paris of 1949, when I had been a student there, and in St-Paul-de-Vence. I told Micheál of my meetings with Orson on the Pasolini set and how pleased he had been to hear that I had seen the plays he presented in Paris during the summer of 1950. Micheál roared with laughter and brought out a copy of another book he had written, and which he gave me, after writing a dedication. The book is called *Each Actor on his Ass*. On its first pages, it told of how he had left Hilton in Paris to cope with helping to direct Orson's own adaptation of *Doctor Faustus*, in which they had cast an unknown black singer named Eartha Kitt, whom they had discovered in a Parisian boîte.

Micheál went upstairs to take Hilton something to eat and tell him that Peter's friend had seen that play. When he came back he served Irish delicacies he had prepared for us, and Peter entreated him to tell me the story of how they had "discovered" the young Orson Welles. It was a fascinating story: Micheál and Hilton had founded the Gate Theatre in Dublin in 1928. The young Orson had landed in Galway with only a few dollars in his pocket which he had invested in a horse and cart so that he could tour Ireland as an "itinerant painter". When he arrived in Dublin he came straight to the Gate and demanded an audition. "As I remember him, Micheál told us, "he was a very tall young man with a chubby face, full powerful lips and disconcerting Chinese eyes. He told us he had acted with the Theatre Guild, written a couple of plays and toured the States as a sword-swallowing female impersonator". They cast him as the Duke in a production of Kornfeld's *Jew Suss* which was a huge success. "The next year Orson returned to

America and founded the Mercury Theatre", Micheál told us proudly. *In Put Money in Thy Purse*, Orson wrote the preface in which he said: "(Micheál) is an entertainer rather than a conquistador, a good companion, who could certainly scratch, but who prefers to purr. If he must be excluded from the full title of wit, his lack is ruthlessness and his only fault a preference for being kind".

That's how I too remember Micheál MacLiammóir. Before saying goodbye we paid our respects to a sadly ailing Hilton. I'd never go to Dublin again or want to go. I had grown up adoring Irish giants like Oscar Wilde, George Bernard Shaw and James Joyce, all of whom had been obliged to leave in order to seek literary success. W. B. Yeats was one who stayed on and, with Lady Gregory, founded the Abbey Theatre which Sean O'Casey ended by abandoning too. It had been Yeats who had convinced Micheál to return to Ireland and learn the language. On the flyleaf of the copy of *Each Actor on his Ass*, which Micheál so kindly gave me that evening, it is described as being "translated from the Irish by the author". It was another diary of an Irish actor's travels and his return home. The dedication reads: "John the Baptist on his first visit to our wilderness – Micheál the Archangel". I felt a bit too honoured. Marie Seton had called me a saint (Francis) in the dedication of her book. I didn't feel I had been particularly saintly in my 'dolce vita' years which now seemed to be drawing to a close. Or were they?

My Amarcord

Ingmar Bergman once said "films are either documents or dreams". Fellini would go on dreaming to the end of his life. His best film in years to come would be *Amarcord*, the 'I Remember' inspired by his, and his co-scriptwriter, Tonino Guerra's, childhood in their native region, Romagna, a film full of 'dreams' about a real and imaginary past, like those which, with other fellow dreamers, Fellini had already put into *I Vitelloni* and *La Strada* and into the most fascinating parts of *La Dolce Vita* and *8 1/2*. But Fellini would also make *Orchestra Rehearsal* (1979) and *Ginger and Fred (1986)* which, as well as being great films, were acute documents about his times as well as Fellini-style personal 'dreams'.

Visconti would be less inspired as film-maker in his last years of failing health. *Death in Venice* (1971) was his last masterpiece. It had magnificent performances by Dirk Bogarde and Silvana Mangano, superb cinematography by Giuseppe Rotunno, and a screenplay which reflected as much Visconti's own personal 'dreams' as those of Thomas Mann's original novella. *Ludwig* (1973) was another *Leopard*, but without a Lancaster and an Alain Delon to give it some dignity. Visconti would confirm his genius for opera production for the last time with a breathtakingly beautiful production of Puccini's *Manon Lescaut* at Spoleto in June 1973, conducted by Thomas Schippers, with exquisite set designs by Lila de Nobili and costumes by Piero Tosi, two of Luchino's most treasured collaborators. I had admired so many of Luchino's opera productions over the years but I shared the general view that this sensually overwhelming production was the most memorable since his operatic dreams for Callas. A pity that the same year as that splendid *Manon* in Spoleto he would upset many of his admirers (and the author) with his travesty of Harold Pinter's *Old Times* when he staged it, in Rome's major theatre, the Argentina, as a vulgar boxing match between the three characters. When confronted with an ailing Luchino in his wheelchair, after a preview, and he asked me for my opinion, I could only say generously, "Well Luchino, you found an Italian solution for Pinter". He seemed satisfied. I'd never see him again either. Sadly, but perhaps fortunately, I'd never see Fellini again and be asked for an opinion of his last film, *The Voice of the Moon* (1990), which had left me bitterly disappointed.

I have now reached the point where I have finished writing my personal 'amarcord', which is more of a document than a dream, about my turbulent dolce vita years. Perhaps in this memoir I have been indulging in my own ego-trip into my past? But in the same way that, in my preface, I wrote that I didn't aspire to better the homosexual memorialists of my times, like Tennessee Williams and Gore Vidal, so in this epilogue I don't pretend that my ego-trip can rival in interest those of the two greatest Italian film auteurs of our age. I am a cinéphile not a cinéaste. I hope at least that I have been able to record the serious as well as the frivolous side of what I saw and experienced in those 'dolce vita' years.

Of course my 'dolce vita' in Rome didn't finish in 1964. It was convenient for me to carry on being correspondent for *Films and Filming*, at least into the mid-1970s, and, from 1985 for a decade, I was the Rome correspondent of the trade weekly, *Screen International*. This, and my contributions as a critic for the English language dailies published in Rome, wouldn't earn me much income but would give the pretext to continue my travels in Italy and to exotic foreign places. I'd earn some extra pocket money by playing more cameos in films, many by the director-auteurs I admired.

In addition to the grotesque friar in Pasolini's *The Canterbury Tales*, I'd do two cameos for Francesco Rosi, one in *The Moment of Truth* (1965) filmed in Madrid, the other in *Lucky Luciano* (1973) filmed in Naples. For Paolo and Vittorio Taviani, I appeared in *Good Morning, Babylon* (1987), about two Tuscan brothers, stonemasons, who emigrated to America and found work helping to build the sets of Griffith's *Intolerance*, in a Hollywood recreated in an old studio in Tuscany. For Elio Petri, I cameoed in *A Quiet Place in the Country* (1968), with Vanessa Redgrave and Franco Nero, for which I was working as dialogue consultant. This meant the difficult task of ensuring that the entire film was shot in English as the American co-producers had stipulated, whereas Petri was making an Italian film and often used Venetian actors who didn't speak English. He didn't care that Vanessa refused to accept last minute changes to the script. "Tell your compatriot," he'd say to me, "that I'll dub her anyway into Italian". For Eduardo De Filippo I cameoed in his 1976 TV adaptation of his stage play, *De Pretore Vincenzo*, playing an American tourist whose wife gets her bag snatched in a Naples Street and is subsequently seen in a dream sequence as a saint in Paradise!

I'd always regret that I'd never been asked to do a cameo for one of Italy's most celebrated director-authors and comic actors, Nanni Moretti, who would change the face of traditional Italian comedy and also becme a notable Italian public figure. I had been one of the first critics to discover Nanni already when he made his first shorts, in Super 8, in the 1970s and we had become good friends in those years. Perhaps however it was a good thing that we lost touch later otherwise he might have cast me as one of the elderly cardinals in his *Habemus Papem* (We Have A Pope, 2011) where I would have been obliged to play volleyball with the other cardinals in the Vatican courtyard and would have risked having what could have probably been a fatal fall. I had anyway already played a cardinal in *Francesco* (1989), Liliana Cavani's film about Saint Francis in which Mickey Rourke, surprisingly cast as the Saint, gave a deeply moving performance and was an inspiring actor to work with. I am not particularly proud to remember that I played a pseudo Prince Rainier monarch in a preposterous Italian comedy called *Roba da Ricchi* (Things for Rich People), directed by

Sergio Corbucci, a director destined to be turned into a cult by the Anglo-American punk-realism generation, thanks to his spaghetti western, *Django* (1966) of which, to my astonishment, The Museum of Modern Art in New York conserves a print listed among the cinema's immortal masterpieces. An original painting of me in regal attire, made for the film, hung for many years in the entrance to the offices of the producer. I am much less proud to remember that I also appeared in *Caligula*, a film by a director whose early films I had admired before he joined the eroticist brigade, Tinto Brass. He and Gore Vidal, his scriptwriter, disowned the film as it was re-edited by its producer, Bob Guccione.

I'd be very proud, however, of my cameo as a Scottish farmer in a kilt in *Another Time, Another Place*, a film about Italian prisoners of war in Scotland. It was made in 1982 for Channel 4 but distributed in cinemas worldwide. I collaborated on the preparation and shooting on the Black Isle near Inverness. It was the first feature by Michael Radford, with whom I had collaborated on the making of two memorable documentaries filmed in Naples for the BBC. And I'd introduce him to Massimo Troisi with whom he'd co-direct *Il Postino* (1994), for which he'd win an Oscar nomination.

A kilted John Francis Lane in Radford's *Another Time, Another Place*.

In 1975, I was honoured by the President of the Italian Republic by being made a Chevalier or Knight of the Order of Merit of the Italian Republic. The President of the time, Giovanni Leone, was a Neapolitan but he had nothing to do with my being honoured except to sign the certificate which, with the medallion, were presented to me by the Italian ambassador at a luncheon in my honour during a subsequent visit to London. I would discover that the person responsible for my being honoured was the director of the Italian Cultural Institute in London, a Neapolitan who knew what I had done to bring Italian cultural events, and particularly those of Naples, to the UK.

Early in the 21st century, RAI International filmed an interview-documentary about me in my home in Southern Italy. The director, Nicoletta Nesler, called it *A Life in Cameo*. Of my many cameos shown in the RAI film was the one from *Fellini's Roma* (1972). In the final sequence, I am seen at a table in a Trastevere restaurant toasting Gore Vidal who declared: "What better place than Rome in which to await the end of the world!". In the end, neither Gore nor yours truly would stay to await that event in Rome. For reasons of bad health we'd both abandon the Eternal City. Gore would end his days in California. I'd remain in Italy and am ending my days in Norman Douglas's Old Calabria.

In 2010, at the garden party and ceremony at the Villa Massimo in Rome, where the Stampa Estera was celebrating the 50th anniversary of the Foreign Press Association's Film Award, of

At a Trastevere restaurant with Gore Vidal in *Fellini's Roma*.

which I was the only surviving founding committee member, I was invited to present our special anniversary award to Gina Lollobrigida. Before the ceremony began, Gina and I had a nostalgic chat about mutual acquaintances. In presenting her with the award I amused the colleagues of today by recounting that when, as a new member of the Association, I had asked a seasoned colleague what stories out of Rome were always sure copy he had told me "The Pope and Gina Lollobrigida".

After the tragic murder of Pasolini in 1975, I had gradually abandoned my promiscuous lifestyle and, thanks to that fact, in the late 1970s I would meet the companion with whom I'd spend the rest of my life, a much more precious friendship than those I have recounted on these pages. After my accident, in a Trastevere street in 1994, I'd take refuge in his lovely home in the hills around the ancient city of Cosenza where he lived with his family. Our loving union would be more one of souls than of bodies. We would be at each other's side in adversity and in good times. I would accompany him to Houston, Texas for a risky heart operation and he'd come to my rescue every time I had accidents before I left Rome. It would be in the quiet of Nando's home that I'd find the peace to write this memoir. In dedicating this memoir of my Roman 'dolce vita' years to my friend I ask his pardon for not writing about the mostly 'dolce' if sometimes 'amaro' times we'd spend together.

Grazie Nando

Nando and family with John Francis Lane

Preface:

Anthony Steel was starring in *Checkpoint*, with Stanley Baker.

Chapter 1

p6: Edward Alleyn (1566–1626). Played the title roles in the very first performances of Marlowe's *Faustus*, *Tamburlaine*, and *The Jew of Malta*.

p8: *Le silence est d'or*. Maurice Chevalier as a filmmaker caught in a love triangle in twenties Paris.

L'aigle à deux têtes (The Eagle Has Two Heads). An anarchist poet seeks to assassinate a reclusive Queen. JFL saw the first production, directed by Jacques Hébertot. Antonioni filmed it as *Il mistero di Oberwald* (1981).

Toralv Maurstad starred as Grieg in *Song of Norway* (1970).

p9: College founded in 1945. L'Herbier and Georges Sadoul were on the staff. A character in Jacques Becker's *Rendez-vous de Juillet* has an IDHEC diploma. 'On Studying the Film' by JFL S&S April 1950 p93-94.

p17: Stringers are paid only for what is printed. They are promoted to being paid a 'retainer', on the way to becoming salaried correspondents.

p18: Chiarini's films include *Patto col diavolo* (Pact with the Devil, 1949).

p19: Mann stayed at the Hotel des Bains in 1911. Visconti filmed Mann's novella, *Death in Venice*, which takes place in and out of the hotel. The hotel closed in 2010.

p20: Diana Dors's Venice stunt earned her a co-starring role alongside Vittorio Gassman in *La Ragazza del Palio* (The Love Specialist, 1958),

Doctor at Sea. Comedy starring Dirk Bogarde who had more success on the Lido in Visconti's *Death in Venice* (1971).

The Deep Blue Sea. Anatole Litvak's adaptation of Terence Rattigan's play about a suicidal woman at the end of a love affair. Vivien Leigh co-starred.

Though Linda Christian's marriage to Tyrone Power in Rome in 1949 was hailed at the time as the "wedding of the century", she was having an open affair with Purdom, with whom she co-starred in *Athena* (1954). They married for one year only in 1963.

The Cicada (Poprygunya/ The Cricket (1955) from a short story by Chekhov. Starring Lyudmila Tselikovskaya and Sergei Bondarchuk.

p21: *Interrupted Melody*. Eleanor Parker as opera star Marjorie Lawrence and her battle with polio.

The Kentuckian. A frontiersman and his son head for Texas.

p22: Carl Dreyer's *Ordet*: Henrik Malberg as a devout widower with three sons in rural Denmark, from the play by Kaj Munk.

The low standard of the films, and the foreign interference, caused an outcry in the Italian press and later in the Italian parliament. JFL, F&F November 1956 p15.

Chapter 2

p24: *Il Generale della Rovere*. De Sica as a petty thief hired by Nazis to impersonate a Resistance leader.

Giordano Bruno (1548-1600). Domenican friar burned at the stake for advancing the theory that the Earth was not the centre of the Universe. Gian Maria Volonté and Charlotte Rampling starred in a 1973 biopic by Giuliano Montaldo.

p27: Magnani's weepie was *Suor Letizia* (The Awakening, 1956). A boy stirs maternal feelings in a Naples nun. Directed by Mario Camerini.

See 'Tolstoy's 'War' as Vidor Makes It', F&F March 1956, p8-9, 13.

p29: *The Little Hut*. Directed by Mark Robson. Adapted from André Roussin's *La petite hutte* (1947).

p30: Sinatra's Spanish film was Kramer's *The Pride and The Passion*.

p31: *Love is a Many Splendored Thing*. Directed by Henry King. The song, written by Sammy Fain and Paul Francis Webster, was performed by The Four Aces and won the Academy Award.

p33: *No Highway (in the Sky)*. From the novel by Nevil Shute, potboiler with James Stewart as an aeronautical engineer.

p37: JFL's obituary of Guglielmo Biraghi was published in *The Guardian*, 27th April 2001.

p37: *Drifters.* 1929 film about Britain's North Sea herring fishery and its transformation into an "epic of steam and steel".

p38: André Bazin. Co-founder of *Cahiers du cinéma.* Truffaut's *Les quatre cents coups* is dedicated to him.

La Terra Trema. Adaptation of Giovanni Verga's novel *I Malavogli.* A fisherman tries to break out of enforced poverty in Sicilly.

Senso. A Venetian Countess (Alida Valli) falls in love with an Austrian deserter (Farley Granger) during the Third War of Independence.

Bigger than Life. James Mason as a drug-addicted school teacher in a film Mason also wrote and produced.

p39: Grierson's 'Festival at Edinburgh' and JFL's 'Venice Pictures', were published in the same F&F Nov56 issue p14, 33; and 15, 16.

p41: *Legend of the Lost.* A trio hunt treasure in the desert of Timbuktu.

Chapter 3

p48: Piccioni is noted for his work with Risi and Rosi.

p49: The interview would be published as a Dawn Addams' by-line: 'My Life as Chaplin's Leading Lady', F&F Aug57 p12-13, 15.

The Boy Friend. Twenties-style musical by Sandy Dennis, which would form the core of a musical-within-a-great-film by Ken Russell in 1971.

p50: '*Bread, Love and...*" Gino Lollobrigida starred with De Sica in the first two films in the series. Directed by Luigi Comencini.

p51. Hathaway did make a masterpiece, *How The West Was Won* (1962).

p60. Jean Marais. Famous for his performances in Jean Cocteau's *Beauty and the Beast* (1946) and *Orphée* (1949).

Chapter 4

p65: Ken Hughes's *The Trials of Oscar Wilde* (1960) starring Peter Finch.

p69: *Thursday's Children.* Poetic documentary about a school for deaf and dumb infants in Margate. Narrated by Richard Burton.

Lindsay Anderson's *Declaration* essay is "Get out and push!", about the responsibility of the individual to challenge established systems. Stuart Holroyd's is called 'Emergence From Chaos'. Osborne, Amis, Tynan and Wilson were among the other contributors.

p70: for extracts of Zavattini's Diaries see F&F May 1958 p11, 32.

p78: Corrado Pani can be seen in Visconti's *White Nights* and *Rocco and his Brothers*.

p80: 'Volare' won two Grammy Awards and sold 22 million copies.

Chapter 5

p81: *Kanonen-Serenade*. German allies force a cargo boat captain to instal a cannon. For more about the making of the film, read 'A Day By The Sea', by JFL, F&F June58 p33.

p83: Steve Cochran's most celebrated performance in American films is as James Cagney's psychotic henchman in *White Heat* (1949).

p84: "thousands of Romans were becoming potential communist voters demonstrating at Cinecittà against the *Ben-Hur* company which, the night before, had 'ordered' many thousand more extras than were needed. The extras are only getting paid 18s for eleven hours work under gruelling sun, but for many Romans that is a day's living for a whole family."
JFL, F&F August 1968 p31

The Brothers Karamazov (1958), directed by Richard Brooks and starring Yul Brynner and Claire Bloom.

p85: *Lust For Life* (1956). Quinn won an Oscar for his performance as Gauguin. Kirk Douglas was nominated for his performance as Van Gogh.

Nero's Big Weekend (Mio figlio Nerone). Directed by Steno. JFL's 'The Italian Laughter Makers' was published in F&F May 1958 p9-10, 34.

p87. *Bitter Rice* (Riso Amaro). Mangano, strides the rice-fields of the Po Valley to where Vittorio Gassman comes hiding. Giuseppe De Santis directed. Oscar-nominated for Best Foreign Film.

p88: *The Millionairess* by George Bernard Shaw. It would be filmed with Peter Sellers and Sophia Loren (1960, directed by Anthony Asquith).

p95: *The Rickshaw Man* (Muhomatsu no issho) by Hiroshi Inagaki. Rickshaw driver, Mifune, falls in love with a widow and helps her sickly son.

Les Amants (1959). Moreau as a bored mother who revives her spirits by having an affair.

Ascenseur pour l'échafaud (1958, Lift to the Scaffold). Lovers plan to kill an industrialist who is the wife of one and the boss of the other.

Chapter 6

p96: Emmer's art films include *Il dramma di Cristo* (1948), *Piero della Francesca* (1949) and a three-part film on *Leonardo da Vinci* (1952).

Like many short films of the period, Read's film about Henry Moore can be seen on youtube.

p105: Arena's boxing film was *Un uomo facile* (The Defeated Victor).

p106: JFL's profile of Cristaldi was published as 'Golden Boy'. Nov58 p5.

p108: F&F Italian Special issue - April 1959 - contained articles by Fellini, De Sica, Antonioni, Lattuada, Castellani and JFL; and features on Rossellini, Zavattini and Gassman.

Chapter 7

p112: *The Four Just Men*: wrong-righting adventures of four men who met in Italy in World War Two. De Sica starred in nine of the thirty-nine 30min episodes. Basil Dearden was one of the directors. Alan Bates and Judy Dench were among the guest stars.

De Sica's article: 'British Humour? It's the same in Italy' F&F Ap59 p10.

p113: Fellini's article: 'My Sweet Life' Ibid. p7.

Europa '51. Bergman suffers from mental health in the wake of her neglected son's death.

Antonioni's article: 'There Must Be a Reason For Every Film', Ibid p11.

p115. 'Moo' was booed at it first night at the Royal Court, 25th June 1957. JFL took the part originally played by Robert Stephens.

Chapter 8

p119: *I soliti ignoti*. Gassman leads a bunch of amateur thieves in a meticulously planned safe-breaking escapade. Directed by Mario Monicelli.

p121: Mingozzi's feature films include *Flavia* (1974) and *L'Iniziazione* (1987). See 'The Cinema of Gianfranco Mingozzi', F&F May 1974, JFL.

p124: Renato Marmiroli founded the 'European Monarchist Movement'.

p126: Louise Rainer, from Reinhardt's Vienna ensemble, was the first actress to win two Academy Awards.

p129: *We, the Women* (Siamo donne, 1953). Five-part portmanteau film, one part of which was directed by Visconti and starred Magnani.

Chapter 9

p132. Loren and Ponti solved the problem by becoming French citizens and marrying in Sèvres in 1966.

Oliver Reed Alped an elephant in *Hannibal Brooks* (1968, Winner).

p133: *Les quatre cents coups* (The 400 Blows). Jean-Pierre Léaud as an unloved boy in Paris.

Le beau Serge. Jean-Claude Brialy as a cynical city sophisticate hosting his studious country cousin, Gérard Blain.

Come Back, Africa. Exposé of apartheid in Sophiatown.

The Savage Eye. Divorcee sinks through an L.A. lowlife of strippers, cults and death. Ben Maddow, Sid Meyers & Joseph Strick directed.

Eve Arden would reprise her wise-cracking role in *Grease* (1978).

p134: *Ashes and Diamonds* (Popiól i diament). Zbigniew Cybulski as a Resistance fighter ordered to kill a communist leader on the last day of the war.

The Train (Pociag, Night Train). A woman shares a compartment in a night train with a man who may be a murderer.

La Grande Guerra. Gassman and Sordi as non-conformist conscripts in World War One.

p140: *Hercules Unchained*, the second of Reeves' three Hercules films sold more tickets in Britain than any film released in 1960. F&F Jan61 p29.

p141: *Where Angels Fear to Tread* was filmed by Charles Sturridge in 1991 at the end of the Merchant-Ivory boom.

p142. The Archimedes film was *L'assedio di Siracusa*, starring Brazzi.

p143: *La notte brava*. Brialy, Terzieff and Franco Interlenghi scheme with two prostitutes to sell stolen guns.

p145: *Moraldo in the City*. The screenplay was translated in English by John C. Stubbs and published by University of Illinois Press.

Chapter 10

p147: *Via Margutta*. In a bilingual role, JFL speaks Italian with an English accent. Gérard Blain, Yvonne Furneaux and Spiros Focás star.

p151. Roger Casement. Irish humanitarian who reported human rights abuses in the Congo and Peru, and who negotiated a non-invasion treaty with Germany in 1914. Executed by the British for treason, who quoshed appeals for clemency by circulating diaries which portrayed him as a promiscuous homosexual.

p153: Domenico Modugno: 'Mr. Volare Finds He's Become an Actor', F&F Jan60 p10, 32. Modugno's main contribution to cinema was probably his discovering and promoting Franco Franchi and Ciccio Ingrassia.

Risate di gioa. Two needy actors join a professional pickpocket for jewel thievery in Rome on New Year's Eve.

p156: *Under Ten Flags* (Sotto dieci bandiere). A British Commander, Laughton, takes on German battleship captained by Van Heflin.

p158: *Divorce Italian Style*. Marcello Mastroianni as a Sicilian baron who falls in love with his cousin, played by Stefania Sandrelli. Germi was also nominated for the Best Director Oscar; Mastroianni for Best Actor.

Chapter 11

p161: See JFL's 'Roman Scandals' F&F April 1960 p29, 32, 33

p164: JFL's location report of *The Guns of Navarone* was published as: 'Big Guns'. F&F August 1960 p28-29, 32.

p165: *Notre Dame de Paris*. Gina Lollobrigida co-starred with Quinn. The Hakim brothers produced.

p167: *Never on Sunday*. A Pygmalion story of a prostitute and a scholar. Nominated for six American Academy Awards. It won for Best Song.

Chapter 12

p176: Salerno would play the detective in *The Bird With The Crystal Plumage* (1969), the first film by *Paese sera* film critic, Dario Argento.

The festival director declined to read out a telegram saying Visconti's producer, Goffredo Lombardo, rejected the award. F&F Jan61 p3.

Justice est faite. Valentine Tessier on trial for the mercy killing of a terminally ill man she loved.

p178: *Come September.* Hudson learns that his villa is used as a hotel, at which Sandra Dee and Bobby Darin fall in love.

The Wastrel. A speedboat accident with his young son causes Van Heflin to reconsider his West Indian life with his Italian wife.

p180: Michael Truman. Director of TVs *The Saint* and producer of five Ealing films including *The Maggie* (1954).

p181: The third Italian Special Issue of F&F (Jan1961) contains articles by Fellini 'The Bitter Life - of Money' p13, 38; Antonioni 'Eroticism - the Disease of Our Age' p7; Visconti 'The Miracle That Gave Man Crumbs' p11; & Pasolini 'Intellectualism ... and the Teds' p17, 44.

p182: Damiano Damiani directed an adaptation of *La Noia* (1963), with Bette Davis, Horst Buchholz and Catherine Spaak.

JFL's translation was printed on p14, 44; his article on Antonioni on p9, 45; In the same issue he also wrote about 'The New Realists of Italy': Bolognini, Vancini Pontecorvo, Rosi and Rossi, p20.

p185: *Three Coins in the Fountain.* The fountain is the Trevi. The tossed coins come from three American women looking for love. Brazzi co stars.

Chapter 13

p188: *A Man For All Seasons* dir. Noel Willman. Scofield subsequently won an Oscar for his 1966 film performance directed by Fred Zinnemann.

p189. JFL saw *The Caretaker* at the Duchess Theatre. Donald Pleasence and Alan Bates starred. Pinter's *The Birthday Party* (May 1958), *The Room* and *The Dumb Waiter* (March 1960) had already played in London.

p192: Lisa Gastoni acted in 31 episodes of *The Four Just Men*; the Ugo Gregoretti part of *RoGoPaG* (1963) and had a box-office hit with *Grazie, zia* (1968), Salvatore Samperi's film about a boy infatuated with his aunt.

Dilys Powell, film critic for *The Sunday Times*, called *La Dolce Vita* a: "panorama of a man's progress through a corrupt society".

p194: *On the Wall.* Dir. Peter Duguid. Norman Rossington starred.

David Storey's *In Celebration; The Contractor, Life Class, Home, The Farm* were first directed at the Royal Court by Lindsay Anderson.

Sequence. Oxford University Film Journal founded and edited by Lindsay Anderson to champion the 'good' cinema of Ford, Flaherty and Cocteau and to attack the 'bad' cinema of Britain - Rank, Powell, Reed.

p195: Baron Corvo (Frederick Rolfe). English Uranian. Mostly remembered for his novel *Hadrian the Seventh* (1904).

p201: John Le Mesurier found fame in Britain as Sergeant Wilson in TV's *Dad's Army* (1968, and screened almost continually since).

Chapter 14

p202: A fine interview with an articulate Warren Beatty: F&F, April 1961 p7, 8, 32: 'The first ten seconds - They shape the Way Ahead'.

p209: Richard Burton and Mastroianni starred in a fictionalised account of the Massacre, *Massacre in Rome* (1973, dir. George Pan Cosmatos).

p211: In *Anger and After*, John Russell Taylor, writing of Wood's film work, says his translation of *Fellini Satyricon* was "a masterpiece of invention, if nothing else".

p213. This juxaposition didn't happen. In the film Christ is crucified at the moment of a real-life total eclipse of the sun.

p214: *Salomé* starred Margaret Tynes. Thomas Schippers conducted.

Chapter 15

p218: De Seta's short films include several in impressive colour cinemascope, including *Pescherecci* (1958) and *Un giorno in Barbagia* (1958).

De Sica's *The Last Judgement* starred Sordi, Gassman, Aimée, Mangano, Fernandel, Manfredi, Stoppa, Mercouri, Palance, Ventura and De Sica.

The title change to *Rome Adventure* was prompted by the box-office success of the Cinerama travelogues, such as *Cinerama Holiday* (1955), *South Seas Adventure* (1958) and *Holiday in Spain* (1962).

p221: *Ballad of a Soldier.* A teenage soldier travels across Russia to see his mother. Directed by Grigori Chukhrai. The screenplay was nominated for an Oscar.

p222: *Accattone:* "The polemics have yet to die down over *Accattone,* which the censors have been obliged to show with only a few dialogue changes. The initial banning of the film had provoked the biggest outcry since *La Dolce Vita* and has, of course, increased its commercial value. Elizabeth Taylor, hearing so much talked about the film was considering buying the American rights... *Accattone* has been doing business at the box-office on the same level as *The Guns of Navarone.*" JFL, F&F Feb62 p37.

p227: *Cronaca familiare.* A Rome journalist (Mastroianni) is told that his young brother (Jacques Perrin) has died.

Of *Maciste in Hell* , Phil Hardy writes in *The Aurum Encyclopedia of Horror* (1985): "The film's only point of interest is strictly anecdotal: the prestigious English film journalist and promoter of all things Italian, John Francis Lane, appears briefly as a coachman."

p229: JFL's obituary of Freda was published in *The Guardian* 24.12.99. He points out that Freda "had a knack for launching talent, such as Gassman (who played Casanova in Freda's *Cavaliere Misterioso,* 1948), while designers like Beni Montresor and Filippo San Just began their careers with him."

p230: *Eve.* Novelist, Stanley Baker, falls for Jeanne Moreau in Venice. The film's American publicist tried to hype it up as *La Dolce Vita* of Venice. It flopped badly and was heavily re-edited by the producers.

Jules et Jim. Truffaut masterpiece with Moreau in love triangle with a Frenchman and an Austrian on the eve of the First World War.

In addition to *Accident,* Pinter wrote the scripts for Losey's *The Servant* (1963), *The Go-Between* (1971) and an unfilmed script of Proust's *À la recherche du temps perdu.*

p231: *Boccaccio '70* 's publicity claimed it was the most expensive film ever made in Italy. Visconti, De Sica and Monicelli also contributed episodes, though De Laurentiis cut Monicelli's contribution for the film's premiere at Cannes, prompting outrage from the Italian press.

p232: Frank Wolff, second-billed in Kazan's *America, America* (1963), played Claudia Cardinale's 'husband' in *Once Upon a Time in the West* (1968).

Chapter 16

p236: *La Dolce Vita* got Oscar nominations for Director, Screenplay, Art Direction, Costume Design. *West Side Story* won ten Oscars that year.

A Violent Life (Una vita violenta). Directed by Paolo Heusch and Brunello Rondi.

p237: Citti spent thirty-eight days in jail.

The New Angels (I Nuovi Angeli). Based on a collection of stories, *The 20 Year-Olds Are Not Madmen*, by Mino Guerrini.

p239: Bresson's *The Trials of Jeanne d'Arc* starring Florence Delay.

p240: *O pagador de promessas*. A man pledges away his lands in honour of his donkey's health.

p243: *Chips with Everything*. The biggest box-office success of any Royal Court Theatre production that year, though the management had turned it down until a commercial impresario agreed to share the costs. John Dexter directed.

p244: Alberto Sordi gives "workers" the finger in Fellini's *I Vitelloni*.

p246. Vitti's cheerful roles included *Modesty Blaise* (1966) by Joseph Losey and the rather more significant *Dramma della gelosia* (1970) by Ettore Scola, with Marcello Mastroianni and Giancarlo Giannini.

p247: *Il Conte Ory*. Thomas Schippers conducted. Saul Steinberg designed.

p248: Among Williams' rewrites of *Milk Train* was *Boom!* (1968), a film version starring Elizabeth Taylor and directed by Joseph Losey.

Chapter 17

p252: *The Adventures of Gerard* (1970). Peter McEnery as a Cavalry Colonel in Napoleonic Wars comedy. Eli Wallach played Napoleon.

Mastroianni and Loren would however act together on the screen in a dozen hit films from *Peccato che sia una canaglia* (Too Bad She's Bad, 1954) from the story by Moravia, to Robert Altman's *Pret-a-Porter* (1994).

p253; Lampedusa's novel, *Il Gattopardo*, was published in 1958.

p255: Colquhoun's article was published in F&F Oct62 p10-11.

p258: *The Naked Island* (Hadaka no shima). A boy falls ill on a small island occupied only by his family. Taiji Tonoyama starred.

"The audience is noisy, impatient. When Werner Herzog presented his film, *Stroszek* at Taormina in 1977 he described the audience, realistically and without meaning to be offensive, as 'savages in the arena'." JFL F&F.

p260: *Anima nera*. Gassman as a newly married man in Rome who can't escape his rent-boy past.

Chapter 18

p263: Of the Zeffirelli production, Miller wrote: "The Italian one with Monica Vitti was interesting. This was no great departure for them, apparently, from plays by Pirandello, from plays by numerous other European writers, where people were able to verbalize what they were feeling. So Zeffirelli put Monica Vitti on stage with Giorgio Albertazzi who created an ambience of such intense search, that I looked at it and I thought, the emotion is all there... When we – Americans, and the British – begin to try to think on stage, we get very remote. When the Italian does it, he never for a moment separates this from the fever of thinking." from *Conversations with Miller* by Mel Gussow, p90.

p264: Barbara Steele. English actress. A cult star of horror films, particularly Mario Bava's *Black Sunday* (1960) and Riccardo Freda's *The Horrible Dr. Hichcock* (1962).

p265: Tamara Lees usually played royalty and mistresses. Her films include *La donna più bella del mondo* (1955, with Gassman and Lollo).

Spiros Focás. Appeared in *Via Margutta* (1960) and played one of Rocco's brothers in Visconti's great film.

p266: Georgia O'Brien has a role in Benigni's *Johnny Stecchino* (1991) and is the subject of a documentary by Mingozzi.

p269: *L'Ape Regina*. Ugo Tognazzi as a middle-aged man on the eve of marriage to a virgin played by Marina Vlady.

El cochecito. An old man craves a motorised wheelchair so he can keep up with his friends.

Ettore Garofolo also plays an angel in the recreation of Pontormo's 'Deposition' in Pasolini's *La Ricotta*.

p279: See JFL's 'The Trial of Orson Welles' and 'Pasolini's Ride to Calvary', in *Film & Filming* March 1963 p70, p68-70.

p281: Giorgio Bassani was responsible for steering through the publication of Lampedusa's *The Leopard*. His own novel, *The Garden of the Finzi-Continis*, was filmed by De Sica in 1971.

p282. Bertolucci had made the documentary *La via del petrolio* (1966).

p283: *The Two Colonels* (I due colonnelli). Steno (Stefario Vanzina) edited the Rome humorous magazine, *Marc' Aurelio*. His hiring of the young Fellini as an illustrator and writer enabled Fellini to move in Rome.

Chapter 19

p290: Written under Austrian occupation, *Attila*'s line, "Take the rest of the world but leave Italy to me" always draws cheers from Italian audiences. A recording of Christoff's performance in Florence is still in print.

p291: Tarkovsky's penultimate film, *Nostalghia* (1983) was made in Italy. Co-written with Fellini's longtime collaborator, Tonino Guerra.

De Laurentiis's whiskey was earned. *Barabbas* was a box-office hit.

p292: JFL's 12,000 word 'Oh! Oh! Antonioni' starts: "In the room dedicated to the post-war Italian Cinema at the 'History of the Cinema Exhibition' held recently in Milan, a display card quotes Fellini saying that "the chief characteristic of neo-realism is that it doesn't just want to contemplate the world but also to transform it'."

p294. A photobook of Claudia Cardinale, with thoughts by Moravia, was published in 1963.

Chapter 20

p308: *La Vedova Scaltra*. A cultured Venetian widow tests the sincerity of four suitors.

p313: *The Fall of the Roman Empire*. Produced at a cost of $18 million by Samuel Bronston. Anthony Mann directed. Sophia Loren starred.

p314: This was *Gidget Goes to Rome* (1963). Directed by Paul Wendkos.

"...and as for talking to young, oh so young, Jimmy Darren and his dumb blonde ex-beauty queen wife, even on the subject he likes best, pop music, it was hard going." JFL F&F August 1960 p28.

p318: Giuliano Vasilicò *The 120 Days of Sodom* opened at the Roundhouse on 11th October 1974.

p319: *Oh, What A Lovely War!* starred Murray Melvin, Avis Bunnage. It opened at the Stratford East on March 19th, 1963.

p320: *Twang!*, starring Jimmy Booth, closed after 43 performances.

Chapter 21

p322: *Icarus XB 1.* Directed by Jindrich Polák from the novel by Stanislaw Lem. Tarkovsky's *Solaris* (1972) would also be from a novel by Lem.

p326: Tom Courtenay took over the role of *Billy Liar* from Albert Finney in Anderson's original stage production and Schlesinger's film.

p326: *Le cocu magnifique.* A village scribe writes love letters for illiterate villagers, many of which are addressed to his wife.

p328: *Le feu follet.* Maurice Ronet as an alcoholic who decides to end his life. From the novel by Pierre Drieu La Rochelle.

p329: *Omicron.* An alien learns about Earth by taking over a dead man's body. Lots of Richard Lester-style camera-play and editing tricks.

Il Circolo Pickwick (6 episodes, 1968). Starring Mario Pisu and Leopoldo Trieste.

p330: The Cousteau film was possibly an early version of *Le monde sans soleil* (World Without Sun).

West and Soda. Feature-length absurdist Western.

p332: *Tom Jones.* Directed by Tony Richardson from the novel by Henry Fielding. It won four Oscars for Best Film, Best Director, Best Screenplay (John Osborne) and Best Music (Addison).

The Rover (1967). French-English rivalry in the Mediterranean, with Quinn as the "rover of the outer seas". Produced by Bini.

Chapter 22

p344: *Bienvenido Mr. Marshall.* Spanish desert town citizens get ready for visitors from the United States in the hope of winning Marshall Grant funding.

p347: see 'Lindsay Anderson, The Diaries', edited by Paul Sutton.

The Wars of the Roses. Comprising *Henry VI, Henry VI, Henry VI* and *Richard III.* Adapted by John Barton with a cast that included David Warner, Peggy Ashcroft, Ian Holm, Janet Suzman.

p348: *Tonight* was a half-hour current affairs programme which ran on weekdays on BBC 1. It was first presented in 1957 by Cliff Michelmore.

Daubeny's autobiography was published as *My World of Theatre* (Jonathan Cape, 1971).

Epilogue

p352: Quoted from Bergman's *The Magic Lantern*, as translated by Joan Tate (1988).

Ludwig. Helmut Berger as the mad King of Bavaria from his crowning in 1864 until his death in 1886.

Harold Pinter was so incensed by Visconti's adaptation of *Old Times* he called a press-conference in Rome to condemn it.

p353: *The Voice of the Moon,* with Roberto Benigni as a lunatic, and a film-killing disco scene set to Michael Jackson's *The Way You Make Me Feel.*

In *Lucky Luciano* JFL has a few lines with holding a glass of champagne at a news conference for the title character played by Gian Maria Volonté.

p354: *Roba da Ricchi.* Three tales of lust, cheating and suicide in Monte Carlo, with Laura Antonelli.

The Tinto Brass films are the ones in Venetian dialect, including *Chi lavora è perduto* (1963), a political autobiographical story about a young Venetian anarchist; and *La Vacanza* (1971) starring Vanessa Redgrave.

p355. *Il Postino* received Oscar nominations in five categories: Best Film; Best Director; Best Screenplay (Anna Pavignano, Michael Radford, Furio Scarpelli, Giacomo Scarpelli, Massimo Troisi); Best Actor and Best Music (Luis Bacalov). It won the prize for Best Music.

A caricature of John Francis Lane by Federico Fellini

INDEX

383

385

389

Also Published by Bear Claw Books:

THE BIOGRAPHY OF KEN RUSSELL
VOLUME ONE

BECOMING
KEN RUSSELL

BY PAUL SUTTON

The full story of Ken Russell's rise through ballet, photography, and amateur films to become a professional independent filmmaker. Using hundreds of exclusive interviews with Russell and his colleagues, and thousands of unpublished documents, this details the day-by-day, almost frame-by-frame, making of Russell's first 35mm films, short films that redefined the meaning of 'English Cinema' and which contain the origins of scenes and images from Ken Russell's most famous films.

978-0-9572462-2-5   AMAZON KINDLE
978-0-9572462-6-3   PAPERBACK

VOLUME TWO - KEN RUSSELL, TO AND BEYOND ELGAR (DUE 2014)

KEN RUSSELL's
DRACULA

I've come up with a reason why Dracula would want to live forever."

Written between *Tommy* and *Altered States*, Ken Russell's screenplay for Dracula was one of Hollywood's best kept secrets. It has been used to inspire two hit films and an internationally successful ballet.

978-0-9572462-0-1   AMAZON KINDLE
978-0-9572462-1-8   PAPERBACK

Tim Dry
Falling Upwards

Tim Dry's virtuoso memoir of a life in arts. It rises and falls through the worlds of art school and mime and New Romantics pop to the cinema of Star Wars and the theatre of Steven Berkoff; hallucinogenic drugs; internationally-prized photography and a globetrottery of commercials. From a childhood encounter with a UFO to playing an alien in the cult film, *Xtro*; from seeing The Beatles as a boy to befriending Angie Bowie and performing in front of 100,000 people with Gary Numan. Tim Dry breaks into a theatre to see Kate Bush; makes a highwire appearance on stage with Duran Duran; photographs Mick Jagger; is paid to go berserk as a robot in Germany; has a week-long near nude scene in a film with Ann-Margaret; and presents a food programme on Channel 4. All this and much, much more.

978-0-9572462-6-3   Paperback (June 2013)

Kevin Sutton
Orphans of the Underworld
A Punk Memoir

"There were five of us – Fairy Jane, French Christine, Olly Wood, Cosmic Mark and myself; We were such a bizarre group of teenage castaways, estranged from our own families, we banded ourselves into a kinship group of our own making and together we lived free and uncontained."

5311606R00222

Printed in Great Britain
by Amazon.co.uk, Ltd.,
Marston Gate.